KT-144-622

Secrets My Mother Kept

Kath Hardy

Kath Hardy grew up on a council estate in Dagenham in the 1950s and 60s, the second youngest of ten children. She was a teacher for more than 30 years, before becoming an education advisor. She now lives in Suffolk with her husband, and has two grown-up children.

KATH HARDY

Secrets
My Mother Kept

HODDER

First published in Great Britain in 2013 by Hodder & Stoughton
An Hachette UK company

1

A CIP catalogue record for this title is available from the British Library

Paperback ISBN 978 1 444 76325 6
Ebook ISBN 978 1 444 76326 3

Typeset by Hewer Text UK Ltd, Edinburgh
Printed and bound by CPI Group (UK) Ltd, Croydon, CR0 4YY

Hodder & Stoughton policy is to use papers that are natural, renewable
and recyclable products and made from wood grown in sustainable
forests. The logging and manufacturing processes are expected to
conform to the environmental regulations of the country of origin.

Hodder & Stoughton Ltd
338 Euston Road
London NW1 3BH

www.hodder.co.uk

To Mum and Aunty, the towering forces in my life, who both in their own way shaped me into the person I am today.

Contents

Prologue

I remember wishing it wasn't so cold, but at least the sun shone through the breaks in the clouds.

'The sun shines on the righteous,' Aunty used to say.

It was four weeks since Mum had died. Standing still and straight next to my siblings, I thought of those who were missing: Marge, Marion's identical twin, and Mary, a year older, both in Australia with their families; my secret sister Sheila in the Isle of Man . . .

The priest stood next to the grave and said the prayers of internment in a soft clear voice. Mum was cremated soon after she died and now we were burying her ashes on the small family plot, next to her mother and father and older sister 'Aunty'. The only marker was a small plain wooden cross and the plot was overgrown with rough grass. I wished we had decided to scatter her ashes somewhere beautiful and not in that barren East London graveyard with its dilapidated statues and neglected monuments.

No one was crying except for me, and I wasn't crying for Mum, I was crying for myself.

I had begun to notice the changes in Mum during my weekly visits. She had lost weight, and was shrunken and grey. She had never had many wrinkles, but now her eyes were old and tired, and although she was only seventy-three, she looked frail and ill.

'Kath,' she said softly as I took her up a cup of tea, 'I need to clear out the cupboard in here.'

I looked at her lying in that bed and, to my shame, felt angry. In a few weeks I was having an operation – a serious one. It was my turn to be ill now; I needed her to look after me. Why was she talking about tidying the cupboard? It was blocked in by the wardrobe and no one had opened it in years.

'Mum, can you drink this?' I offered her the cup, but she turned her head away. Mum's bed was in the box room. I had slept most of my childhood nights in that room. First my sister Mary and I had slept together in a big double bed that took up most of the room. Once Mary had left home I shared the same bed with Mum. I used to dread the rare occasions when I was told to change the sheets because I didn't like to see the black speckles of mould that bloomed where the sheets touched the damp walls. There was a large air vent in the external wall but Mum covered it in plastic bags to stop the draughts and I guess that was why the walls were always running with moisture. The bedroom window looked out over our street, Valence Avenue. It was one of the main through routes in Dagenham. It was lined with tall horse chestnut trees, which we would scramble under every autumn searching for conkers.

Inside, the paintwork was peeling, and there was never any carpet on the floor, so when I got out of bed in the mornings my toes would freeze. As well as a double bed there was an old 1930s-style wardrobe and dressing table that had been donated by a well-meaning relative, and squeezed into the remaining space. These held a strange mixture of my things and Mum's and smelt of mothballs and damp. I still dream about that smell, and that room.

After Mary had left home she would sometimes send little presents home for Margaret and me. A pair of socks, a bar of soap, a flannel – small things, but I treasured them. We didn't really have things of our own, so I would squirrel these treasures away in my drawer of the dressing table. I never used any of them – they were far too special to use – I just got them out to touch and look at from time to time. There was no light bulb attached to the fitting that dangled from the centre of the ceiling because Mum couldn't afford to replace it. Consequently home-work had to be done sitting at the top of the stairs under the landing light. Downstairs was always much too noisy and busy and there was never any room for books.

As I stood in that room as an adult, it seemed to me that for all the happy memories, the walls were permeated with secret sorrows.

I hadn't got round to sorting out the cupboard while Mum was alive, but several months after the funeral I agreed to help my older sister Josie clear Mum's room. She and our sister Pat had never married and still lived in our old childhood home.

We began to sort through all the assorted junk and paraphernalia. Josie was looking hot and flushed, and I was worried about her.

'Are you sure you're okay, Josie?' I asked. 'We can stop for a rest if you like.'

She shook her head.' No, I'm fine.'

Her hair was fine like Mum's had been, but she dyed the grey. Josie had always been a very neat person, and was usually well groomed and conscious of her appearance. Her fingernails were always manicured and her hair perfectly styled. The one thing she had never been able to control was her weight, and it was this that was now making her breathless.

Cobwebs dangled from the top and sides of the cupboard, and my mind spun back fourteen years to when I had not long been at college, and my jewellery box mysteriously disappeared from the dressing table. Patrick, my then boyfriend, had bought me some large gold hoop earrings for my twenty-first birthday, a gold ingot pendant and some pretty gold and silver bangles. When I had questioned Mum about it she told me she had put the box in the cupboard to keep them safe. At the time I'd believed her totally, and it was only later that I realised that she must have sold them. Still, I watched closely as Josie groped about in the cupboard.

'What's this?'

She reached to the back of the shelf and pulled out a dusty old bag full of yellowing envelopes. They were all written in the same unfamiliar sloping hand, all with different postmarks, some dated from before I was born, but all addressed to me, Kathleen Stevens. I swallowed as I realised that she'd found something far more precious than that old jewellery box. Something that would have the potential to change my life; to help unravel the mysteries that had dogged it.

I

The Mummy Lady

Thinking back now, my memories of Dagenham began towards the end of the 1950s. I remember a patch of blue sky and someone singing 'Lulla Lulla Lullaby' in a soft, sweet, sad voice. I don't know how old I was, or who was singing, but the melody, though simple, was haunting. Rationing had ended several years before, and food was plentiful for those who could afford to buy it. However we were poor. Crushingly poor. We lived in the same house that our grandparents had moved to in the 1920s, but Dagenham had already begun a downward slide. The once well-kept red brick houses were starting to deteriorate, and many of the original tenants had moved on.

I don't suppose growing up as the second youngest in a single-parent family of ten is ever a bowl of cherries. Trying to do that as a Catholic in 1950s Dagenham was even harder. Pat was the oldest sister I knew, and I loved her to bits. She had shiny black hair and twinkling brown eyes that I could see through her glasses. To me she was all powerful; her strong arms kept me safe and she knew the answers to all my questions. Well, nearly all. I remember her taking me on a special visit one day. I suppose I must have been about three and my only younger sibling, Margaret, would have been about eighteen months old.

As Pat carried me, I wriggled in her arms. I could walk perfectly well; I wasn't a baby! The building we approached was tall, grey and forbidding. I decided to hang on to Pat after all. As we entered through the big doors there was a man who talked to us and then sent us towards the stone stairs. Pat carried me up them and I wondered where we were going. We had to wait with a lot of other people for the bell to ring so Pat took me over to the window to look out. I saw Margaret waiting outside with my other sister Josie; suddenly she looked up from my sister's arms with such a sad look on her face. I felt very important to be the one who was allowed inside.

The bell rang and we moved through the big swing doors. There were chairs and little tables, all empty and waiting. The doors at the other end of the big room opened and the ladies came in.

'There's Mummy,' whispered Pat, and walked over to the lady.

She kissed me on the cheek and gave me a sweetie. 'Hello darling,' she cooed, as Pat handed her an envelope. A tall man came over. He had a funny hat and he took the envelope from the Mummy lady, opened it, looked at it and then gave it back. She and Pat talked while I looked around at the other ladies and their visitors. Then the Mummy lady stroked my face and suggested, 'Why don't you run and say hello? They might have something nice for you,' and being a compliant child I slipped off Pat's lap and did as I was told.

''Ello sweetheart,' one lady said. She looked quite scary and big, with red raw hands and face, but she gave me a sweet so I took it and hurried on. Most of them were sitting at their own little tables, but others were dressed all the same in jackets with shiny buttons on them, and stood around the walls of the room watching everyone like nosey birds. Some of the ladies gave me a sweet, others just patted my head and some spoke to me, but I didn't go near the standing-up ones. I carried on without uttering a sound, just walked solemnly round to each in turn, round the big room with its shiny floor and cream painted walls and its unfamiliar smell.

Years later, Aunty used to stir her tea, look at the bubbles and say, 'Secrets and lies go to the sides and money stays in the middle,' and she would look slyly over at my mum, who would pretend she hadn't heard.

Our council house had been new when my grandparents had moved there in 1926. Granddad died before I was born and

Granny died when I was three, so I don't really remember either of them. I grew up in that house with my mum, two brothers and six sisters and Mum's older sister Edie, or 'Aunty' as we always called her. Strictly we were a family of ten children, but we never counted Sheila. Sheila was the oldest and had gone with her dad when he and Mum had split up during the war. I had never met her, and the only reason I knew she existed was because Aunty would sometimes say to my sister Pat, 'You're just like your sister Sheila.' Pat never answered and would just look away.

Aunty and Mum didn't talk to each other except through us. Even though they were sitting in the same room as each other it'd be 'Tell your mother I'm going out!' or 'Ask Aunty if she wants a cup of tea.' The only direct communication they had was during ferocious arguments – the kind that makes your insides feel like they're falling out. Sometimes Aunty would throw things. She was smaller than Mum, with a thick head of tight curly hair that had been black, but was increasingly grey as the years passed. She would periodically have it permed at the hairdressers round the corner, and would come home looking like a poodle. She rarely washed her hair between times, preferring to rub olive oil into her head. She said it helped with her 'screws' which is what she called her arthritis. Her eyes were a deeper blue than Mum's but they still sparkled. Sometimes they sparked with mischief, as she loved to irritate people, especially Mum. We were never allowed to use bad language, even 'bum' was considered a swear word, but Aunty took great joy in flaunting that rule. If she was just in a playful mood she would talk about burps and farts, but when she was in a temper about something the language would get a lot more colourful!

One day we were sitting at the table and Aunty was shouting from the scullery. She came in like a whirlwind and turning towards Mum screeched, 'I don't care what yer bloody well say, I know what's been going on,' and she slung the teapot full of scalding tea on to the table where it landed, spewing out the hot liquid all over poor Mary.

'There was money in me drawer, and now it's gone!' she continued, spitting the words out, while we children looked on, open-mouthed.

I wasn't very old before I began to understand that lots of things about me were different from other girls and boys I knew.

Our mum was different from other children's mums. She was a lot older and spoke differently. Her voice always sounded posh. She had grey hair and was overweight, and her clothes were old and poor quality. She also smoked a lot, although this was the one thing she had in common with many women at that time. She would send us across the road to the shop to get ten Olivia when she had a bit of money or five Player's Weights when she was hard up.

Mum often had a bottle of PLJ by her bed: Pure Lemon Juice, guaranteed to make you slim. I realise now how desperate she was to recapture her youthful good looks. Though we sometimes only had boiled potatoes for dinner, or a big suet pudding with golden syrup if we were lucky, she would have her PLJ and her cigarettes.

She inhabited a fantasy world for much of the time – one where she was as young and beautiful and glamorous as any film star. The secrets and lies that dominated my childhood were the smokescreen that made her life bearable.

2

School

As we got older we all knew that there were things we were never allowed to talk about, and questions we weren't allowed to ask. There were so many things we didn't understand.

My younger sister Margaret was always the shy one. She was tiny with huge brown eyes like chocolate drops fringed with thick black lashes. We both had our hair cut in a pudding-basin style, although hers was black and mine was brown, and we shared the same bumpy nose. We used to whisper to each other about secret things. She would ask me, 'Where is our dad?'

I told her he died in the war because I didn't really know. I was the big sister and it was my job to boss her around, know all the answers and to always look after her, so I made things up.

Mum wasn't well when I was due to start school so I had started at the nearby state primary school instead of the catholic school all my siblings had attended. At the time I didn't question the decision, but many years later I was to discover the shocking reasons why it had been made.

From the age of six I had to move to St Vincent Roman Catholic primary school so that I could prepare for my First Holy Communion. There were two infant classes and four junior classes in our school, which was built as a long corridor with classrooms leading off. Everything seemed to be painted the same sickly green colour. There was also a hall, which was used for PE and school dinners, and an office where the headmaster sat. The playground was concrete and seemed very big and frightening. At break times there would be hundreds of children racing round, kicking footballs, playing two balls against the walls, skipping, doing handstands and headstands, shouting and running and roaring. My favourite game was Two Balls. We had special rhymes that we sang as we played: 'One two three and a downsey, four five six and a downsey, seven eight nine and a downsey, ten and a downsey, drop the ball.' And then the next girl would take over. And the rhyme would begin again. We would repeat this over and over replacing 'downsey' with 'over' or 'under' and changing the way we threw the balls to match the words. Skipping was another game I enjoyed. Two girls would hold one end each of a long rope and they would turn it, each of the other children taking turns to run in and skip. There was also French skipping which was quite complicated and involved double ropes and jumping in and out skilfully; this was far trickier and took lots of practice to become proficient.

Margaret and I didn't usually stay for school dinners, preferring to walk the fifteen minutes home. We always hoped that Mum would let us stay off for the afternoon, and she often did. We liked to have soup for lunch – always Heinz from a tin.

Once a fortnight it would be family allowance day. Mum would call out to us, 'Come on you two; we've got to go to the Post Office.'

We would run to join her, and holding a hand each she would whisk us over the road to the shops.

'If you stand and wait nicely,' she would say, 'we'll go and get same bananas and some rolls from the bakers and have banana rolls for lunch.' We would squirm with anticipation, and once the 8 shillings was collected, make our way to collect the promised feast. We didn't usually go back to school on family allowance day. If it was hot then we would sometimes be allowed a frozen Jubbly, an icy prism of orange heaven, and very occasionally Mum would also buy us a tiny box of Cadbury's Milk Tray chocolates, with a few nestled inside.

Some of the other children took packed lunches and others had free dinners. My older sisters had had free dinners, but when Margaret and I started at St Vincent's, Marge had pleaded on our behalf. 'Don't make them have free dinners. They're disgusting, and everyone knows you get free dinners because the teacher calls it out.'

Mum had given in; she was always softer with Margaret and I than with the others.

I thought the children that took packed lunches were the luckiest. They had a little box or bag and inside their mum would have packed the things that they liked: a little sandwich, a sausage roll, an apple and sometimes a slice of cake. But there were some children who just brought a plastic bread bag with the toast crusts left over from their breakfast. I didn't envy them.

We grew to hate school. It was an unfriendly place and most of the teachers were very strict and shouted a lot. We didn't go to school that often. Although Mum did her best to persuade us to go, we also did our best to persuade her to let us stay at home. Usually we won.

When I moved into the juniors we had a young Irish teacher who had some modern ideas. One day he brought in a tape recorder. He told us that we were going to come out to the front of the class to read our writing and he was going to record us on to the tape so that we could listen to ourselves. I felt quietly confident. I was one of the best readers in the class and even though my work was untidy I usually got at least 8/10 for my writing. I had been really careful with my writing today as I had something especially exciting to write about. I listened patiently as each child's turn came and went. When it was my turn I carried my workbook up to the front and stood next to the teacher nervously. He pushed the button on the tape recorder and nodded at me to begin. I began to read, but unfortunately had a bad cold. I didn't have a hanky and so tried to control the snot running down my nose by sniffing it back up every minute or so. Some of the children began to giggle but I didn't take any notice I was concentrating so hard on reading my writing carefully. When we had all finished our recordings were played back for us to listen to. Mine sounded awful . . .

'My cat Tiddy' sniff, 'has got 4' sniff 'kittens', sniff. 'Me and my' sniff 'sister look' sniff 'after them' sniff. 'We' sniff 'are going' sniff 'to keep one' sniff 'when it is grown' sniff 'up but' sniff 'the other one' sniff 'will' sniff 'go to a new' sniff 'home' sniff. The result of my runny nose had been exaggerated by the tape resulting in an explosion of laughter from the whole class including my teacher. I wanted to disappear! It would be a very long time before I could read out loud again.

Mum thought that children who played out in the street were 'guttersnipes', but she did let us walk to and from school on our own. My friends Hannah and Jane would sometimes knock for me on the way.

There were still some old bombsites near us, and a favourite game would be clambering through them to see what we could find. Today Hannah had another idea.

'Let's play "Knock Down Ginger".' She turned to Jane. 'You go and knock on the door and we'll hide here.'

Jane did as she was told, while Hannah and I ducked down behind the fence. As soon as she had knocked, Jane flew back down the path and joined us to watch and wait. After a minute or two, a lady with a baby in her arms opened the door and peered out while we crouched down laughing our heads off. This was a game that we played often, but sometimes the person who opened the door would catch sight of us and shout out and occasionally even chase us along the road.

More scary than that was the Milk Float Game.

The horse-drawn milk floats of my sisters' childhood had now disappeared and been replaced with electric versions. These could pick up a fair bit of speed on a straight road. We would wait for the milkman to get on board and then run behind.

'Jump!' we would encourage each other, and we would leap onto the back of the float and hang there for a free ride.

When I return to Dagenham now to visit my sister, who still lives in our house, I sometimes walk around the familiar streets remembering the games and the children that I played them with. I also remember the stark mixture of tension, fear, excitement and fun that was part of my childhood, and it helps me to understand and make sense of my life now – despite all the unanswered questions.

3

A New Friend

The most popular girl in my class was called Christine. She had short brown bobbed hair with a ribbon tied round it, and was always dressed in clean clothes. I was desperate for her to be my best friend.

'Christine is coming round to play!' I announced proudly. Mum just lifted her eyes to heaven. I looked around me. I wanted Christine to play in our back garden with me but was acutely aware that it was completely overgrown. It didn't seem to matter when Margaret and I played out there. In fact it made it more exciting, as we had very fertile imaginations. One of our favourite games was being explorers. We would play until the summer sun set red and gold over Mr Stan's corrugated garden shed, and I'd nudge Margaret and say, 'Look! Aurora borealis!' I must have heard about the northern lights from the television or from my sisters. Either way, I knew they were something exciting!

The only flowers that were visible in the garden were a few white flag irises and a big bushy pink dog rose, remnants of our grandfather's days. Most of the space was now covered in a dense layer of weeds and grass, almost as tall as we were. The thick scratchy heads of couch grass were difficult to cut with a pair of old blunt scissors, but that was all I had. I needed to 'tidy up' the garden before Christine came to play and so knelt down and slowly began to cut. My sister Marge came out into the garden.

'What are you up to?' she asked, watching me with a curious expression.

'Gardening.'

'Why?'

'Because my friend is coming to play.'

Marge smirked, 'You'll be lucky!' and she went back inside laughing. The sun was hot on my back but I didn't mind. I must have stayed there for a long time, because I remember how the grass and stones began to cut into my knees, and how my fingers ached from working the scissors.

Marge was right – Christine never did come to play. She told me her dad had forbidden her to come.

'He says I'm not allowed round your house cos he knows your dad. He works with him at Ford's.'

This was a bolt out of the blue for me. *My* dad?

I met her words with silence. I was used to not knowing things, used to things not making sense, and I was also used to keeping quiet. I just stared back, swallowing the disappointment and trying not to care.

Margaret and I continued to enjoy our garden throughout the summer, and played lots of pretend games, building homes with the sheets on the line, draping chairs with old bits of cloth, and using them as 'Indian tepees'. Other favourite games involved steeping flower petals in water to make perfume, and collecting stones and grass to make a 'dinner' from anything else we could find. There was one time when we took this a little too far. Mum had said we couldn't have a bath because she couldn't afford the gas. Bath time was usually only once a week on a Sunday and we would use each other's water. By the time it got to our turn it was an interesting grey colour. On this day we had decided we wanted our own bath. We whispered to each other in the garden, and then proceeded to plaster our faces, arms and legs with as much mud as we could find.

'Have I got much on my face?' I asked Margaret.

'No, I can't see much,' she lied, so I layered even more of the brown-grey mixture across my cheeks.

Mum came out to call us in for bed and let out a screech.

'You naughty girls!' she shouted, and bent down to take the slipper off her foot. Our mum never smacked us, but in that second we saw such frustration and anger that our instincts told us to run. How well I remember diving up the stairs with Margaret a step behind me, followed closely by Mum, slipper in hand. We ran into the bathroom and slid the lock across and stood inside breathing heavily, our hearts racing.

'Come out of there now, you naughty girls!' Mum said angrily. But we stayed where we were. It seemed like an eternity until we heard her going back downstairs but in reality it probably took no more than a minute or two for her anger to subside and for her to see the funny side. We got our bath that night. Mum sometimes bought us Matey bubble bath when she had some money. We loved it and would sit in the bath for an age, playing with the suds until our fingers and toes were as wrinkled as prunes. That would only be in the summer time, because the bathroom in our house was painfully cold in the winter. Margaret and I usually had our bath together, and I can remember our sister Mary trying to persuade us to get out of the barely warm water onto the freezing floor.

'If you don't get out soon the witch will get you,' she warned.

'I don't believe you,' I retorted, 'there's no such thing as witches.'

'There is!' Mary continued, lowering her voice. 'She lives under the bath, look you can see her peeping out now.'

Margaret and I jumped out of the water like flying fish, to be grabbed roughly and rubbed dry by our impatient, shivering sister. For a very long time that witch haunted my bathroom visits, and having to go to the toilet with the 'witch' waiting to pop her head out from under the bath was terrifying.

During the harshest winters Aunty would go the oil shop round the corner to our house and buy paraffin for the tiny stove that she would put in the bathroom to stop the pipes from freezing. The smell was acrid and permeated the whole house but it did take the chill off the air upstairs. The only room that was heated in the winter was what we called the kitchen but which in effect was our living room.

I mentioned being different; the rooms in our house were certainly called different names from those in my friends' houses. They had a kitchen instead of a scullery, and their living room was what we called the kitchen. When Granny and Granddad had moved to our house when it was newly built, that was indeed what the rooms were used for. The scullery had been where the laundry was done. There had been a huge copper for heating the water, a Butler sink perched on two enormous stone pillars and a mangle for squeezing the water out of the clothes before they were hung on the line to dry. The cooking was done in the kitchen on a black lead range. Although this changed over the years, the rooms retained their past names like ghosts.

Most of the families around us were relatively poor but the homes of my friends were usually clean and tidy and most important of all they were warm. One particularly icy winter morning I went to knock for my friend Hannah who lived across the road so that we could walk to school together. Margaret was staying at home but I wanted to go to school because our class were putting on a play called *Alice in Wonderland*. Our new young teacher had cleverly said that I could play the part of the Red Queen and say, 'Off with her head!'

'But,' she said, 'you will have to be sure to come to school every day so that you can practise . . .'

Hannah's mum glanced at her watch when she opened the door to me, but welcomed me warmly. 'Come on in and wait, Hannah is just having her toast.' She led me into their little kitchen and as I entered I was hit by the smell of the bread toasting under the grill. Hannah sat at the little table with her clean clothes on waiting for her toast and tea.

'Would you like some toast, dear?' asked her mum.

I took in the scene before me: the simply furnished but cosy room, the clean table, the fresh toast being placed on Hannah's plate, its delicious smell wafting across to where I stood watching. We never had breakfast. Mum wasn't usually up before school time, so I had just got myself dressed and come out as usual.

I looked solemnly at Hannah's mum and shook my head. 'No, thank you.' We had been taught to be polite, but I really don't know why I refused her kind offer, when what I wanted

most in the world at that moment was to be Hannah with her
fresh buttered toast, her hot cup of tea, her school socks warm-
ing above the oven and her mum, smiling.

Our primary school wasn't very far but it took us about
fifteen minutes to walk there. The route took us up past the
local corner shops at the junction of Becontree Avenue across
into Haydon Road and we would then come out at the top
where the C of E church was opposite the Catholic church
that neighboured our school. There was a good selection of
local shops then. We had two greengrocers, butchers, post
office, bakery, two sweet shops and a newsagents. There was
also a fish and chip shop, an oil shop and a grocers on the
corner and next to that our favourite shop of all: the toy shop.
Margaret and I were often sent on errands to the shops as
soon as we were deemed old enough, which was when I was
about seven.

We passed the greengrocers just opposite our house on our
way to school. They ran a raffle every month, so when a customer
shopped with them they would give them a raffle ticket. The
monthly prize was always a lovely big basket of fruit and vegetables. I don't know whether my mum was extremely lucky, or the
lady who owned the shop was very kind, all I do know is that we
seemed to regularly win that basket of fruit and vegetables and
it made a big contribution to our larder!

That wasn't the only contribution the greengrocers made
to our family, but unfortunately the other was less welcome.
Although we rarely had breakfast, we would occasionally get
a penny for an apple to eat on the way to school. On one
particular day when we went into the shop the lady said very
kindly to me, 'Just wait there a minute.' She went out to the
back of the shop and returned with a warm, damp flannel
and then proceeded to wash my face and neck. I was
outraged! I attempted to pull away but she held me fast as I
wriggled.

'Just hold on – there that's better,' she said.

I was so angry and embarrassed! The poor woman

undoubtedly meant well and I was probably filthy, but it was a while before I ventured into that shop again.

The one shop I really didn't like going in was the corner shop The lady and man who ran it were always very unfriendly to us, and would follow us round, watching us carefully. It was the beginning of the supermarket era and although there were still certain things which you had to ask for, like cheese, butter, bacon and eggs, many things were displayed on the shelves for you to choose from.

It was only years later that I learned why those shopkeepers were so suspicious of us and the reasons were to shock me to the core.

4

Outings and Weddings

Although my primary school was pretty old and dilapidated, I do remember some things with great happiness and nostalgia.

One morning after Miss Jones had taken the register she said she had something to tell us. We looked at each other in anticipation.

'Children, next Monday we are going to High Beech for the day.' Some of the boys made silly noises, while we girls just smiled at each other happily.

I smiled along with the others but wasn't really sure what or where 'High Beech' was, but it must be something good.

'You will all need a packed lunch, and there will be orange squash available for you to drink,' carried on our teacher, 'but we will also have to learn some special rules to make sure we have a good time.'

I couldn't wait to get home that afternoon, so that I could tell Margaret and Mum about going on an outing.

'Can I come?' asked Margaret hopefully. She was off school again and had been helping Mum put the washing on the line. We both liked helping Mum with the washing, even though it was hard work. We didn't have a washing machine, so Mum would fill the big Butler sink full of hot water from the ascot that hung on the scullery wall. It was a gas water heater and I hated it because when you turned the tap on it made a really loud booming sound as the pilot light ignited the gas. This had taken the place of the old copper that had heated the water when my sisters and brothers had been young. Then Mum would pour in the Omo powder. It had a very strong odour and was a bright blue colour, but it made lots of bubbles, and had a nicer smell than the bar of soap Mum used to have to grate into the water. Sometimes I was allowed to stand on a chair and rub the clothes up and down the glass and wood washing board, which had thick ridges in it to help get the clothes clean. Once the clothes were washed and rinsed, the task of trying to remove as much water as possible from them began, so they would dry quicker. There was a big old mangle which Mum would pull out from the corner, and Margaret and I would feed the clothes through while Mum turned the handle. This then pushed the rollers round and squeezed the water out from the clothes. The only problem was that if you were not extremely careful your fingers could get 'mangled' along with the clothes, which we learnt to our cost was very painful!

Pegging the clothes on the line was the best bit of all, particularly if it was a windy day. We would take the basket into the garden and Mum would let the line down so we could reach. We would then be allowed to peg the smaller things out ourselves, but needed Mum's help with things like sheets.

Today though, I had been too late to help. The washing had been done and Mum and Margaret were just finishing putting it on the line.

'You can't come, because it's only for juniors,' I said to Margaret. I felt guilty when I saw her face fall. 'Don't worry. Your class will go on an outing too.'

Margaret and I sat in the kitchen in front of the television and Mum switched it on so that we could see *Watch with Mother* (although 'Mother' rarely sat with us). Every day of the week had a different show and we each had our favourite. Mine was *Picture Book* on a Monday and Margaret's was *The Woodentops* which was on Friday; we quite liked *Andy Pandy* though, and of course there was *The Flower Pot Men* and *Rag, Tag and Bobtail*.

Although Mum occasionally walked us to the park in Goodmayes, we didn't go out very often. So when I thought about our school trip, back came all my usual anxiety about having the right kind of lunch, the right kind of clothes and whether I would need the toilet. I would guess that over the next few days Miss Jones told the class about where we were going and what we might see, but I stayed at home for the rest of the week planning for the outing. I had to make sure that everything was ready.

On Saturday Mum took us to the shops in Green Lane.

'Do you want cheese spread or Spam for your sandwiches?' she asked. I wanted cheese spread, I never did like the sweaty, bland flavour of Spam. I was also allowed to choose a special cake from the baker's and on Sunday evening helped Pat to pack my lunch up in some greaseproof paper ready for the morning.

Bright and early on Monday I was beside myself with a mixture of happy anticipation and growing dread, especially when I arrived at school to see a big coach parked outside. As I went in to class, Christine turned to me. 'Where's your coat?' she asked. 'Miss Jones said we have to bring a coat in case it rains, so you probably won't be allowed to come.' I looked anxiously around to see if anyone else had forgotten their coat, but no, even though it was May I was the only one in just a cardigan.

To my utter relief a boy called Stephen burst into class. He went straight to the teacher and said, 'My mum says to tell you I ain't got a coat.'

Miss Jones turned to him, 'Don't worry, Stephen. The sun is shining; I don't think it is going to rain today so hopefully we won't need our coats.'

With that, I let out an inward sigh of relief and let myself enjoy the day – a day of dappled sunlight, warm orange squash and the sort of wild freedom that would never pass a health and safety checklist!

Later that year my Godmother Julie had announced that she was getting married and I was to be a bridesmaid. Julie was the same age as my sister Pat and they were very close friends. She was an only child and her Mum was my Aunty Maggie, one of my mum's older sisters.

One Saturday as the time of the wedding drew nearer, Julie came over to pick me up. 'We are going to get you fitted for your dress today'. I was a quiet, shy and subdued child, so I didn't dare to ask the questions that were buzzing round in my head. Would my dress trail along the floor like a princess's? What colour would it be and would I wear a tiara?

Julie's friend was making my dress and my tummy did somersaults as we approached her front door. I hadn't had any breakfast and it was well past lunchtime. Julie didn't realise that I hadn't eaten, and as we went inside the house I began to feel headachy and nauseous.

'Come on then' said Julie kindly. 'Jump up on the chair so we can get you measured.' I tried to do as I was told but I wobbled and nearly fell.

'What's the matter with you then' said Julie's friend catching me with one hand.

'Oh she's probably over excited' said Julie oblivious to the fact that I was dizzy with hunger.

My dress was made from shiny pale green satin and had little puffed sleeves. It sat just above my knees, and had a flouncy petticoat, which wasn't particularly flattering as my legs were rather short and quite plump!

A few weeks later Julie arrived to take me shoe shopping.

'We're taking you to meet Carol the other bridesmaid and you can get your shoes together,' Julie told me as she picked me up.

Carol? I thought, who is Carol? No one had mentioned another bridesmaid.

'You can get to know each other and have a little play.'

We drove for what seemed like an age and finally arrived in Hayes where Carol lived. Her Mum welcomed us in and said kindly 'Carol, why don't you take Kathleen up to your room to play while Mummy and Julie have a chat, we'll call you down for lunch when it's ready.'

Carol had a room all of her own and didn't have to share it with anyone. I looked around me in wonder. It was the most beautiful room I had ever seen. It had pink flowery wallpaper and clean crisp white paintwork. At the window hung curtains full of white daisies like the ones I had seen growing in the park, but best of all, there on the floor, was the fluffiest, pinkest, softest rug I had ever seen! It was glorious, and I wanted to sit on it forever and run my fingers and toes through it.

'Do you want to play babies? Or we can play with my dolls house? She pointed to the shelf at one side of the room. I looked at the toys on the shelves, the assortment of teddy bears on her bed and at the rows of books neatly stacked on a tiny bookcase, and thought that she must be the luckiest little girl in the whole world.

After lunch we walked to the shoe shop. My eyes fell on a pair of shoes that sparkled. They were covered in glitter and sequins. I crunched up my eyes and wished with all my might, but at the same time was too timid to make my preferences known to the grown ups.

'I think these ones will look best next to the green' said Carol's Mum picking up a pair of dull cream satin shoes that had a small bow on the front, but Carol said 'Oh no please Mummy, the sparkly ones are the nicest, please, please, please.' The adults exchanged looks and smiled. Julie picked up the sparkling shoes and said 'Do you know Carol I think you're right, the sparkly ones are definitely the best, do you like them Kathleen?' I nodded so vigorously that my head almost left my shoulders and I couldn't stop myself from smiling broadly.

I knew then that wishes could come true. With my new green satin dress, sparkling starlight shoes, shiny flicked up hair and green feather headband, I would look like a princess and this time when people looked at me, they would be thinking I looked beautiful.

5

Michael

From the end of the Second World War to the early 60s, all young men were conscripted into the armed forces, as long as they passed a medical examination. My oldest brother Michael was no exception. He was called up for National Service when I was about three so I don't really remember him much before he was in the army. It would not be the first time he had been away from home. In fact, as I later discovered, he was already a veteran at living apart from our family.

As the second oldest in the family, he had been born just before the outbreak of war. He was a very beautiful baby with golden curls and a chubby face, but did not have a particularly happy childhood. Mum had already given birth to Sheila a year before, so they were very close in age. Mum and Ron Coates, their dad, had a house around the corner from Granny and Granddad. It was still on the Becontree Estate but was a bit smaller than mum's childhood home. Things started to go badly wrong. They were both quite young, still in their twenties when Mum became pregnant for the third time. War broke out and Ron was working long hours at Ford, and Mum was lonely.

Aunty told us many years later that Ron Coates was a 'womaniser', but we never knew if that was true. It was while Mum was pregnant with their fourth child, Josie, that they finally separated. Michael was five at the time. Today the idea of a single parent bringing up children alone doesn't surprise, shock or horrify anyone, but in 1942 in a Catholic community Mum was stigmatised.

★　　★　　★

After Michael's ten weeks basic training for National Service, he was shipped over to Gibraltar – 'the Rock', as it was known then. He was just over nineteen years old and had already been bringing a wage home. He was trying to help to keep the ever-growing family's head above water. Now all that had changed and he wasn't sure what chaos and calamity he would come back to. Despite his worries about Mum and us, he loved army life and soon metamorphosed from a chubby, shy, anxious teenager into a tall, slim, confident young man. After he had been in Gibraltar for about two years his letters home started mentioning a Spanish girl named Isobel. He sent us photos of her. She was so beautiful; with her dark hair and smouldering eyes, she was the most exotic looking person we had ever seen. Then another letter from him arrived.

'Your brother's getting married,' I overheard Mum telling Pat and Josie. They were in their late teens and had been working since they left school at fifteen.

I was so excited but wasn't sure exactly what it meant.

'Is our brother really getting married?' I asked Pat.

She nodded.

I knew all about weddings since I had been a bridesmaid.

'And will he be coming home now?' I added. The only memories I had of Michael at that time were as a brief visitor when he had occasionally come home on leave.

Pat gave me a look. 'I don't think so; not yet,' she said and changed the subject quickly.

They were married in Isobel's home village near to Malaga but none of our family were able to attend. The fare to Spain would have been as out of reach to us then as a flight to the moon would be now! They did send photos though, and when I looked at them I thought they were like characters from the pictures.

In the same year that Michael and Isobel got married, our class began to be 'prepared' for our First Holy Communion. This meant learning lots of things by heart, which I was quite good at. It also meant making our first confession. We had to confess our sins first so that we would be free from sin when we went to receive Jesus in the communion bread and wine. The problem was we were only six or seven. We didn't have any sins to confess so we made them up. We knew that telling lies, being unkind to our sisters and brothers, swearing and murder were all very bad sins so we confessed them. Apart from murder that is; I don't think any of us confessed to that one!

When the big day came we lined up in the church pew and knelt down to remember our sins and to pray for forgiveness. When it was my turn to go into the confessional box I was quite excited. I pulled the door that was already slightly ajar and slipped in. I could remember the words we had to say to the priest who was in the other side of the box. He couldn't see me and I couldn't see him.

'Bless me Father for I have sinned. This is my first confession,' I began.

The priest said some prayers and then asked me what I had done.

'I have lied, I smacked my sister and I was cheeky to my mum.'

None of this was true, of course, but I had to say something and these sins sounded along the right kind of lines.

The priest forgave me. 'Say two Hail Mary's and one Our Father and don't sin again.'

I left the confession box feeling ten feet tall. I was a forgiven sinner at last!

I was to make my Holy Communion in June. For Catholics, making your first Holy Communion is really important. For a start you get a new white dress and a veil and everyone looks at you and gives you presents. I was so excited.

However, the question of my dress was posing some problems for my family. One afternoon Margaret and I were looking through a big thick catalogue imagining the clothes we were going to buy.

'That white one's nice. And it's not too . . .'

Mum looked over our shoulders. 'Hmm. We'll have to wait and see.'

I bit my lip. What would I do if I didn't have a communion dress? It wasn't mentioned again for a while so I tried not to think about it. Then one day a letter arrived from Michael. That afternoon after school Mum had some news for me. My dress was on its way! Michael's new wife was a dressmaker, and a Catholic as well, so understood the importance of the occasion. She was going to make my dress!

Over the next few weeks she made me a beautiful, simple white dress that she hand stitched and embroidered. It wasn't fancy or frilly, but was made from fine white cotton with narrow white ribbon threaded through it across the bodice, round the sleeves and the hem. It also had a little Peter Pan collar, which I loved. She also made a replica dress for my little sister Margaret to wear so that we would look alike. But Margaret wasn't having a veil; that was special for me.

The day it arrived in the post, carefully packaged in tissue paper, my fingers were trembling with excitement.

Once I had made my Holy Communion it meant that I was old enough to walk in the May processions. These were very big events where all of the little girls and boys who had made their first Holy Communion would process through the streets along with the older children. All would be dressed in white and many of the girls would wear a little veil. I wore mine and felt so proud as we walked past the houses. People would come to their gates and stand watching us as we walked and sang hymns to Mary the Queen of Heaven and Queen of the May. There was very little traffic on the roads in those days so we must have been quite a spectacle.

Afterwards I carefully put the dress away. We didn't get many new clothes. Aunty sometimes bought us a few bits and pieces home from Plessey's where she worked. I think they must have 'fallen off the back of a lorry' and were sold on the factory floor. The other major source of our clothes was a kindly woman called Mickey. She worked in the United Dairies depot near to our house and sometimes Mum would say to Mary or one of the twins, 'Go into the dairy will you? Mickey's got some things for you.'

Mickey worked in the servery. That was the office section in the dairy that kept a record of the milk and other things that the milkmen would take out on their daily delivery rounds. Every now and again she'd send word to Mum that she had some things for us. One day Marge, Marion and Mary were sent into the diary and returned with a suitcase.

'That's huge!' I exclaimed, excitement rising. 'What's inside?'

Marge flung it open. 'Don't touch, you two,' she said bossily. 'We'll tell you which things will fit you.'

We ignored her and descended upon its contents, trying to push our way through the big girls' arms.

'A bra!' Mary said, shoving Marion out of the way. Marion was always the less confident of the twins and I could see the disappointment on her face. Marge picked up a yellow jumper that was probably a few sizes too big. As she held it against her, Mum said 'Just wait a minute, will you? Don't forget Pat and Jo might like some of those things.' Unfortunately most of the clothes were too big for Margaret and me, so we lost interest quite quickly and just looked over occasionally while the contents of the suitcase were shared between our sisters. We had the last laugh though because when our older sisters were at school and work, we would put on their clothes and bounce on the old iron bedstead singing at the top of our voices!

I do remember one Easter having a new little suit to wear. Margaret and I had one each. They each had a pleated skirt and a little matching jacket. We thought we were marvellous when we wore them to Mass on Easter Sunday. Mum told us that she had bought them but that we had to say thank you to Aunty, as she wanted us to think that she had got them for us. Poor Aunty, you can probably guess who actually paid the money for them.

6

The 'Special News' Day

Later that year, Mum told us some 'special' news. It was a damp chilly autumn and some of the luckier children at our school had gone hop picking. Our family never went. Mum said it was 'common' and looked down her nose at those who went, but Margaret and I were always envious at this time of year. All that time off school playing in the sunny hop fields!

It was Monday and Margaret and I had just started to walk home from school for lunch when we spied Mum across the road waiting for us with her headscarf tied tightly round her head and her big black bag over her arm. She never went anywhere without her bag. She even took it up to bed with her at night, and when she was sitting in her chair by the fireplace it would sit firmly at her feet. No one was ever allowed to look inside. Strangely it seemed almost malevolent lying on the floor next to her, daring us to peep inside. I didn't know at the time what Mum kept in there, but knowing now, that feeling makes sense.

'You will never guess what,' Mum said with a huge smile on her face. I looked at Margaret, as her huge brown eyes got bigger.

'What? What? What?!' we screeched. We were quite used to 'exciting news'. I think, looking back, that Mum may have had marginal bipolar as she would swing between extreme highs and lows with a ferocious regularity. Today was going to be a high.

'We've won the pools!' she exclaimed, beaming at us. Mum did the pools religiously every week. She would sit in front of the television on Saturday afternoons with the pools form in front of her, ticking things off in response to the monotonous voice of the commentator 'Arsenal 1, Chelsea 1; Wolverhampton Wanderers 0, Crystal Palace 1 . . .'

'No school for you this afternoon – we're going to see Aunty Maggie to tell her all about it.' We jumped up and down, clapping our hands. This day was getting better and better! Off we walked, Mum holding one of our hands in each of hers, swinging us along Becontree Avenue to the bus stop in Bennetts Castle Lane. The 145 or the 148 would take us to Aunty Maggie's house in Seven Kings. She lived there with her husband George, a small kindly man who worked at Plessey's with Aunty.

We had to sit upstairs on the bus so that Mum could have a cigarette. I raced to the empty front seat and Margaret followed. This was always our favourite place as we could pretend we were driving the bus. Today as the bus started to move I noticed the first few raindrops splattering onto the windows. We spent the whole journey talking about what we were going to do with all of the money we had. Pat and Josie could give up work, we would all have new clothes, and I could have a party and invite all the girls at school. By the time we got to Seven Kings it was pouring with rain. Our coats were quite old and poor quality but Mum had a battered old umbrella that the three of us huddled under to keep dry as we walked to Aunty Maggie's house.

'Don't jump in the puddles,' Mum said cheerfully, 'your feet will get soaking,' but we slyly splashed just the same, giggling together either side of Mum.

Aunty Maggie and Uncle George had bought their own house in a neat Victorian terrace on a quiet road. I knew that house well. I often came to stay for a few days and would be given my own room to sleep in. Every time my Aunty Maggie would take me to the big cupboard in the kitchen and when she opened the door inside would be an array of neatly stacked clothes including various quilted dressing gowns, or house coats as they were often called then, which had belonged to Julie. I would be given one to wear and then allowed to bring it home with me. Once I got home the 'housecoat' always seemed to vanish. I don't know where they went, but next time I came to stay I would be given another one. They had a dog called Trixie, who was a cross between a border collie and a few other things, and pretty snappy. Aunty Maggie and Uncle George were constantly warning me not to put my face too near her but I never listened. Margaret and I had no fear of dogs. We had always had a dog and whatever dog we had it was always called Pongo. The Pongo we had at the time was getting very old. She had a chronic skin condition that meant her hair fell out in huge clumps and my sister Pat would have to smear a foul smelling green sticky ointment over her back. The sight of the green slimy ointment together with the potent smell of wintergreen always turned my stomach.

In the front room at Aunty Maggie's there was a piano and a glass cabinet that held all of their treasures. There were small china animals, a tiny teapot ornament and a variety of knick-knacks that they had collected over the years from seaside holidays. I was sometimes allowed to play with them as long as I was careful.

On the 'exciting news' day we arrived rather damp and chilly at Aunty Maggie's front door. We knocked and waited, listening to Trixie barking and flinging herself at the door. When the door opened Aunty Maggie was standing looking a little surprised to see us.

'Flo – what are you doing here? Why aren't the children at school?'

'They're not very well,' Mum replied as we were ushered into the tiny back room that was warmed by a black coal-fired stove.

'A bit daft to bring them out in the rain then,' muttered Aunty Maggie, as she took our coats and gave them a good shake. 'I'll put the kettle on.'

Why wasn't Aunty Maggie happy to see us? She would soon cheer up when she heard we had won the pools. Perhaps Mum would buy her something special. On the bus Mum had pointed out the house we would be moving to. It was very large and we would all be able to have a bedroom each. There was a big garden with lots of flowers at the back and Margaret and I would have a bike. And I was definitely going to be allowed to get a horse. In fact I could probably have two! This had been my dream forever. I loved horses. I had once been allowed to have a ride at the funfair on a Shetland pony and had fallen hopelessly in love with it. Since then I had been horse mad. I painted and drew horses continually, longed for a *Pony Annual* every Christmas and played horses in the garden with Margaret. We had a stable each where we kept them. My favourite was a golden palomino named Champion. We would build jumps for us to ride the horses over. I almost always had a clear round, but Margaret often got faults for knocking the jumps down. The horses were in reality just sticks, but to us they each had a name, colour and personality and we loved them – so much so that once when my brother Peter had come out into the garden to play with us and had accidentally broken one of the sticks, I was heartbroken. I cried my eyes out while Peter tried to console me.

'It's only a stick,' he said. Little did he know that he had just killed Blaze, my second favourite horse!

This time it would be different. I was going to get a real horse now. I couldn't wait. The excitement was running off my skin like the raindrops. Margaret and I were given a biscuit and a drink of milk while Mum and Aunty Maggie had their tea.

'Yes, eight draws – all came up,' Mum said happily to Aunty Maggie. 'Only problem is that we won't get the money for a while. It takes time you see, to get it sorted out.'

I looked up and saw a strange look cross my auntie's face. She didn't look very pleased at our good fortune. In fact, she looked rather resigned and serious.

'I haven't got any spare money Flo,' she said firmly.

Mum's face took on the pinched look that I had seen before. It usually meant she was going into one of her moods. Her eyes would change too, and become more distant and worried look-ing. 'Just until the winnings come through,' she said, but Aunty Maggie was shaking her head.

She went over to the mantelpiece and took down one of several tins. Each was labelled differently: 'electric', 'gas', 'fares' and so on. The one that she reached for said 'food'. She took it off the shelf and handed Mum some money from inside.

'I don't want it back, Flo, but I haven't got any more.' She then went over to the kitchen cupboard and filled a bag with an assortment of tins and packets. These she also handed over to Mum.

Mum looked down sadly as she took the bag. 'Time to go,' she called to us and home we went.

Through the years of my childhood Aunty Maggie was a stoic support for Mum and us and I don't know what we would have done without her.

By the time we got home that afternoon, Mum's mood had changed. She hadn't said much on the bus, but instead had looked out of the window as if she could see something we couldn't. She didn't talk about winning the pools anymore that day, so neither did we.

I would see that sad, faraway look often on my Mum's face throughout my childhood, but it wasn't until I was a mother myself that I actually saw her cry.

7

Overcrowding

One day Mum told us that Michael was coming home!

'Is he going to live at our house?' I asked.

'Yes and he's bringing Isobel with him.'

'Is Isobel our sister?' Margaret whispered to me.

'No, she got married to Michael,' I said knowledgably, 'and guess what? She's going to have a baby!' At this news Margaret jumped up and down; she always loved playing babies best of all. I didn't let her play that game often because I thought it was boring. I liked action games where we would explore unknown territories or come across a band of renegade Indians.

'Will the baby live here as well?' she asked excitedly.

'Yes in yours and Josie's room.'

Margaret's look of excitement now became one of perplexity. 'But where will we sleep?'

I was relishing my superior knowledge now and took great pains to explain what was going to happen. The only reason I knew was that I had overheard an argument the night before between Aunty and Mum. I had crept out of bed to go to the toilet and had heard Mum talking downstairs.

'Tell your aunt that we're going to have to move the settee round to the other side so we can open it our more easily.'

I heard Aunty sniff loudly.

Then I heard Pat's voice saying: 'Michael and Isobel will need the back bedroom.'

'What are you talking about?' Aunty spat back.

My stomach lurched.

'Tell your aunt that Kathleen and Margaret are going to sleep in the bed settee with me.' Mum's voice had taken on a prim and proper air now.

I heard something being slammed down hard.

Aunty's voice got louder. 'I'm bloody well fed up with this!' She was shouting now. 'How am I supposed to get ready for work in the mornings with them all 'anging round the place?'

'Well they're coming here and that's that,' Mum retorted. She didn't often challenge Aunty. Aunty had a ferocious temper and we seemed to spend our lives avoiding awakening it. I was frightened by Mum's tone of voice and the fact that she wasn't backing down.

'Well you can sodding well *all* get out then,' Aunty retorted. 'And good riddance. P'raps I'll get a bit of peace then!' I heard a noise of something landing with a crash. Marion, Marge and Mary had all crept out of the bedroom they shared with Aunty. We huddled silently on the landing listening to the commotion below. I held my breath, hoping Aunty would calm down and stop shouting at Mum. Aunty slammed out of the room and stamped up the stairs; we slunk in the bathroom doorway as she charged into her bedroom. It was then that I noticed little Margaret had crept out to join us and was standing trembling, hanging on to my arm.

'It's all right,' I whispered, 'they've finished now.'

I always had to pretend to be brave for Margaret's sake. I was the big sister. I would always look after her, even when inside I was quaking with my own fears.

Mum got her way that time. Michael and Isobel did come to live with us for a while until their first daughter Vicky was born and they were given an army flat in Woolwich. How we all fitted into that house is completely beyond me now: Michael and Isobel in the back bedroom, Aunty, Marion, Marge and Mary in the big bedroom, Peter in the box room, Mum, Margaret and I on the bed settee in the kitchen and Pat in the front room. Poor Josie had to sleep in the tiny narrow hallway on a camp bed covered with coats as there were no spare blankets.

I needed the toilet one night, and was gently trying to squeeze past her little bed. As I began to make my way upstairs I stopped.

'Do you like sleeping out here?' I asked her innocently. 'Don't you feel cold?'

'No, not really.' She laughed. 'Well, maybe just a little bit – go on up you go.'

I stood watching her for a moment, then feeling the draughty fingers of cold from the front door chill my legs and feet, ran to the toilet as fast as I could before hurrying back to the warmth of my bed, and Margaret and Mum, my living hot-water bottles.

Of course that was before the Peter problem happened.

Mum was always exasperated by Peter. He refused to conform and follow the rules like the rest of us. He often teased us younger children.

'Give me your hand,' he commanded.

I trustingly obeyed.

'Here's the tree,' he pointed to my upturned palm, 'see here are the swings' (pointing to the base of my thumb) 'and look,' he spat into my hand, 'there's the pond!'

I screamed. 'Yuk! You're disgusting!'

'Peter, what are you doing to those children?' Mum would shout.

He'd just laugh as he ran out of the door.

Another time Mum had ordered him to take me for a walk. I don't know how old I was, but must have been quite young.

'Now make sure you keep an eye on her, and don't let her wander off,' Mum instructed. 'Now why are you taking your bike?' she shouted after us as Peter led me down the path. 'Don't you go putting her on the crossbar, she might fall!'

As soon as we were round the corner and out of sight, Peter lifted me up onto the crossbar.

'But Mummy says you're not to.'

'Oh don't worry about that,' Peter said and off we flew. As the wind blew into my face and I screamed with joy, I loved my brother even more than before.

I didn't understand why, but it seemed that Mum had not lived in Valence Avenue much when he, Mary, Marge and Marion had been little children. Certainly she never held, kissed or cuddled any of these 'middle' children the way she did Margaret and me. Life in our house was always chaotic, and she would send them out at any opportunity. Occasionally they would be made to take Margaret and I along. I clearly remember their annoyance when they had to take us to Sunday Mass, and can remember wondering why they didn't want us to go with them.

Peter was always going missing. He would disappear for days sometimes, even when he was still quite young. 'He's gone to find his father in Ireland,' Aunty would say, and Mum would ignore her and look the other way.

Aunty had always favoured Peter, probably because Mum had left him in the care of her and Granny from when he was quite small. He was like her own child, and she certainly treated him differently from the rest of us. She would always stick up for him against Mum and take his side in any conflict, and there was plenty of opportunity for that.

Now he had grown up from a scruffy bedraggled little boy into a handsome young man with a pretty large local female following. One Friday afternoon when Peter was about seventeen, there had been a flurry of activity all day. As Catholics, we were not allowed to eat meat on Friday so if Mum had enough money we would sometimes have fish and chips for dinner. This usually meant that Aunty would have fish and chips and the rest of us would share several bags of chips and maybe a wally or two – a large pickled gherkin – or a piece of cod roe. On this particular Friday I remember Mary, Marge and Marion were already home from school and we were waiting for my older sisters Pat and Josie to get back from work.

'Put the kettle on, the girls will be home soon,' was a familiar refrain from my mum. You could almost set your watch by it, twenty past five every weekday. Today though there was something different. Mum seemed agitated, and we had been made to 'clean up'. Those two simple words always struck dread into our hearts. Clearing up was not easy in our house. There were too many people and too much furniture and there was far too little space. Over time the house had become more and more cluttered, which resulted in it becoming more and more untidy and ultimately very dirty. We had a large settee across the corner in the kitchen. This was quite old and had become saggy with constant use. To make it more comfortable, Mum would pile newspaper under the seat cushions. These would periodically slide out on to the floor and have to be pushed back under. There was also a gap at the back of the settee where it crossed the corner. We thought this was extremely useful, as whenever we had to tidy up the kitchen we children would just throw everything behind the settee into the yawning gap. The problem was that every now and again the gap filled up and began to overflow. That morning Mum had suddenly announced, 'We'll have to pull out the settee.' That struck terror into our hearts. I hated those times. You never knew what you were going to find. There would be some old friends of course, like the odd toy that had been lost, or a friendly forgotten sweet still in its sticky paper bag, but mostly there would be less welcome finds, such as pieces of mouldy food, crusts of bread, dirty clothes and other items of detritus that had accumulated. Worst of all, though, were the silverfish. These little creatures seemed always to be present. They sound so pretty, don't they? But I hated them. They would slither so quickly that I would just catch them out of the corner of my eye, them and their friends the woodlice. The room was eventually tidied and cleaned to Mum's satisfaction. Pat and Jo had arrived home, tea had been made and poured, but there was a tense atmosphere in the house, which wasn't helped by Aunty's arrival at six. An air of expectancy hung over everyone. We were hungry but didn't dare to mention food. Suddenly there was a loud knock on the door.

As Mum stomped out to answer it, Pat turned her chair, which was directly in front of the television, so that her back was set to the rest of the room. Josie hovered around getting out cups and saucers that I didn't even know existed. Plates of sandwiches appeared, which was also very unusual. The only sandwiches I remember having were those that we took when we went on outings, which were usually sweaty and soggy. Mum came through the door leading a woman and a man, closely followed by Peter and his girlfriend Linda.

'Go and play you two,' said Mum, shushing Margaret and me out of the room, 'Marge, take them upstairs will you? And Marion, you go too.' We dutifully did as we were told until we got to the top of the stairs, where Marion and Marge stopped and knelt down to try to listen.

'You two go in the bedroom,' said Marion.

'But I want to hear!' I grumbled.

'Go in the bedroom and shut up,' said Marge. 'Mum will tell you off if she catches you listening.'

'Well, you're listening too!' I said as I was bundled roughly through the doorway. It was no good though, once in the bedroom it became impossible to hear what was going on downstairs. The man and woman seemed to stay for ages, but it was probably no more than half an hour. We didn't get any visitors at our house, apart from family and the tally men, so this was very unusual.

It wasn't long after this that Peter and Linda got married in a register office. Linda had their first daughter six months later. They were still both just seventeen years old when they moved with their new baby into the box room, which now made eight adults, five children and two babies living in a three-bedroom house with just one tiny scullery for cooking and laundry, one kitchen to live and eat in and one toilet and bathroom between us.

8

Feast or Famine

Food played a big part in my childhood. Mum definitely signed up to the feast or famine philosophy of eating. She was a good cook and could conjure up amazing meals within our limited means when she was in the mood. Roast breast of lamb was a favourite, and I learnt to cook this for the family from a very young age when Mum was unwell and unable to come downstairs. I would run up and down to the bedroom picking up instructions from Mum. 'If it's getting too brown turn the gas down to number 5' or 'put the potatoes into the oven now and turn the gas up to 7.' This would go on throughout the cooking period so that the dinner was all ready by the time Aunty came home from work at six o'clock. Of course my cooking generated a lot of washing up. That was supposed to be Margaret's job, but inevitably as she was only a little girl it built up and the scullery was always a complete mess by the time dinner was served out. Pots, pans, dishes, plates, spoons would spill out of the old Butler sink, over the wooden draining board and on to the cupboard shelf. All surfaces would be covered in a mound of clutter that was always left to the twins to deal with later.

Another more unusual favourite was curry. Now I know that curry is commonplace right across the country today, but in the late 1950s and early 60s it was considered a very exotic dish and none of the other families I knew ate it. I suppose the reason we did was because our Granny was born in India, where her father was stationed. He had fled Ireland to escape from the potato famine in the 1850s and spent the majority of his life serving in the British army. We had curry usually once a week, cooked in a huge metal pot on the gas stove. The memory of the smell of curry powder frying with onion and meat still makes my taste buds tingle. Mum would throw in copious amounts of chopped up vegetables, and leave it to simmer for most of the afternoon. The aroma would fill the house and Margaret and I would stare longingly at the bubbling concoction, desperate for it to be ready, mouths watering, tummies rumbling. We would often have it cold for breakfast the next day, when it seemed to taste even better.

Marion, Marge and Mary did most of the household jobs when I was very young. Pat and Josie were absolved as they went to work and earned wages. Aunty never did household chores for the same reason and Margaret and I were too young to do them properly, although we liked to try.

Over the years we all learnt to cook. Mum taught us how to behead and gut mackerel, scrape the scales off the skin, and dip it in white flour ready for frying; how to rub flour and fat together to make smooth creamy-coloured pastry, used to top rich-smelling beef and kidney pies. We would help Mum to concoct aromatic stews and soups, my favourite being a rich salty pea and ham soup. Those were the good times of course, when there was enough money, but there were also too many days when there was no money at all. Those were the days when we ate a plate of boiled potatoes, or a bowl of porridge, or a lump of suet pudding for our dinner. Once, when there was no money for the gas meter, my sisters had to cook the porridge in a big pot on the coal fire.

'I don't want it,' I cried, pushing the bowl away and refusing to eat the sooty grey slush that it contained.

'Don't be silly,' Marion said, crossly. It had been a long day and Mum was in bed ill. The ice was starting to form inside the windows upstairs; it was a bitterly cold winter and the only warm room was the kitchen, with the coal fire scorching the knickers drying in front of it. They were poked through the wire of the fireguard, and the rest of the wet clothes hung from the picture rail that ran around the walls. There was a damp feel to the air and it must have stunk of coal and cigarette smoke, but you don't notice the smell when you live with it. As a teacher I could always tell which children lived in families with smokers. Their book bags always had that same smell.

Mum had been unwell and so the twins had been kept off school to look after us. We must have been a handful, especially along with all the other household duties they would have been required to do.

Seeing my sulky face, Marge tried an alternative tactic. 'Don't be silly. Don't you know that porridge is best when it's cooked on the fire?'

I began to consider this information.

They ate their porridge with manic enthusiasm. 'Mmmm yummy! This is sooo nice,' Marion mumbled through mouthfuls of thick porridge.

'I want some!' I said, reaching out for my bowl and wolfing down the whole lot. The problem was from that day onwards I always refused to eat porridge unless it was cooked on the fire, which exasperated my family on many occasions.

The gas and electric meters were hungry monsters in our house. Mum would feed them with shillings whenever she could but they were never satisfied and cold food and darkness were their cries for more. Every three months the electric man or the gasman would come to empty the meter. This was a bit of a red-letter day as because of the way the meters were calibrated households always overpaid, so there would usually be a sizable rebate to come. Margaret and I would wait expectantly in the kitchen while the meter was emptied. Then there would be a knock on the kitchen door that would indicate the gas or electric man was ready to go. Outside in the scullery, underneath where the gas and electricity meters were screwed to the wall, would be a pile of shilling coins sparkling with promise. This would definitely be a banana roll day if we were lucky!

Of course there were also the desperate days when the meter would have been broken into and there would be no money inside. This happened more than once, and I can remember the meter man questioning Mum sharply. We never knew how those bad people got in to take the money, or how they managed to break into the meter without Mum knowing.

We had no fridge when I was a child. Perishable foods, meat, fish tended to be bought on the day they were going to be used, or certainly not long before that. Items such as eggs, cheese and milk would be stored in the huge larder, which was built into the wall next to the front door. It had stone walls and was very dark with just a tiny ventilation grill at the back. Food did keep quite well for most of the year but in the summer Mum would try to keep the milk cool by putting it in a bowl of cold water. When Isobel came to live at our house the occupants of the larder slowly began to change. The smells were different now. Strange-looking sausages appeared and were hung in there. These added a new aroma, rich and spicy. Isobel showed Margaret and I how to eat melon, even sucking the seeds, splitting them with our teeth to chew out the insides. She also made tortilla with pota-toes and eggs, turning these simple ingredients into a feast of flavour, which we devoured with relish.

The house was even more chaotic now than it had been before. Meal times were complicated, and sleeping arrange-ments were even more so. We now shared the bed settee with Mum in the kitchen, which meant that we stayed up very late every night. When the bed was put down, Margaret and I would snuggle up on each side of Mum. I remember so clearly how Mum would unfold her arms so we could rest our heads there. She always did this even when I shared her bed as an older child in the box room. It must have made her arms ache, but she never moved me away.

One bonus of having both Michael and Isobel and Peter and Linda living with us was that they both had tiny babies. Once they were born, Vicky in December and Carolyn in January, my brothers' search for a place of their own began in earnest. This meant that Margaret and I spent even longer periods of time away from school. We were allowed to play with the cast-off bottles, dummies, nappies and other baby paraphernalia. Mum even showed us how to 'swaddle' our dolls in some old material she found for us. Margaret was in her element.

Soon after the babies were born, my brothers both managed to find flats of their own. Michael was given an army flat in Woolwich and Peter found a small flat on the ground floor of a converted house not far from my Aunty Maggie in Seven Kings. Mum would often take us to visit them but most often we went to see Michael, or rather Isobel and baby Vicky. The journey from Dagenham to Woolwich seemed never ending. We would walk to the bus stop to catch the 62 and then get the 106 from Barking. For me, the journey was fraught with danger. Would people look at us? Would they say something horrible to Mum? Would they shout at us and would Mum have to shout at them? There had already been so many times in my young life where exactly that had happened. Everything could turn on a sixpence, and happiness could descend into chaos with a single look, word or action.

There was one time when Margaret and I had been playing happily upstairs. Mum was just about to serve up dinner. It was one of the 'plenty' days. We were having meat pudding. The savoury smells from downstairs were wafting up to us and our tummies were getting excited at the thought of the feast to come. Aunty, Pat and Jo were home and Marion and Marge were doing their homework on their laps at the top of the stairs, under the landing light.

'Shush,' Marion complained to us. She always had the hardest homework as she'd won a scholarship to a very posh grammar school in Hackney called St Victoire's. When the time had come for her to start she still hadn't got her special grey uniform and the tailored stripy blazer that was a requirement. The girls who were there on a scholarship had been sent grant cheques to pay for their uniform, and so they were to collect them direct from the school office. When her first day came she was called with the group of three other scholarship girls to go and collect it. When she came forward the lady looked down through her glasses at the label on top of the neatly folded pile.

'I'm sorry, dear,' she said kindly but with a knowing look in her eye, 'I'm afraid you can't take yours today; it hasn't been paid for yet.' Marion slunk back to class with a dreadful dawning awareness that tomorrow she would be the only girl in the class with the wrong clothes. When she came home and told us, Mum was furious.

'What do you mean she wouldn't let you have your uniform?' she said angrily. 'Just you wait; I'll write you a letter.'

It had taken more than a letter, Mum made many visits to the school and many protestations to the head teacher before the school accepted that the grant cheque had never arrived and Marion was allowed her uniform.

Today she had brought it home, and so was determined that this was a new start. Tomorrow she would look like the other girls, she would have done all of her homework and she would be able to walk into school without feeling that everyone was looking at her. She had even saved her bus fare by walking the three miles from the station so that she could buy some celebration sweets on the way home. It was going to be a good day.

Suddenly there was a sharp, loud *bang bang* at the front door. When Mum opened it the shouting started.

'I want me bleeding money!'

I recognised the man from next door. Margaret and I sat huddled together on the stairs, terrified. Mum was soon joined by Aunty and Pat and they all began to shout together. Then the man's wife Vera arrived on the doorstep.

'You promised! It's been over free bleeding weeks naw!' she bellowed and began swinging for Mum. The noise reached a crescendo and suddenly Mum pitched forward, clutching her chest.

Aunty let out a cry. 'Flo, oh no! Flo are you awright?' Pat supported Mum, who looked as though she was going to pass out, but the shouting carried on. I wanted to run to Mum, but was holding tightly on to Margaret who was now crying.

'It's all right. It's all right. It's all right,' I kept repeating, while I rocked back and forth, feeling as though my limbs were turning to liquid, and my tummy sinking in on itself. Aunty gave a huge push and managed to slam the door on the man and woman.

'Flo, Florrie,' she kept repeating as Mum slowly started to recover herself. Aunty was panicking as she always did. 'Paddy, get the doctor! Flo, Flo, oh my gawd, you awright Flo?'

Pat calmly led Mum into the kitchen, sat her down and then went to put the kettle on. We stayed on the stairs trembling for a while and then crept down and peeped into the kitchen; seeing Mum sitting on her usual chair by the side of the fire, we rushed over to cuddle her. Marion and Marge had stayed at the top of the stairs but now made their way quietly down, their eyes big and round. No one enjoyed their meat pudding that night.

9

Margaret

Margaret had stopped eating. She was getting thinner and thinner and deep black rings appeared underneath her eyes. Mum was beside herself with worry.

'Come on now, have a drop of tomato soup just for me.' Margaret turned her head away. Nothing anyone offered her could tempt her to eat. She was six years old but looked about four as she began to shrink and disappear before us. Her eyes, always big, now took on the appearance of dark brown saucers set in her bleached white face. Her hair had always been much darker than mine, and this seemed to exaggerate her sunken features.

Mum took her to see Dr Stanton. We sat in the crowded waiting room with its cream-coloured, sterile walls. The chairs were hard and were lined up close together in rows so that there wasn't enough room to move between them easily without having to push past people. I kept close to Mum but noticed one of the girls from my class at school just across the other side of the room with her mum. She had a big handkerchief held to her nose and kept coughing. We seemed to be there for ages when at last the voice that had been calling the patients one by one suddenly called out 'Margaret Stevens', so Mum got up and we walked towards the doctor's room. As we passed by the girl from my class, she said in a loud voice, 'Why is your sister called Margaret Stevens instead of Margaret Coates?'

As Mum pulled me forward, I turned and whispered, 'That's our special doctor's name.'

I thought everyone had a special name they used just for when they visited the doctor's; that was what Mum had told us. I wondered why this girl looked at me in such a quizzical manner.

Mum knocked on the door and we went into the room where the doctor sat smoking a cigarette.

'Now then, what's the matter with you, young lady, worrying your Mummy like this?'

Margaret just stared down at the floor. She attempted to bury her head in Mum's ample bosom but Mum turned her back towards the doctor again so he could examine her.

'Well young lady, you look fine to me.' The doctor smiled at Mum. 'I think she just needs fattening up!'

'But she won't eat, Doctor. She just turns her nose up at everything I give her.'

'Well let's give her a tonic and some Senokot granules in case she's constipated – that can sometimes affect children in this way. If she's not any better by next week bring her back.' We left the surgery and walked slowly home.

Margaret wasn't any better next week. Mum had duly cajoled and encouraged her to take the Senokot granules, which had to be mixed with water to make a muddy brown liquid drink. As Margaret would try to swallow it down she would retch and splutter. It was awful to watch and quite often I would hide away with my eyes screwed shut and my hands over my ears so that I didn't have to listen.

Today Mum had bought a special 'variety pack' of cereals to tempt her. This was made up of eight individual packs and was, Mum said, very expensive. Margaret pecked at a bowl of Ricicles, but she didn't really eat very much at all. I sat opposite her at the square wooden table, eating my cereal with enthusiasm, scraping up the last of the milk with my spoon. The kitchen wasn't a large room but it was stuffed with furniture. Apart from the big old wooden table there was a settee and three armchairs: one for Aunty, one for Mum and one for Pat. They had wooden arms and legs and there was a huge, ornate sideboard across one corner. Fitted carpets were still considered a luxury and our kitchen floor was covered in oil cloth, which was a bit like linoleum or vinyl flooring. I was always fascinated by the multitude of tiny circular indentations that were made by the stilettos my older sisters wore, and would sometimes trace their shape with my fingers. There was also a big rectangular grey rug in the middle of the floor which, even though it was quite threadbare and worn, made the room feel warmer. Today, as it was winter, wet washing was hung around the room to dry. Margaret's spoon dropped onto the table suddenly and it was as though she didn't have the energy to pick it back up. Mum stood up and carried her over to the settee – it was too cold for her to go upstairs. She tucked a coat over her, and put a shovel full of coal on the fire.

I was lonely without Margaret to play with. We were only eighteen months apart in age and had always been very close, but now that she was ill I began to be a more solitary child. I had always enjoyed reading, and would find books around the house – often unreturned remnants of my siblings' library visits. The whole family were now blacklisted, so although Margaret and I were sometimes taken to the library, we could never join or take books out.

I don't ever remember learning to read; I just seemed to be able to do it one day. I do know that I was reading quite well before I started school so must only have been about four or five. Books were very important in my life. There were plenty around the house, even though many of them were for adults.

When Margaret was first ill she wasn't yet able to read, so that became my job. Over the years I became adept at reading and sharing books with her. I wasn't scared or nervous when I read aloud to Margaret in the little bedroom she now shared with Josie. It was really quite cosy in there. Josie had stuck lots of posters of Elvis Presley on the walls and she kept the room tidy. Mum sometimes even lit a little fire in the fireplace on the coldest days if we had enough coal. We read the Katy books, *Little Women* and *Jo's Boys*; we devoured quantities of Enid Blyton and cried over *Black Beauty*. We explored some old poetry books that we found, and I sang the words to old songs and tunes that we half remembered. I would like to pretend that I did all of this because I was such a kind sister, but that wasn't the truth. I did it because I was tormented with jealousy. Margaret was the centre of attention. She was tiny, vulnerable and listless and so my Mum, Aunty and all of my sisters did their best to cheer her up. This meant that she got special little treats, one of which was a box of chocolate kittens each individually wrapped, which I coveted. I longed to be 'special' and wished many times that it was me that was ill, but I hid my feelings from everyone. The best way for me to get the attention I craved was to be the kind big sister. So I was.

Margaret was ill for several years. Over that time she had periods when she seemed to get better for a while, and things would be almost back to normal. We would play out in the garden again and get up to our usual mischief, but then she would suddenly go back downhill and slip back into a state of decline. Her body took on the appearance of an undernourished waif and Aunty would joke, 'Don't stand behind the lamppost or we won't see you.'

We started calling her 'Maggie Aggie Baggy Pants' and that name stuck with her until adulthood.

When you live with someone and see them every day you aren't always aware of their decline but looking back at photos it is clear that she was shrinking away. The doctor couldn't find anything wrong with her and I suppose these days she may have been diagnosed with an eating disorder or a more general 'failure to thrive'. The causes and symptoms were varied and sometimes vague, but for Margaret I believe it was a kind of saddening.

10

A Family Christmas

It would soon be Christmas. The preparations were always very exciting. Mum would buy us some little 'make your own' Christmas cards which we would spend hours colouring and spreading with glue and glitter. We would make one each for everyone in the family, taking great care with each of them and carefully writing: 'To ... Merry Christmas from Kathleen and Margaret xxx'. We were also allowed to make paper chains from strips of paper – long looping strings of colour to hang around the walls and from the ceiling. Then the most exciting day would arrive and Pat would go to the market near where she worked in Poplar to get the Christmas tree. It would be placed in the same corner every year and we would cover it in all the old decorations. We would sing Christmas carols, and Mum would let us dance around the room like angels, and act out the Christmas story for our sisters.

On Christmas Eve the greengrocer would deliver a big box of fruit and vegetables which would include things we rarely saw other than at Christmas. There would be tangerines, oranges, grapes and bananas, all in copious quantities. The smell of the oranges would drive us wild but there was a strict rule that nothing could be tasted until Christmas morning. One year I gave way to my greed and crept downstairs to where the fruit box was standing in the passage and took a tangerine. It was the sweetest fruit that I have ever tasted, but the guilt that followed the eating was very bitter indeed and it was a sin I never confessed but certainly never repeated!

On this particular Christmas morning my excitement was uncontrollable. As my eyes snapped open it was still dark outside. Mum never went to bed on Christmas Eve. She always dozed in her armchair so that she could keep an eye on the turkey and the Christmas candle that had to be lit at midnight and would burn for twenty-four hours.

Margaret had joined me in bed with her pillowcase and we emptied them with gusto. We looked longingly at the sweets and fruit, but didn't eat any. We would be going to Christmas Morning Mass soon and we weren't allowed to eat before receiving Holy Communion. Mum never came to Mass but Aunty did. She attended every Sunday but would sit the other side of the church from us children. Perhaps she needed the peace!

Our tummies would rumble all through Christmas Mass, but we knew that Mum would have slipped some Quality Street into our pockets to eat on the way home and this always got us through.

We always had turkey, and the smell of it roasting in the oven when we got back from Mass sent our taste buds into overdrive. When Pat picked it up from the butchers there was always a concern that it wouldn't fit in the oven. We had to have a big bird as there were so many of us to feed and it usually weighed about 27 or 28lb. We would hold our breath while Mum covered it in streaky bacon rashers to keep it moist and slid it carefully into the oven. There was always a sigh of relief to see it actually fit! She would never cook the stuffing inside. We always had Paxo sage and onion and it would be cooked in a separate dish on Christmas Day. Christmas dinner was the only day in the year that I can remember us all sitting down together to eat. This was a huge logistical feat. The big table would be pulled into the centre of the room and we would have a tablecloth! The armchairs and settee around the edges would be joined by additional chairs retrieved from around the house. Mum would usually sit at the head of the table near the kitchen door so that she could get in and out to the scullery where the cooking was done. The rest of us would fit where we could. There was always a rush not to sit in front of the coal fire, as you would start to feel your back scorching halfway through the meal. We had crackers on the table which would be pulled early on so that we could don the paper hats from inside. Pat would always carve the turkey before we sat to eat, and the dog would sit hopefully next to her. We would watch as she carved perfect thin slices of meat, licking the juices from her fingers and occasionally throwing Pongo a piece of the meat as she cut. Josie would put our plates in front of us and then the sliced turkey would be brought in on a dish by Mum joined by a huge tray of crispy roasted potatoes and parsnips. Of course there were always copious quantities of brussels, peas and carrots and a huge jug full to the brim with Bisto gravy. Mum always made her own Christmas pudding, which we would set alight with a drop of Aunty's brandy. Mum never drank alcohol and neither did the rest of us, except for Aunty. At Christmas we did have non alcoholic ginger wine though, which was hot and spicy and singed our throats and was Mum's special favourite.

That year, after the Queen's speech, Pat and Jo announced that they had devised a game called 'The Tomb of Tutankhamun'. We were ushered out of the kitchen into the hallway.

'Stay there and no peeping,' Josie said.

We heard screams and laughter as one by one my big sisters disappeared into the room. Then it went eerily quiet. Margaret and I wriggled with anticipation. It was my turn to go in next. I crept fearfully through the door. The room was dark. The curtains had been closed and the light was off. There was a white sheet draped over one corner of the room and Mum, Aunty and my sisters were sitting round it. Suddenly I heard a voice which sounded a bit like Josie but deeper and much, much scarier.

'This is the tomb of Tutankhamun.' I shivered. 'You must follow the light and bow down and worship him. Go to the white sheet and say three times – "I bow to the tomb of Tutankhamun." '

I giggled nervously. Marge pushed me forward towards the sheet. I followed the light, which was in reality a torch held by one of my sisters behind the sheet. I bowed once and my sisters helped me to say the words. I did the same again and then on the third bow as I lifted my head and continued to follow the light to the top of the sheet, an arm sprang out from behind clutching a big wet sponge which was thrust into my face. I screamed loudly and jumped back to fits of uproarious laughter!

Goodness knows what poor Margaret was thinking when she heard this outside, knowing it was her turn next. I just remember feeling very glad that my turn was over and I would now get to be one of the watchers when she came through the door. Being the older sister had some consolations.

Over the years that game would be repeated every time there was a new addition to the family. Mary, Marge and Marion's boyfriends all had to endure this initiation to the Coates family.

11

Aunty, Mum and the Empty House

'Who's been going through my drawers?' Aunty shouted down. She had just got in from work early as it was a Thursday and she was clearly in one of her worse moods. She had stamped straight up the stairs when she arrived and was now banging around in the bedroom she shared with Marge and Marion. Since Michael and Peter and their wives had found flats of their own, the house was a bit less crowded. Mary and I shared a double bed in the box room, Margaret was in the back bedroom with Josie, and Pat had the front room downstairs all to herself. Mum still slept on the bed settee in the kitchen. She looked a bit worried now and raised her eyes to heaven. While she put the kettle on, we sat quietly, holding our breath to see what would happen next.

Aunty stomped down the stairs.

'Ask your aunt if she wants a cup of tea,' said Mum.

'I don't want no bloody tea – someone's been in my drawers again,' she shouted. She plonked herself down on her chair in the far corner near the window and crossed her legs. I watched nervously as her leg begin to swing agitatedly. This was always a sign that we were in for a stormy time.

Mum went out to the scullery to make the tea, throwing the words over her shoulder: 'No one's been in anyone's drawers.'

Aunty sniffed loudly, which was another sign that she was very cross. Today was rent day. Every fortnight the council man would come to collect the rent. When Granny had died the tenancy had been passed to Aunty as the eldest daughter in the house. This was very lucky for us as it meant that we at least always had a roof over our heads. Aunty had realised long ago that if she were to keep it that way she would need to find a way of paying the rent, as she knew if she left it for Mum to do, the money would disappear before the rent man arrived. Her solution was to give it to one of her friends who lived several houses along. Her name was Mrs Timberlick and we sometimes went with Aunty the night before rent day to take the money along. Mrs Timberlick's house was easy to recognise. Although most of the houses in Valence Avenue were very similar, it was the gardens that set them apart. Mrs Timberlick's had the most beautiful hydrangea bushes tumbling over her front garden, all around the gate and up the path – bluey pink balls of petals which bobbed about when the wind blew through them.

Sadly Aunty's fears for the rent money were well founded. Mum had a habit of acquiring money when she was desperate, and not worrying too much where it came from. There had been many incidents over the years that had caused arguments and tears in the family, and they were almost always about money. Every Monday before Peter had got married, Mum would take Peter's only suit to the pawn shop. She would get a few pennies for it and then she wouldn't give poor Peter the pawn ticket until he had handed over the majority of his wages on a Friday, after which he would then have to go and redeem it before he could go out with his friends at the weekend. It would drive him mad with anger and there were bitter arguments between him and Mum which often ended with Mum threatening him with a saucepan or some other kitchen implement. Peter was so annoyed once that he put a bolt and padlock on his bedroom door, but that didn't really help as it soon got mysteriously broken off.

The pawn shop was in Green Lane, which was about twenty minutes' walk away. The entrance to the pawn shop was down a short alleyway, which was quite dark, almost as though it were hiding its secrets. It had a sign outside with three balls hanging, which fascinated me. Mum would usually leave us waiting outside while she went in, but occasionally we would be allowed inside. It seemed to be full of objects of every shape and size, including big piles of clothes all laying on top of each other. It also had a musky, mothball kind of smell which stung my nose and made me want to sneeze. I always wondered how the man could see what he was doing as it was so gloomy in there. I don't think Mum ever got very much for the suit, but when you have a huge family of mouths to feed every little bit extra helps.

Mum was always looking for ways to get more money. Although she was able to claim social security, it wasn't a huge amount, and it certainly didn't allow for any extras. When the lady came from the social, Margaret and I were always sent upstairs. We would desperately try to hear what was being said, but we never knew what took place during those meetings.

Many of the items of furniture around the house had mysteriously disappeared over the years. One by one anything that was worth anything had been sold. Granny would have been sad to see her piano disappear from the front room, which used to be the parlour. Aunty Rene, one of Mum's older sisters, had been a really accomplished pianist and the whole family had nice singing voices. Of course in days before television singing around the piano had been a favourite family occupation, but that was all finished now. The piano had long gone, along with the wind-up gramophone and the pretty china that had belonged to Granny.

The only things left were bits and pieces of furniture that we had been given or found. Mum never really bought anything for herself except for her cigarettes. Her clothes were always poor quality and old, and her shoes were worn and usually in need of repair. She wore slippers most of the time, and if she went out would wear a headscarf tied tightly under her chin. By the time my memories began, the constant worry and stress that must have made up her life had started to take their toll, and she looked older than her years. Her hair was silvery grey and had begun to thin, but her skin was still as soft as a baby's. I can remember as an adult stroking her arm when she was near the end of her life, and wondering at its smoothness.

One of the ways that Mum managed to provide the things she thought we needed was to get things on 'tick'. This in effect meant buying from a door-to-door salesman, who would encourage Mum to 'have now pay later'. Over the years these debts grew to mammoth proportions, and the weekly problem of deciding who she could pay this week must have been a constant pressure on her. Occasionally there would be a knock at the door and there would be a man with a parcel that would always contain some unnecessary item that we would rush to unwrap. At the time, Margaret and I thought it was wonderful. Looking back, it must have been a kind of addiction for Mum, or an antidote to the dreary monotony and tedium of her life. She always wanted to give us things, to be the gift giver, the supplier of everything wonderful and exciting. The sad thing was that she didn't need to buy anyone's adoration, loyalty and love. She got that for free.

When Mum was cornered by her worries, and I suppose overwhelmed by the trap her life had become, she would sometimes tip over into flight mode. The first time I remember it happening was when she had just got back from the phone box over the road. We didn't have a phone in the house until I was a teenager, but my Mum's sisters did. Aunty often took us with her when she went to phone Aunt Maggie. She would sometimes make us wait outside, but more often we were allowed to squeeze in with her. She would dial the number saying 'RIP rest in peace' and laugh. It was ages before we worked out the reason for this was that Aunty Maggie's code was Rippleway which was abbreviated to RIP. She seemed to talk for an age, and Margaret and I would jiggle and wiggle about getting more and more restless. What did she have to talk about that took so long? Sometimes she would joke to Aunt Mag, 'They're laughing at me these two – saucy monkeys.'

When she was in a good mood she might placate us with the promise of some penny sweets from the sweetshop next to the phone box. There was an exciting array to choose from and we would spend an age on using up our thruppence.

Once Mum came out from the phone box very upset.

'Someone has taken my purse,' she wailed. 'We'll have to go to the Police Station,' and off we trundled to Chadwell Heath.

She was crying desperately as we went inside.

'My purse has been stolen,' she wept to the kindly police officer behind the desk. 'All of my food money was in it,' she continued, only stopping periodically to dab at her eyes, and bend to give us a cuddle, as we had 'caught' her distress and now stood crying too.

'All right madam, try to keep calm now,' the police officer said soothingly, 'then perhaps we can try to help you.'

'I went to phone my sister,' she told him, 'and must have mistakenly left my purse in the phone box, then when I went back,' here she burst into fresh tears, 'when I went back it had gone!'

The police officer lent forward and gave her a fresh hanky.

'There, there madam,' he said. 'Just leave it with us and we'll see what we can do.'

He wrote down the details and promised Mum that they would do their best to find the culprit, but Mum could not be consoled.

'You don't understand,' she whispered through her tears. 'That was all the money I had for the children's food. What am I going to do now?'

I don't know quite what happened next, but Mum was eventually handed an envelope, and she thanked the police officer profusely, and cheered up considerably as we walked all the way back home.

'You see,' she told us, 'the police are so kind, they always help you when you're in trouble.'

There were also times when she went to the phone box on her own. Once when she returned, her mood was black and bleak. She had that same look in her eyes again, the one that made her look like a different person, the look that took her away from us. Josie had got in from work and gone straight up to bed. She often did this; in fact she spent long periods of time in her room, listening to music on her little radio and writing stuff down in little notebooks. Pat was sitting in front of the television and Marge and Marion were trying to do their homework on the stairs before they were asked to help out. Mary had gone round to her friend Helen's house straight from school and Margaret and I were playing out in the garden. It was the beginning of the autumn and was starting to get dark and a bit chilly. Mum blew in through the front door and we heard her shouting at the twins: 'Where's Mary?'

'She's gone round to Helen's,' one of them answered.

'What on earth for? I need her here – Marion go round and get her now.'

'I can't Mum I've got to finish this homework for tomorrow.'

Mum stomped through to the back door. 'You two inside now,' she said roughly. We looked at each other; we weren't ready to stop playing so we just carried on. 'I said now!' she shouted. This was unusual; Mum rarely shouted at us and never with so little cause.

'Marion, Marge get down here,' she repeated, 'I want Mary home now.' The twins descended the stairs resentfully. They grumbled their way out of the house to walk the ten minutes round to Helen's house. By this time Margaret and I had come inside and were snivelling at having to leave our game. As they left, Mum walked into the kitchen and looked around her. Aunty wasn't yet home from work, the room was untidy and cold and there was no dinner cooking; the damp washing was hung around the walls as it had been raining earlier and she hadn't been able to put it on the line in the garden.

Pat murmured, 'Don't shout at the littluns. They're upset now.'

Mum spun round and snapped: 'I've had enough. I'm going out.'

'Where are you going?' Pat asked, shocked. Mum didn't usually go anywhere in the evenings unless it was to the phone box and she had just got back from there.

'I don't know, just out.'

Pat's face lost its colour. 'Why? What's wrong?'

Mum moved towards the door. 'I'm fed up, I'm fed up with all of it, and with the lot of you.'

Margaret ran to her and hung on to her coat. 'Mummy, don't go,' she cried, but Mum just shook her off and left, banging the front door behind her.

Margaret broke down in sobs, so I tried to comfort her. 'She'll be back soon,' I promised, but inside I was terrified of what might happen next. Pat went upstairs to talk to Josie and then the twins came back with Mary.

'What's happened?' asked Mary, at which I started crying along with Margaret, because I really didn't know.

Mum storming out become a recurrent theme throughout my childhood, and even though our experience showed us that she would usually return after a few hours, it didn't stop me feeling terrified that this time it would be different and she wouldn't come back. After all, I'd heard stories of how she'd disappeared for weeks at a time when my sisters were young. Sometimes Josie or Pat would go to look for her if she hadn't come back by night-fall. They would usually find her wandering around, or some-times pretending to wait for a bus, just standing at the bus stop smoking and thinking. When she came back, she would be quiet and absent for a while, with that same faraway look in her eyes, but it never lasted long. She always did come back, because I guess by that time she didn't have anywhere else to go.

Mum didn't usually get up to see us off to school in the morn-ing, but one summer morning she was up early and called to us to get out of bed.

'Come on you two, you have to go to school early today.'

We grumbled down the stairs; going to school was bad enough without having to get there early. As we reached the kitchen we were shocked to see Aunty still at home. She usually left for work at Plessey's at about 6.30 each morning so wasn't usually around by the time we rolled out of bed.

'Tell your Aunt that Julie is picking us up in the car at half past,' Mum said. We flicked our eyes at Aunty. We were so used to this way of theirs of talking through us children that we some-times didn't even bother to repeat the words, because it was blatantly obvious that they had heard what each other were saying, but I was shocked. Mum and Aunty *never* went out together.

Aunty sniffed 'Tell your mother that I'm ready now,' and she went out into the passage to get her coat, even though it was promising to be a warm day. We were ushered out of the door even though it was only 8.15 and were left to wonder where they were going that was so important that they were going together – and with our Aunty Maggie's daughter Julie.

Margaret looked at me as we wandered slowly towards Becontree Avenue. 'Where is Mum going today?'

'I don't know. I expect they're going to Aunty Maggie's house.' I didn't really believe that was where they were going; social visiting wasn't something that Mum and Aunty ever did together, and anyway they would have gone on the bus, not been picked up in a car.

'They might be going to the shops,' Margaret suggested as we carried on walking. This again was highly unlikely, as the only shops Mum ever went to were the local ones, or occasionally to Green Lane. She rarely even went as far as Ilford or Barking and again she would have gone by bus. It was a puzzle.

School dragged on throughout that day. I was in junior 4 now and we were knee-deep in spelling tests, comprehension and maths, question after question, tables after tables. Outside the sun was shining, which only heightened our wish to escape. By playtime, when we were released from the confines of the classroom, it was as though the top had come off the pressure cooker. The boys in particular would go wild, tearing madly around the playground.

By the end of the day I had almost forgotten about the puzzle of Mum and Aunty's trip out, so when Margaret mentioned it on our way home, I didn't pay much attention. I was too busy thinking about the homework Miss E had given me, which I really didn't want to do. When we arrived at our front door we gave the usual family knock and waited for Mum to open the door as always.

No one came.

Margaret looked at me worriedly. 'Why isn't Mummy opening the door?'

I knocked again, louder this time, 'She might be upstairs,' I said, trying to hide my concern from Margaret as I always did. Still no reply. I knocked again, and this time we opened the letter box to look inside. Pongo was barking and jumping up at the door but there was no other movement. I waited for a few minutes and then tried once more.

'What shall we do?' Margaret started to cry.

'Don't worry, they'll be home soon.' But it felt strange and uncomfortable to be standing outside our own front door desperate to get in. Suddenly I had an inspiration. 'I know, we can go and knock at Mrs Timberlick's house.' Margaret agreed it was a good plan so off we walked. We opened the front gate and walked up the path. I knocked and waited. We heard a sound from inside and the door slowly opened. 'Hello my dears,' said Mrs Timberlick kindly. 'What's the matter?'

'No one's home,' I answered carefully. The kind old lady ushered us into the front parlour where she told us to sit ourselves down.

'Would you like a drink? Orange squash?' she offered, but we both declined politely even though we were incredibly thirsty. There we sat for what seemed like an age until finally Mrs Timberlick suggested we pop down to see if Mum was home. I held my breath as I knocked on the door and said a little prayer. My prayer was answered. There was Mum, distracted and upset, but not because of us. In fact she hardly seemed to be aware of us as we went inside. There was an air of sadness and silence and Aunty had very red eyes.

Our big sisters had all returned from work and so I went over to Marge and asked 'What's happened?' only to be told, 'Shh, Uncle John has died.' This sounded very sad, but I had never met Uncle John. He was Mum and Auntie's oldest brother and lived in Birmingham.

I had heard Aunty talk about him from time to time, but Mum always looked away or changed the subject when his name was mentioned, as though she were ashamed. We weren't allowed to ever show our feelings, or to talk about them either, so the rest of the evening was spent with very little being said, but a lot being felt by both Mum and Aunty. Every so often I would catch Aunty looking over at Mum with what looked like an angry look in her eyes.

It wasn't until many years later I found out why.

12

The Wages Mystery

When I was about seven my sister Mary got a job in the General Post Office (GPO). She was to be trained to be a telephonist. None of my sisters had been able to stay on at school past the age of fifteen as their wages were needed as a contribution to the household budget; none of them ever complained but it must have been hard. Mary was always very popular and attracted lots of attention from the local boys; she sometimes flirted back but she was never serious about any of them. Then she came home from work one day looking very excited and just a bit flushed.

'I've got a date,' I heard her whisper to Marge and Marion. There was only a year difference between Mary and the twins, so they often confided in each other.

'Who with?' Marion asked.

'A young bloke who works opposite me in London. He looks quite sweet.'

'What's his name?'

'Dave,' Mary replied a little dreamily.

Suddenly Marge put her hand over her mouth, 'Oh God, are you going to tell Mum?'

'Course not,' said Mary, 'she doesn't need to know. I'll tell her I'm going to the pictures with Helen.' Mary had been friends with Helen since primary school. She also came from a big Irish family, and Mary would often go round to her house to whisper and giggle about grown-up stuff.

'Do you think you'll get away with it?' asked Marion.

'I don't know but I'm going to try.'

I was outraged! How dare they do things that would upset

Mum? I wondered if I should tell Mum, but decided against it. It might make her go off again.

Mary and Dave began courting and Mum seemed to accept it quite well. This was very exciting for Margaret and I because Dave had a motorbike and sometimes he would drive it to our house from his parents' home in Leytonstone.

One night Mary told us that Dave had a surprise for us. When he knocked on the door, and Mary came running downstairs to open it, we peaked through the banisters to watch them. Dave looked up and said, 'Do you two want to come for a ride?'

We looked at each other in disbelief. *A ride?*

Mary laughed. 'Get your coats on then; it will feel cold.'

Mum shouted out from the kitchen: 'What are you doing?'

'We're just taking the littluns for a ride round the corner.'

'Oh no you're not,' Mum said firmly. 'They're too little; they might fall off.'

'It's okay, Mrs Coates,' Dave reassured her, 'I've put the side-car on.'

When we got outside it was dark and a bit windy, and a few drops of rain were starting to fall.

'In you go then,' said Dave as he opened the flap of the side-car. We clambered inside and squashed together as he zipped it up. It was very cosy, and smelt of petrol and grease. As Dave started the motorbike up, Mary climbed on the back and suddenly we were away! It was probably only about five or six minutes that we drove for but it was one of the most exciting things we had ever done. The bike was very bumpy and wobbly and as we turned the corners it felt like we were going to topple over on our side, but we loved it. When we got home we couldn't stop laughing and talking about it. Dave had suddenly become our hero, Mary was our favourite sister, and Mum was beginning to be won round – but that wasn't to last for long.

Being a GPO telephonist was a high-status job and Mary enjoyed it. She was taught how to work a 1A lamp switchboard, which was quite a complicated piece of equipment, but she was clever and quick to learn and she was also making lots of new friends. Mary had a sparkling personality and was always the centre of attention. She was both funny and kind to us younger children. The stories that she told us were always exciting and I can remember one time her sitting on the back doorstep with Margaret and I and telling us a story about fairies in the clouds and witches in the coal cellar. She also taught us to catch raindrops in our mouths and to splash in puddles. Once she started getting serious with Dave she wasn't around quite so much, although Mum had very strict rules about courting. Mary had to be home by 9.30 p.m. if she saw Dave in the evening, which meant there was very little they could do other than go for a walk. Sometimes they hurried home from work so they could make the early showing at the pictures. This was tricky as it depended how long the film was as to whether they got home in time, and if they didn't there would be hell to pay! Mum would stand waiting at the front gate with her arms crossed and an angry look on her face. Mary decided it just wasn't worth it and so they often left before the film was over just to make sure they were back on time.

One day Mary had a very bad cold. She still went in to work, travelling on the train from Chadwell Heath into Liverpool Street station. It wasn't a long journey, but was stuffy and damp and by the time she got home that evening she was feeling worse. Mum told her she should stay at home the next day but Mary didn't want to. She had arranged to meet Dave at lunchtime, and was looking forward to seeing him, but Mum was insistent.

'You need to get rid of that cold otherwise it could turn to pneumonia.' Mum always worried about illness getting worse. I suppose she had experienced life before the welfare system and the National Health Service and knew that when little ailments were ignored they could progress into something much worse. She had lost her own little brother Peter when he was just two. He had caught diphtheria which was a terrible, and sadly common, disease before the vaccination was developed in the 40s. One day the poor little boy had a cold and a cough, then he developed a high temperature and within the week he began to struggle to breathe. He died not long after. At the time it wasn't only diphtheria that was to be feared, but also polio, tuberculosis and pneumonia. Things were better for our generation. Antibiotics were seen as the great cure-all and had almost eradicated the complications that had often accompanied childhood diseases such as measles, whooping cough, mumps and chicken pox. Those parents that had grown up in the pre-antibiotic age were still fearful at the mention of some of these diseases. I clearly remember Aunty's reaction when Mum brought me home from the doctors one day having been diagnosed with scarlet fever. Mum had managed to calm her down, repeating the doctor's reassurances, and Aunty was then further placated at the sight of the pink bottle of penicillin that had been prescribed.

Whenever Margaret or I were ill, Aunty would always go over the road to the greengrocers and buy us a huge shiny Jaffa orange, which was a very expensive and unusual treat. Mum would tuck us up on the settee and cover us with a coat or a blanket, cut the orange in quarters, and then give it to us to suck, one piece at a time. Being tucked up in front of the fire with orange juice trickling down our chins was almost as good for us as the penicillin.

Mary was older and her experiences of being ill were different. Mum had not been around for much of the time when she and the twins were small. They never knew where Mum went, only that she was often absent for long periods of time. She would come back to visit periodically, but they would view her as a visitor rather than a mother. Much later as adults we would be able to piece together her likely destinations and begin to understand why she went but for the young Mary, Marion and Marge, Granny and Aunty were the care-givers. Granny was an old lady by that time, and Aunty was out at work, so being home ill was a very different experience for them. For sixteen-year-old Mary, the prospect of being stuck at home with Mum, even with an orange for company, didn't compete with going to work and seeing her friends and meeting up with Dave, so she got up the next morning, got ready and went in to work. Mary's cold did indeed get worse. A lot worse. She developed a very severe throat and chest infection, which was slow to respond to the antibiotics she was prescribed. She ended up being off work for almost four weeks. At that time Mary was paid weekly, but as she was unwell, this was to be sent to her as a weekly postal order. The first Saturday came, but no postal order arrived.

'I don't understand,' said Mary, 'I'm sure that they are supposed to send it off on Friday – sorry Mum.' All of my working sisters gave Mum the majority of their wages. She desperately needed it to feed us and pay the weekly callers who continually harassed her for the money she owed. The girls would need to keep their fares of course, but after that and a shilling or two for an occasional pair of stockings, the rest went to Mum.

Mum reassured Mary, 'It's fine love, don't worry. I'm sure it will come on Monday.' Nothing came on Monday, nor the following three weeks.

'I expect you will get it in one go when you are back at work,' soothed Mum. Mary was so grateful that Mum wasn't angry. She knew that money was very scarce and didn't like letting Mum down like this. She planned to give Mum the money as soon as she was paid, and even thought how nice it would be that she would be able to give Mum a little extra as there would be three weeks' worth of fares and stocking money left over. When Mary finally recovered sufficiently to return to work, she was really excited. It would be good to see everyone again, especially Dave, who had brought round a bunch of flowers for her, even though he hadn't been allowed inside to see her. She got dressed carefully on Monday morning, backcombed her hair and even put on a little bit of a lipstick that she had managed to buy one week. The train journey to London felt fresh and new and Mary was feeling so much better, even though Mum had reminded her that the first thing she must do was to go and tell the wages people that she hadn't been paid for the four weeks she had been off sick. Mary arrived at work keen to return to her switchboard, but before she did she made her way to the wages office, and let them know about her wages not being sent. They looked puzzled but promised to look into it for her. Mary worked through the morning, and managed to find a few minutes to catch up with her friends.

'Dave has really missed you,' said Hannah. 'He keeps popping over trying to see if you are back yet.' They laughed together, Mary feeling happier by the minute.

At lunchtime she made her way over to the entrance of the building where Dave worked, hoping to catch sight of him as he went out to lunch. Suddenly there he was, beaming at her.

'Hiya,' he said, 'have you got time for a sandwich?'

'Yes, but I can't be too long, I need to go back to the wages office to see if they have managed to sort out my money.'

After a sandwich and a cup of tea, Mary left Dave with a promise of a date the following evening, and went to the wages office before starting her afternoon shift at the switchboard. She knocked on the door, and was asked to come in. The wages clerk was trying to smile and be helpful, but she was obviously uncomfortable about something.

'Mary, I'm really sorry but Mrs D wants to see you,' she said quietly, looking down at her shoes.

Mary was worried; had she done something wrong? Was she going to get the sack for being ill for so long? As Mary went through to Mrs D's office, she had a horrible feeling that something was not right.

'Hello Mary, are you feeling better now?' asked Mrs D kindly.

Mary nodded and waited.

'Mary, we are a little bit confused about your wages, dear,' Mrs D continued. 'Is there anyone else at home who might have signed for the postal orders? A brother maybe?'

Mary flushed. Peter was married now, and in his own flat, but she knew he would never take her wages anyway.

'No, not really,' she whispered, feeling a sinking dread. What was she going to tell Mum? If they were saying that the wages had been sent, there wouldn't be any extra money today, and

Mum was expecting it. What would she say? What would Mum do? She looked up at the kind but serious face of Mrs D.

'But I really need my money,' Mary continued. 'My mum needs it for food, and I haven't been able to give her any keep for four weeks now.'

Mrs D's look hardened, 'Mary, I am really sorry but I am afraid we are going to have to tell the police about this, because someone has taken your postal order, signed for it and cashed it every week.'

At this Mary started to cry, she didn't know what to do, but the thought of the police being told filled her with fear. What if they didn't believe her and took her to prison?

'Look dear,' said Mrs D, seeing Mary's obvious distress and confusion, 'why don't you go home and talk to your mum about it before we do anything else?'

Mary nodded and thanked her.

When she got home that evening, she was surprised that Mum didn't go mad.

She did look angry at first. 'Are you sure they said they were going to call the police?'

'Yes, I don't know what to do. Mrs D told me to talk to you about it.'

A strange look came over Mum's face and then she turned away to pick up her empty cup. Shrugging her shoulders, she said in a resigned voice, 'Well just leave it, then. It's not worth causing trouble over,' and walked into the scullery.

Mary was so very relieved; she was happy to let the matter drop.

13

A Family Holiday

Margaret's health had improved dramatically. The doctor had finally managed to have her referred to the London Jewish hospital in Stepney. The hospital had been founded in the middle of the nineteenth century to serve the growing Jewish immigrant population. This enabled their patients to adhere to the strict Jewish laws and traditions while being cared for. In 1947 the hospital was taken over by the newly formed National Health Service. I am not sure why Margaret was sent there, but through the years clues that have been revealed have shaped my suspicions.

Margaret was nearly nine by this time and had almost become resigned to being the sick member of the family. When Mum took her to the hospital Margaret was distraught.

'I don't want to go,' she wailed.

Although Mum must have been upset herself, she managed to hide it.

'It's only for a little while and when you come out you'll be all better.' This was wildly optimistic but Mum was always an expert at convincing people of the most unlikely outcomes.

'Can Kathleen stay with me then?' Margaret pleaded, her huge eyes taking on a pathetic desperate look. Mum didn't answer.

After Margaret had been weighed and measured the nurse called her colleague over to take her to the ward. Margaret clung on to Mum's arms as the nurse gently extracted her and led her towards the big doors. As she disappeared from our sight she was still crying for Mum. Today parents are encouraged to stay with their children when they are in hospital and being comforted by a loved one is recognised as being an essential part of recovery, but in the 60s this was not the case.

Margaret was subjected to a barrage of investigations including kidney tests, but they all came back clear, and the doctors became more and more perplexed. Finally they noticed that she had very enlarged tonsils and it was decided that these should be removed. I can still remember her crying silently after the operation because she was in so much pain, and the look of disgust on her face when the promised ice cream arrived in a flavour she wasn't expecting.

Whether it was the removal of her tonsils that triggered Margaret's improved health we will never know, but improve it did.

It was now only a week or so until the summer holidays. I was due to move to my secondary school in September and was very nervous. New situations always equated to anxiety. I was always fearful of not fitting in, being different from the others, not having the right clothes, shoes, things . . . I also knew that meeting new people meant answering difficult questions. Questions I never knew the answers to. The last few terms at primary school had not been easy for me. I was in the top group in my class, but did not attend regularly. Despite this my teacher was hopeful of me passing the 11-plus exam that all children took at that time to decide whether they would win a place at a local grammar school or would have to attend the secondary modern. I was also entered for a scholarship exam for the Ilford Ursuline Convent School, which took several scholarship students each year from its local community. My sister Pat had won a scholarship there and Mum was hopeful that I would do the same.

On the day that I attended for the exam at the Ursuline School I was very nervous. They had big girls there to show us where to go. Everything was quiet and clean and shiny. So shiny in fact that I slipped over. A kind nun in a long black habit came and helped me up.

'Hello,' she said, 'up you get. These floors are so slippery, aren't they?'

I scrambled to my feet, feeling very silly and embarrassed.

'What's your name?' she asked.

'Kathleen Coates,' I whispered back.

A look of recognition crossed her face. 'Ahh yes, your sisters came here didn't they?' I looked back puzzled. My sister Pat had come here but no one else.

'Yes, I remember them – Sheila and Patricia; lovely girls and very clever.'

I stared back and nodded. *Sheila?* My secret sister Sheila had come here?

'I'm sure you'll do well if you are as bright as they were,' she added.

I wasn't. I failed both the 11-plus and the entrance exam to the Ursuline, so secondary modern it was.

I remember going with my mum to the launderette shortly after the results had come. 'How did she get on then?' the lady had asked.

'Oh she passed both,' answered Mum, 'but I've decided to send her to the Sacred Heart Convent instead because I think she'll prefer it there.' I was very confused. Had I passed? I was sure I hadn't because when Mum opened the letter she was upset and I heard her telling Pat that I would have to go to the secondary school now with all the rough girls. I suddenly felt ashamed. Mum had lied to the lady because she was disappointed in me and didn't want everyone to know that I wasn't clever enough to go to grammar school. I was already a failure and I wasn't even eleven until August.

I was looking forward to the six weeks holiday though. That wonderful feeling of freedom, of not having somewhere you should go or be. When I arrived home from school Mum opened the door humming. This was a good sign. When we were staying off school with one of our 'mysterious' ailments she would often teach us songs, and sometimes sing while we danced around the room. We would dress up in old pieces of fabric draped around us and we would become graceful butterflies while she sang, '*Butterflies white, butterflies blue, butterflies golden and heliotrope*

too,' and we would swoop around flapping our wings. I also
loved to read poems from the books that were lying around the
house and would sometimes try to match them to music and
make up dances for us to do. There was one very mournful
poem that I loved by Walter de la Mare:

> No breath of wind, no gleam of sun,
> Still the white snow whirls softly down

which I matched to the tune of 'Greensleeves'.

'Guess what?' Margaret said, flying to meet me as Mum
opened the door. 'We're going on holiday!'

'What?'

'We're going on holiday!' she repeated louder this time in
case I hadn't heard.

I dropped my school bag on the floor. 'Are we, Mum?' I
asked, afraid to believe it. We had never been on holiday before
– well, not in my memory. I had seen photos of myself holding
hands with Pat and Josie as I tottered between them on a sandy
beach when I must have been about a year old, but of course I
didn't remember that. Something bad must have happened
there because Mum never wanted to talk about it; I was only
ever shown that photo furtively, when Mum wasn't around.

Now, nearly ten years later, here was Margaret telling me that
we were going on holiday and Mum was nodding and smiling to
confirm it.

'Where are we going? When are we going? Who's coming?'
The questions came spilling out. Mum came and sat down in
the kitchen on her chair and lit a cigarette, 'We are going at the
end of July, which is in a few weeks, and we are going to a place
called Ilfracombe.' That sounded like a funny name to us but it
also sounded exotic and exciting. We started giggling. We were a
pair of gigglers, at least that was what Mum called us. Usually it
seemed to annoy her, but the more she told us off the more we
giggled; it must have driven her mad. But not today; today she
was in one of her good moods.

'We will all be going and Mary is staying here with Aunty to look after the cat.'

'Are we taking Pongo with us?' I asked worriedly. Pongo was supposed to be my dog. Old Pongo had died, but it wasn't long before Mum had brought home a new puppy. This one was black and white and I loved her. She was Pat's and mine, and I took my responsibility very seriously. That dog loved us back, and would always sit on Pat's lap when she was home from work, and I would squeeze next to them on the same chair. I was a bit too big to do that now, but I still adored playing with Pongo and she would rush to meet me when I got home from school.

'Yes, Pongo is coming with us,' Mum reassured me as she stroked the dog's head. 'We will get the train to London and then a coach all the way to Ilfracombe.' Margaret and I counted the days, desperate for the holiday to arrive. We talked endlessly about going and longed for time to pass until we got on the train. When we saw some battered old suitcases appear it began to feel more real.

On the Friday evening before we were due to leave, Marge, Marion, Pat and Josie had all arrived home from work. Margaret and I were beside ourselves with excitement, although mine was tempered by the dread that always accompanied anything new. Would people on the coach look at us? Would they say something to Mum?

We left for the station bright and early. Mum had arranged with Mary that she would leave her family allowance and benefits book with her so Mary could draw it out for the fortnight we were going to be away. Mary had agreed to 'loan' Mum the money in advance from her and Dave's savings so that we would have some money to take with us. Off we left for the station, dragging our heavy suitcases onto the 62 bus to Chadwell Heath station.

As we boarded the train I turned and looked around me. Something had to go wrong. This was all just too wonderful and exciting for words! 'I bet the train will break down,' I thought, 'or maybe it will crash and we won't get to the coach in time,' but it didn't and we did. The journey seemed very long. The coach was warm and stuffy, and when it stopped for people to take a 'comfort' break and have a cup of tea we stayed on board. There was no point in going into the café as we couldn't afford to buy refreshments. Mum had made Spam sandwiches and had filled bottles with orange squash for us while the older ones had tea from a flask. As the journey was so long and the coach was so hot, the sandwiches were sweaty and the juice was warm. My head begin to throb and I felt a wave of nausea. I started to feel panicked. What would I do if I needed to be sick? Everyone on the coach would see. For the rest of the journey I was in misery, my head banging furiously. I was trying desperately not to be sick. In the end I managed to make it, but Pongo wasn't so lucky. She vomited, but luckily Pat managed to catch it in her sunhat! I don't think the other passengers on the coach were very impressed and the smell was awful.

We were all relieved to arrive. The coach dropped us in the centre of Ilfracombe and Mum got out the letter confirming our holiday rental.

'Right, let's have a look now.' She read the directions out loud.

The house where we had hired a flat was at the top of a very steep hill and the flat was at the top of a very tall house, so there was a lot of climbing involved every time we went out, but we didn't mind.

Margaret and I were given the bunk beds, her on the bottom and me on the top. The beach was in walking distance, and we went there almost every day. On the first day we passed a seaside shop. It was glorious! Sun hats swung from its awning and buckets and spades tumbled out from its windows, along with shells, paper windmills, wind breaks and all manner of exciting objects. We were allowed to choose a bucket and spade each and a sunhat.

'Can I have the red one?' I pleaded with Pat, as she reached into her purse to find the money. Margaret pointed excitedly at the yellow one and we were both delighted with our acquisitions. We chose pink and blue sunhats that were cone-shaped with pretty fringes all over. My heart skipped a beat when I saw the beach stretched before us for the first time.

'Oh look!' I shouted to no one in particular, pointing to the endless sand and white-topped waves. We had been on day trips to Southend before, but I had never seen such golden sand, so many tempting rockpools.

'Come on,' I said to Margaret, 'I'll race you,' and we tumbled along the sand towards the sea. The sun seemed to shine every day. We had ice creams and sticks of rock, and even had fish and chips, which we ate on the beach as we looked out at the seagulls swirling around us hungrily. We made good use of our new swimsuits and showed off the newly acquired skills that we had learnt from our weekly swimming lessons at school. In the evenings we would all go back down to the beach and play cricket. People would gather round to watch, and sometimes they would clap if one of us hit the ball a long way, or made an impressive catch. We must have looked the epitome of a big happy normal family. Looks can be deceiving.

14

Running Out of Money

The first week of our holiday whizzed past at speed, and everyone seemed to be happy for once. I had now moved to share the double bed with Marge, as I had fallen out of the top bunk on the first night we were there and had bruising all down my left side.

I had screamed my head off, but Pat said, 'Just go for a swim in the sea. Don't you know that salt water is healing?'

The flat we had rented for the fortnight was small, but clean and tidy. There was a table with enough chairs for us all to sit down at the same time, which was a real novelty. Mum would cook an evening meal for us after we had been at the beach all day and we were always ravenous by then. After dinner we would either play cards, snakes and ladders, draughts or sometimes Monopoly, which we had brought with us. We also went to the penny arcades a couple of times. This was a huge treat for us, and we had to decide whether to put the pennies in to see if we could get the silver balls into the right slots or whether to make the laughing policemen roar hysterically.

At night Josie told us ghost stories. She was very good at this, and could make all sorts of strange voices and noises. There is a very fine line between terror and delight and we enjoyed walking that line whenever Josie was in the mood to play with us, and would often go to bed trembling with fear and imaginings. We had watched a Punch and Judy show on the beach one day, and even at ten I remember feeling confused and unnerved by it. It was the one thing we did during that first week that I didn't enjoy. The strange guttural voice of the puppets, and the violent smacking just didn't seem right. Arguments, shouting, chaotic situations, violent outbursts and strange unfathomable, confusing secrets – it was just too close to the truth of my childhood, and ugly Mr Punch haunted my dreams for many years afterwards. But apart from that, I had a wonderful time; my sisters laughed and played around me and Mum was always smiling.

By the end of that first week things changed. There wasn't much food left and the money had run out. Mum had her family allowance and benefits book with her as she had forgotten to leave them for Mary, but she couldn't draw out the money until Tuesday. On Saturday we woke up and the sun had disappeared. Grey clouds had gathered, and with them came a change in everyone's mood. Margaret and I picked up on this and were starting to squabble. Most of our sisters didn't want to go to the beach because they said it was too cold and was going to rain, so we were just sitting in the small flat with nothing much to do except look out of the window hoping for sunshine.

Suddenly Pat jumped up and said, 'Come on you two, let's go for a walk with Pongo.' I put on my shoes eagerly but Margaret wanted to stay at home with Josie who had begun to make some little dolls for her out of a couple of wooden pegs she had found in a basket under the sink. Pat and I headed off towards the beach, but the clouds were getting blacker and it was soon obvious that it was going to rain. There was a loud clap of thunder and I let out a scream, then a jagged fork of lightning seemed to bounce off the sea.

It was really scary but Pat said, 'Oh it's all right, it's just God moving his furniture.' I didn't really believe her but it did make me feel better. By the time we got home we were both soaking wet and so was Pongo.

'Come here Pongo and I'll dry you,' said Pat, as she grabbed the towel from the bathroom and started to rub the dog's fur. Mum was sitting by the window looking out at the rain with that faraway look in her eyes. She almost changed into a different person at these times, and we would all normally instinctively know to adapt our behaviour. But today we were all irritable and hungry. We hadn't eaten since the night before and that had just been a plate of potatoes. Josie told Marion to put the kettle on for a cup of tea but she answered back: 'No! Why should I? It's always me has to make the tea, it's her turn,' and she gestured towards Marge. It was almost five o'clock. Marge got up and went out to make the tea without any fuss.

The room was unusually quiet but I broke the silence by asking, 'When is dinner going to be ready?'

Mum swivelled round and just looked at me crossly. 'There isn't any dinner.' She turned her back on us. I looked at my sisters who were all pretending that they hadn't heard. Margaret started to cry.

'Stop grizzling,' said Mum sharply, and went and got her coat. 'I'm going out.' With that she slammed the door behind her, stamped down the stairs and went out into the rain. Josie and Pat exchanged a look. Josie comforted Margaret, who by now was even more upset.

It was about half an hour later that Mum came back with another large bag of potatoes. 'Here,' she said, flinging them on to the table. 'Twins, come and peel these, and put them on to boil.' When they were cooked Josie brought them to the table and dished them out onto our plates. We had a good plateful each, but they didn't look very appetising sitting in their pale glory alone on our plates, with nothing more than a shake of salt to make them taste of anything. Still, at least we weren't going to bed hungry.

The next day was Sunday and Mum sent us to Mass at the local Catholic Church. Mum never came to Mass, even at home. When we came out she was there to meet us. 'We're going shopping,' she said, and we followed her to a small grocery shop on the corner of the road that was open on a Sunday. As we went inside we saw Mum hand over her family allowance book to the man.

'Right you are then,' he said, 'but only £1 worth.' Mum asked for potatoes, sausages, eggs, baked beans, lard, loaves of bread and margarine and various other items, which the grocer duly filled her bags with. Mum looked at the sweets and asked for two lollypops and then, hesitating, asked for ten Player's cigarettes. Mum lit up as soon as we left the shop and then we walked back up the tall hill, carrying the bag of shopping up the three flights of stairs to the little flat at the top. We were worn out by the time we got in; two days of nothing but boiled potatoes doesn't fill you with energy.

'Let's have sausages and chips for Sunday dinner,' Mum suggested, her enthusiasm returning, and we were very glad that it wasn't to be boiled potatoes again.

On Tuesday Mum retrieved her allowance book from the grocer's shop that also had a post office counter at the back, and drew out her money, paying the man back the money he had allowed her in advance. This didn't leave much to last for the rest of the week, so there wasn't any more ice cream or treats, but we still managed to have a good time and I certainly didn't want to come back home to Dagenham, even to see the cat and Aunty.

15

The Baker Boy

When we got home Dave was at our house with Mary.

'Mum, you forgot to leave your allowance book,' Mary said tremulously.

'Oh I know,' Mum answered, not meeting Mary's eyes but continuing to unpack the clothes ready for washing.

'Margaret must have put it in my bag before we left,' she said and carried the washing into the scullery. I watched Mary and Dave exchange looks, and when Mum returned it was Dave's turn to question her.

'Well, can we have it now? Only we need to get the money back into our savings,' he said firmly.

Mum turned to give him a withering look. 'Don't you speak to me like that,' she spat.

Mary started to cry. 'Mum, please; you know we need it for the wedding,' she pleaded.

'I know that, but you'll have to wait,' she said, turning to leave the room again. As she reached the door she stopped and looked them both in the face. 'And if you're not very careful there won't be any wedding,' and with that she flounced up the stairs.

Dave stood there and watched her go, muttering under his breath, 'Bloody hell.' When Mary started to cry again, he put his arm around her and led her out of the front door.

Aunty was in a bad mood all of the time and there wasn't anything to look forward to any more. We still had four weeks of the summer holiday to go but I knew that at the end of that time I was going to have to brave the new world of secondary school. I was becoming more self-aware and self-conscious. Puberty was just around the corner, and things were happening to my body that felt different and strange.

Mary had felt it her duty to tell me about periods. No one had ever told her and she was determined that I wasn't going to be as afraid as she was when she had thought she was bleeding to death! I was only about nine when she told me, and I had been so impressed with this knowledge that I had decided to pretend that I had one. She had shown me where she kept her Dr. Whites towels and told me that I could take one when the time came. I helped myself, and proudly told Josie that my period had started.

Josie looked shocked. 'How do you know about periods?'

When I said that Mary had told me she looked annoyed.

'You're too young for all that,' she said, but not unkindly. 'Show me the towel.'

I blanched; of course there was really nothing to show, but I went up into the toilet and, feeling a sense of panic, tried as hard as I could to scratch my finger. Finally managing to extract a pinprick of blood and blotting it onto the towel I proudly called down to Josie, 'You can come up now!'

When she saw the towel she smiled. 'Oh okay,' she said, going along with my deceit, 'but I think you might not have another one for quite a while.'

'No,' I agreed, 'I don't think I will.' Scratching my finger until it bled was not something I wanted to repeat any time soon.

By the end of that summer I was more self-conscious than ever. I had put on some weight, and I was beginning to get spots! I was not looking forward to the start of term.

Mum called me in from the garden about a week before school started.

'We need to get your uniform,' she said. 'Come on, we have to go to Lucilla's in Green Lane; that's the only place that stocks it.'

I knew that the uniform was maroon because my sister Marge had been transferred to the school for her last year of secondary education when it was first built. Marge's uniform was long gone, as she was seven years older than me. By the time it came for me to start at the Sacred Heart, she was almost eighteen and had started going out with Ron.

It had been strange how she and Ron had met. He was the young man who drove the baker's delivery van, and delivered bread and cakes all around where we lived. Mum had taken to having a loaf delivered every other day as it saved her going across to the baker's, and didn't cost any more. On this particular day Ron knocked as usual, although he was about half an hour later than normal.

'One sliced loaf,' he said passing the bread to Mum.

'Are you all right?' she asked. 'You look very white,' at which Ron started to sniff.

'I've had a bit of an accident,' he said. 'As I was turning at the top of Martin's Corner, this bloody great Rolls Royce went into the van.'

Mum put her hand to her mouth. 'Oh you poor thing!' Then she started to laugh. 'Fancy that, a Rolls Royce in Valence Avenue! Come in and I'll make you a cup of hot sweet tea.'

Mum led Ron into the kitchen where Margaret and I sat on the floor, our play suspended in disbelief. People didn't get invited into our house. Mum gestured towards the settee, and Ron sat himself down, feeling the cushion slip as he did so, and noticing the pile of newspapers beginning to slide out from underneath. As he tried to push them back under, we began to giggle.

'What are you two laughing at?' he said with a cheeky smile. He seemed very tall to us, and had thick bushy black hair but his eyes looked kind. Mum came back in from the scullery with a large, teaming mug of very hot, very sweet tea.

'Here you are.' She offered him the mug, and as he took it I saw an interesting new look cross Mum's face. Ron stayed and chatted for a while, and Mum told him she had twin seventeen-year-old daughters. When he came to collect the bread money on Saturday, it just so happened that the door was opened by Marge. Mum had taken Pat and Marion to Green Lane with her and left Marge looking after us two. Josie was up in bed as usual. Ron took Marge to the pictures that night and they had been together ever since.

Ron called Mum 'Mrs Lady'. He was so kind to us. Looking

back, I don't know how he put up with it really. Marge and he rarely got to go out on their own; most of the time they had to take either Mum or Margaret or me with them, and sometimes all three of us! We went stock car racing, and saw the cars smashing into each other – that was one of Mum's favourite outings. We also sometimes went to the Chinese restaurant in Ilford near to Plessey's where Marge had now joined Pat, Josie and Aunty working there. There we tasted new kinds of food that tickled our taste buds. My favourite were the fried banana fritters with syrup that were included in the price of the 'Set Menu'. Sometimes Ron just took us for a drive on a Sunday afternoon. Mum thought the world of him and I think he was also very fond of her, even though in later years she sometimes turned into the mother-in-law from hell!

Margaret and I also loved Ron. He was infinitely patient with us, and we must have cost him a fortune. One Saturday we started the Black Cat Café. I wrote out the menu:

egg on toast 6d,
beans on toast 6d,
bacon sandwich 9d,
tea 2d etc.

and then drew a big black cat at the bottom.

When Ron arrived at lunchtime I sidled over.

'This is the menu,' I said thrusting the carefully written list into his hand. He smiled at Marge, who raised her eyes to heaven. Mum was sitting in her usual chair, and Aunty was in the front garden. Poor Ron knew he didn't stand a chance.

'Okay then,' he said defeated. 'I'll have a bacon sandwich and a cup of tea please.' I bustled out to the scullery and prepared his meal for him. He duly paid his bill and was then allowed to take Marge out for the afternoon. The Black Cat Café was opened most weekends that year, and we extended our clientele to serve the rest of my sisters who were around on Saturday. It was a lucrative business for me the cook and Margaret my washer-upper, and kept us in sweets for quite some time.

16

Getting Ready for Big School

I was excited at the prospect of getting a new school uniform. We didn't have many new clothes and often wore things that had been passed down from our sisters or given to us by other people.

Pat and Josie had been saving money from their wages so that I could have the proper uniform. They were so kind. They hardly had any money left over after they had paid their fare and given Mum keep money, but they had carefully put by what little they could in preparation for this day.

The smell of Lucilla's made my eyes water. It was a strong, unpleasant chemical odour that permeated the whole shop. The smell reminded me of the dry cleaner's that my Aunty Maggie worked in. I had occasionally been allowed to help her, and she had given me a few pennies pocket money. I remember feeling very grown-up writing out the collection tickets for the customers until Aunty Maggie had told me off for not being neat enough, and for spelling things wrongly!

The sales assistant at Lucilla's ushered Mum and me into one corner and told me to take off my clothes. I really didn't want to as my underclothes left a lot to be desired and I was very aware that I was starting to grow 'bumps' on my chest. Mum just bundled me out of my things and I stood exposed to anyone who walked in. The lady looked me up and down.

'Hmm, what size do you want her to try?'

Mum looked at me and said, 'Big enough for her to grow into.' I knew what this meant; out from the rack of skirts came an enormous maroon box-pleated skirt with a strange sort of sliding zip that enabled you to tighten or loosen the waistband to fit.

'Try this,' she said, so dutifully I put it on. It was gigantic! Not only was the waist massive but it was so long that the hem almost touched the floor. I tried to protest, but I was shushed by Mum.

'No, that will be fine,' she said, and started to role the waist up to make the skirt fall just below my knee. I think I would have needed to grow to 6ft for it to ever fit properly! We also had to buy a special pair of PE knickers in the same colour, a stripy maroon and gold tie and a white blouse.

'Most people buy three blouses,' the lady said, 'then they can wash, dry and rotate them.' Mum said we just wanted one. Lucilla's was very expensive, and the lady spoke with a very posh voice, but Mum could talk in the same posh voice. In fact she did it better than the lady did. Aunty Maggie had knitted a maroon cardigan for me so there I was, all kitted out and ready for big school. Why then did I still feel that I would be different from the other girls? Why was I frightened that I wouldn't fit in?

As my first day of secondary school approached I got more and more worried. I didn't even know where the school was. Mum told me that there would be other girls at the bus stop in the same uniform, and that I should get off at the same stop as they did and follow them as they walked to school.

That first morning I got up very early. I'd had a bath the night before and washed my hair. It was quite long and very straight and was beginning to get greasy a day or so after being washed. I had borrowed some of Josie's foam rollers and had slept fitfully, because the plastic clips that fastened them had poked into my head throughout the night. My uniform was ready downstairs for me to put on so I crept down trying not to wake anyone. I wanted to be on my own for a while and that was always difficult in such a crowded home. Aunty had already left for work, and Mum was still asleep as I slid out of our bed. Pat and Josie always got up at 7.30 and caught the 8.20 bus so I had at least half an hour before anyone would be up. I went to the sink and splashed my face with cold water. We didn't have a basin in the bathroom, just a toilet and a bath, so we had to wash our face and hands at the scullery sink.

Aunty would have her early morning wash at that sink, and if you got up too early, you could be greeted by the sight of her in her many vests and baggy drawers, poised at the sink, flannel and soap in hand.

Today though she had already gone off to work so I had the scullery to myself. Then I heard a sound on the stairs.

'What are you doing?' whispered Margaret.

'Just having a wash,' I answered, inwardly annoyed that she had followed me downstairs.

'What time are you going?' she asked, joining me on the cold stone floor. Even in September the house could still be quite cold, particularly in the early morning.

'I don't really know, I'll watch out of the window about eight o'clock, I guess, and wait until some girls get to the bus stop.'

We only had one clock, and that always stood on the mantelpiece. It was an ugly 50s object but it did keep good time. Pat had bought me a watch when I was younger. She was often buying me little treats when she could afford them. When I was four I was playing in the garden, jumping over horse jumps that I had made out of bits and pieces I had found in the garden. When I stumbled and fell, dislocating my shoulder, it had been Pat that I cried for. It had been Pat that had to come home from work and taken me to the hospital to have it slotted back in, and it had been Pat who shouted at the doctors and nurses because they hadn't given me any anaesthetic. It was also Pat who took me to London Zoo and to see the Trooping of the Colour to celebrate the Queen's birthday as a treat for being brave. Unfortunately the watch from Pat hadn't worked for years, so now the clock was the only way to make sure I wasn't late for my first day at school. Pat and Josie got up at 7.30 as usual and while Pat had a cup of tea, Josie looked me up and down. 'Come here, Kathleen,' she said as she grabbed my arm and started to unroll my rolled up skirt.

'Look, if you fold it rather than roll it, it will sit flat and not make you look like you've got a spare tyre round your waist!' She showed me how to fold the waistband neatly.

'There,' she said, 'that's better, and what have you done to your hair? Pat, pass me my bag will you?' She took out a comb and tried to flatten the chaotic curls that surrounded my face and seemed to turn in a hundred different directions, giving me a kind of crazy unkempt look.

. I wriggled. 'Oww!'

'Will you keep still? I can't do anything if you jiggle about.' She finally managed to tame my hair into a ponytail that hung untidily down my back. I didn't have a fringe so my broad forehead gave me the effect of having a dome-shaped head! I had practised doing my own tie up so that didn't look too bad, but the cardigan Aunty Maggie had knitted wasn't quite the right shape and had 'leg of mutton' sleeves that were extremely unflattering. The arms were also much too long and I had to roll up the cuffs so that they didn't cover my hands. Finally Josie was reasonably content with how I looked.

'Put your blazer on then,' she said. Now the blazer had been a big issue. Blazers were expensive. You could buy them more cheaply from a local shop but they didn't have the school badge on the pocket. However Lucilla's did stock the badges separately and you could buy these and sow them on to the cheaper blazer. Josie had done this for me, but although she had sewn very neat tidy stitches, it was still obvious that it wasn't the 'proper' badge. I donned my blazer, which had also been bought far too big for me so that it would last the whole time I was at the school. I looked ridiculous, but luckily I wasn't alone. I watched the 62 bus stop across the road from our house start to fill with girls of all shapes and sizes, mostly dressed in uniforms comically big for them – obviously, like mine, bought to last!

17

Little Anne

My first term at secondary school was almost worse than primary. I felt big and lumpy and ugly. My clothes felt uncomfortable and I didn't make many friends. I was put in 1B, which was the middle band, where I think the school placed all the children that they weren't quite sure what to do with. I was considered too bright to be in the C class but my non-attendance at primary meant they wouldn't chance putting me in the A class. So there I was in 1B with a strange assortment of other girls, none of whom I seemed to gel with. It wasn't long before I stopped going to school again. Mum would try to persuade me to go, but her heart wasn't really in it and I think she had too many other things on her mind. Consequently it wasn't long before I was demoted to 1C. Then something happened that changed everything.

I had been friends at primary school with my neighbours Jane and Hannah but they were in the year above me. They were already established at the school, but were kind to me and let me join with them and their friends at lunchtime when we were cast out into the playground to amble around for about an hour before being let back into class. One day in the spring term of my first year I was heading over to join Jane and Hannah's posse. One of the second-years stepped forward and said, 'I think you're in the same class as my sister Anne.'

'Am I?'

'Yes, her name is Anne McMahon.'

The girl's name was Miriam, and she took me over to where her sister Anne was standing surrounded by a group of other girls. Miriam pushed our way through the others and there I stood in front of a very small, neat and tidy girl with very blue eyes, a scattering of freckles across her nose and a perm that made her hair frizzy. I recognised her at once, as she was the most popular girl in our year.

'Anne, this girl is in your tutor group, her name is Kathleen Coates.' Anne looked at me for a few seconds and then must have decided that I was okay. For some completely obscure reason that I have never been able to fathom, Anne liked me.

'Do you want to play rounders at lunchtime?' she asked. I quickly agreed. I played rounders, cricket and all manner of other ball games with my sisters in our back garden, so was quite good at them. When the bell went for lunchtime, she came over to my desk.

'Are you sandwiches or school dinners?'

'Sandwiches,' I replied wondering if this was the right answer. It was.

'Do you want to come with us to eat them then?' she asked and as I nodded my head, she ushered me out of the classroom and down the stairs towards the back entrance of the school. There were a couple of girls who followed us, and a few more who were patiently waiting at the doorway. One girl, Joan, was very tall and thin; she smiled at me. We all left the building together and walked onto the grassy area where we were allowed to have our lunch. There was nowhere to sit except on the low walls that surrounded the building, which tended to fill up very quickly, so there were lots of groups of girls just sitting on the damp grass to eat. Although it was early spring, it was still quite cold and not very pleasant to be eating outside, but we weren't allowed to stay in for lunch except in the winter. Anne led us round the side of the building to where there were some dilapidated greenhouses. These were full of an assortment of old terracotta plant pots of various sizes, half-opened bags of compost and a few neglected gardening tools. Anne looked around us and slid the door of one of the greenhouses open, and we all piled in behind her. It was snug and warm, even if it did smell of old rotting vegetables and stale earth. Once we were inside we found something, anything, to sit on. I managed to perch on a broken piece of wooden staging and sat watching what the others were going to do. They started delving into their bags and bringing out an assortment of lunch boxes, packets and parcels. Anne and Joan both took flasks out of their bags and untwisted the lids. Joan had tea in hers, but Anne had a rich flavoursome-smelling soup. My mouth watered. Then Anne pulled out two chicken legs, which were a delicacy and quite expensive. She also had an iced bun, a bag of crisps and a Topic chocolate bar with peanuts in it. I had cheese-spread sandwiches and most of the others had something similar. Joan got out a huge bottle of lemonade, took a large swig and then proceeded to hand it round to everyone else to have a drink. I wasn't sure I liked the idea of this but felt obliged to take a drop. After we had eaten we went on to the playground at the back and chose rounders teams. My heart sunk at the thought. I was always the last to get chosen, but not this time. There were two teams, one led by Anne and one led by Joan.

Anne chose first of course.

'I'll have Kathleen,' she announced to my complete and utter amazement. I had never been chosen first for a team in my whole life; it was exhilarating, and I determined to play my heart out. When the two teams had been picked, Anne called the players around her. 'Right, I'll go backstop, you go on first base Kathleen, Teresa you bowl. The rest of you spread out, Jane on fourth, Maria on third and Sally right at the back cos you're a good thrower.'

Off we went. Backstop was a scary position to play, because you often got hit by either the bat or the ball, both of which could leave you with a nasty bump. But Anne was brave; she was never afraid of anything. My job on first base was to be ever alert to the batter and the backstop. If the batter missed the ball, the backstop would throw it as hard, as straight and as fast as possible to first base so that the batter would be out. What a responsibility!

We played. I managed to 'stump out' player after player from the opposing team, and each time I did so everyone cheered. By the time it was our turn to bat, they only had two rounders. We started to bat. Anne was a good batter, as were some of the others. When it was my turn to come forward I walked up in trepidation. Would I let everyone down? The hard round ball came hurtling towards me and I wanted to jump out of the way, but instead I held my nerve and hit with all my might. My team were shouting, 'Slog it! Slog it!' and I did. I ran like the blazes round the bases, getting a rounder to cheers from my team.

We won that game, and for the next few months lunchtimes followed that pattern every day, until the weather warmed up and we chose to sit on the grass in the sunshine instead and talk about stuff.

Anne had chosen me as her friend. She chose me. Me, out of all of the other girls that wanted to be her special friend, who followed her around and hero-worshipped her. It was me that she always looked for first thing in the morning when we got to school, me that she invited to her house to play, me that she told her secrets to. More strangely than all of that, it was my house that she always wanted to come to, my mum that she grew to love as a second mother, and my family that she chose to spend the holidays with. Anne really did change my life. She made me realise that I was worth something, and that I didn't need to always be afraid, especially if she was there with me. After that first game of rounders it was obvious that we were going to be friends for life.

Anne was always up to mischief. We began to build a gang of followers of which Anne was the leader and I was the undisputed deputy! The power was heady indeed. For the first time in my life other girls watched to see what I would do so they could copy me. They listened to what I had to say and took notice of me, and did what I wanted them to. This was a new experience for me, but not for Anne. She was the youngest in a family of six children. She was very small and petite for her age, and in fact had been in hospital for growth problems. Anne was spoilt by both her brothers and her sisters, and in particular by her dad, an amiable old Irishman who had such a broad accent I could never understand him. When he came home from work he would call out to her, 'Nan, Nan, cunya make ya da acuppata, darlinnow sweetart Nan?' and he was the one adult she would always look truly pleased to see.

I remember the day he passed his driving test.

'Dad's going to drive us to swimming,' Anne announced proudly. It was raining hard, and Barking pool was outdoors, but that wasn't going to stop us. We piled into his old Ford Anglia, swerving all over the road as he put his arm out through the window to wipe the rain off the windscreen because the wipers were broken. Anne's mum was very different. She would always make a big fuss of me when I called round insisting that I had a cup of tea and a piece of cake, but there was just something not quite comfortable about being in their house. It was a beautiful home with lovely things in it, which had been bought with the compensation money Anne's dad had received after an industrial accident. Before that they had lived in a council house on the some estate as us.

One day Anne said, 'Can you come around to my house straight from school today?'

'Okay, but why?'

'Wait and see,' she said running up the stairs two at a time with me trailing behind her. I knew Mum wouldn't be worried if I was late home as long as I was back before six, as she knew that I would sometimes go to the park with my new friends.

When Anne and I arrived at her house after school, we went up to the bedroom she shared with Miriam and there on the side was a record player.

'I've got some of my dad's old Irish records out,' she said pulling a huge 78 from its paper sleeve. 'It'll help us learn the words.'

'Why do we need to learn the words?'

'So we can sing to the old people, of course,' she answered incredulously, as though I should have been able to read her mind.

So that's what we did. I would love to be able to count the number of hours we spent listening to those old Irish rebel songs but it must have added up to whole days. We would often go swimming in Barking outdoor pool straight after school and then go back to Anne's where we would sit and sing along to those records, time and time again. We did learn the words and had great fun singing, even developing a strong Irish accent as we went along, but I never really thought we would actually go and sing to an audience of people.

Anne and I would usually meet at Becontree Station to walk to school together. We caught the 62 bus from opposite directions and both got off at Becontree. We would sometimes meet other girls and would all walk together to school. On this particular morning I got off the bus as usual and saw Anne waiting for me. She had a big grin on her face.

'Kathleen,' she started as I got off the bus, 'my sister has sorted out for us to sing on Friday night.'

'What!' I said, incredulous. 'You must be joking?'

'No, I'm not. We're singing at the Irish social club in Barking.' Anne smiled at me, and although I was terrified inside I knew that I would go and I knew that I would sing, because Anne wanted me to.

I had arranged to go round to Anne's house straight from school to get ready. My sister Josie had found an old green velvet corduroy dress at home that had a white lace collar and luckily it almost fitted me. When I took it out of my bag, Anne was delighted.

'You look like a real Irish girl in that,' she claimed, so off we went. We must have looked like a strange pair – me in my oversized green dress, looking clumsy and plain, and Anne, petite and pretty in her green Irish kilt and white jumper. We sang our hearts out that night! We sang 'Sean South of Garryowen', 'The Bold Fenian Men', 'Black Velvet Band', 'Spinning Wheel' but best loved of all was the song Anne sang as a solo, 'Danny Boy'. She held the notes so pure and true. By the time we finished there were few dry eyes in the hall and we withdrew to an intoxicating burst of applause.

18

Making a Stand

Although I was so much happier at school, things were tough for other members of the family. Isobel, my brother Michael's wife, was struggling to look after her baby Vicky, who was nearly eighteen months old, and now she was pregnant again. She couldn't read or write even in her own language and couldn't speak more than a few words of English. My brother Michael had become fluent in Spanish during the time he was in Gibraltar and so that was the language in which they communicated. Isobel was becoming more and more isolated and looking back she was probably also depressed. She came from a tiny rural village near to Malaga called San Roco, and had left behind her large close-knit family. Everything she knew and understood made no sense in her cold, bleak, adopted country. Michael worked long hours as he was now in the catering corps and was training hard to become a chef. They had a telephone but it was expensive to ring Spain, so she wasn't able to talk to anyone at home very often. The other servicemen's wives tried to be friendly but the language barrier hampered their friendships and so Isobel became more and more lonely. Mum came to the rescue.

'Mary, I want you to go and stay with Isobel until the baby's born,' she ordered. Mary was quite happy to do this; I suppose it was a kind of escape.

'All right Mum,' she said, 'I'll need to get my things packed up.' And so it was arranged.

This had the added benefit for Mum that she didn't need to feed Mary, although Mary was still obliged to send her 'keep' to mum every week. At first it seemed like a good arrangement.

Mary was happy staying with Michael and Isobel and Vicky, Mum still got her 'keep' money and Isobel had a willing helper in Mary during the long lonely evenings.

Unfortunately after a while things began to change. Marion and Marge were given the job of going up to wait outside Mary's work on a Friday so that she could hand over the majority of her wages to them to take home to Mum. At the same time she and Dave were desperately trying to save a few shillings here and there so that they could get married and try to find a flat of their own. Their savings had taken a dent after our holiday, and the 'misunderstanding' that had caused such an argument on our return. Saving was difficult, as after paying Mum her keep, Mary was only left with enough money for fares and the odd pair of stockings.

One day Michael saw Mary fishing in her purse for a spare few pennies.

'Why are you still sending Mum money? You live here now; just give me a few bob towards your food and stuff and you can keep the rest to save for the wedding.' This started Mary thinking; she had never questioned the fact that her wages in effect belonged to Mum, but now she wondered. Could she keep the money? Would it really be possible? She desperately wanted to get married as soon as possible, but that day seemed as far away as ever. Dave didn't earn a great deal, so between them their savings were growing very slowly. Mary made up her mind: she would do it!

The next Friday came and as Mary left the building where she worked, her heart was in her mouth. He knew Marion and Marge would be there waiting for her, and she also knew that if she was ever going to be able to get married she was going to have to stick to her guns. Although it was only five o'clock when she came out into the busy street, it was already beginning to get dark as winter had almost arrived. She saw Marion wave from across the street while Marge was looking in a shop window. 'Mary!' shouted Marion. 'Over here.' Mary slowly went to join them, a feeling of dread overwhelming her.

'Look,' she said, 'I'm really really sorry but I can't send any money this week.'

'Why not?' said Marge, who had now turned to join the conversation.

'I just can't afford it,' answered Mary quietly.

'Mum's going to go mad. What are we going to tell her?' asked Marion.

'Just tell her I can't afford it anymore.'

'Does that mean just this week or never?'

'Never,' said Mary with conviction. It was as though she had just made a very important decision, the first grown-up decision of her life apart from agreeing to marry Dave.

When Marge and Marion arrived back in Dagenham that evening, they were very withdrawn as they came into the house.

'What's wrong?' said Mum, who was always very astute at picking up on all our moods and vagaries.

The twins looked at each other but neither spoke.

'Come on, out with it,' said Mum, starting to get agitated.

'Mary said she can't afford to give you any more money,' blurted out Marge. Mum's face became red and then went a strange white colour.

'Right,' she said quietly, 'we'll see about that,' and she went out into the scullery to get the dinner out. Margaret's big brown eyes turned to me questioningly but I just carried on combing the dog.

The next morning was Saturday, so everyone was home. Mum told Pat that she was going to go over to Michael's.

'What, today?' asked Pat. Although Mum visited Michael's at least once a week, she rarely went on a Saturday as we were all home.

'Yes today,' she snapped back. 'Margaret, Kathleen, get your coats on.'

We ran to get our coats and join Mum as she left the house, and walked towards the bus stop. It was bitterly cold even though it was only November, so waiting for the bus seemed endless. Mum would always say, 'If I light a cigarette the bus is sure to come along,' so we would always be trying to encourage her to have one more, because we thought it was like a magic spell. The odd thing was that it did always seem to work – well almost always. At last the bus arrived and we boarded, heading upstairs as usual. Mum lit up her cigarette and Margaret and I settled into one of the seats nearby. The bus was quite crowded but we managed to find a seat together. Eventually after the usual changes and the trip across the river on the ferry we were almost at Michael's. By that time it must have been about midday and our tummies were grumbling loudly. We very rarely ate breakfast so we were still waiting for our first meal of the day. Michael and Isobel's flat was on the first floor and the stairs were on the exterior. It was an ugly 1950s block with concrete landings on each floor. Mum banged on the front door and we heard a baby crying. The door opened and there was Mary, looking as shocked as I had ever seen her.

'Oh,' she let out a little cry. Mum bustled us in through the door. Michael was sitting at the kitchen table with a large sandwich in front of him, Isobel sat opposite with Vicky on her lap and Mary's place was next to this, her half-eaten sandwich on a plate. Margaret and I looked at the food hungrily.

Michael got up. 'Mary, put the kettle on.'

Isobel watched over the top of Vicky's head, which was covered in golden curls.

'I'm hungry,' I whispered to Mum, tugging gently at her arm.

'Shush, wait a minute,' she answered.

Mary filled the kettle as Mum sat in the place she had vacated. She looked at Mary and said, 'You're coming home,' and as Mary tried to protest, Mum turned to Michael.

'If she's not home by Monday night, I'm informing the army that she's been living here for more than the allowed three months, and you'll be in deep trouble.'

With that she stood up, scraping the chair across the floor and grabbing our hands, dragged me and Margaret out of the door, both of us casting a longing, backwards look at the unfinished food on the table.

Mary didn't want to come home. She had tasted freedom, and glimpsed a different kind of life. Michael and Isobel were quite poor, and their flat was small and cheaply furnished, but for the first time in her life Mary had her own bedroom. She was allowed to go out with Dave a few nights a week or he would sit and watch television with them after Vicky had been put to bed. The only rules Mary had to follow were to help out Isobel with the washing up, keeps things tidy, and play with Vicky in the evenings before she was put to bed. It was quiet and uncrowded in the flat compared to our house, and she was allowed to see her friends without it causing an argument. She definitely wasn't going home. Michael came up with a solution. He had a friend who ran a pub down the road, and he let out a small room in the attic. Michael suggested that Mary live there and just come to the flat in the evenings for her meals and to keep Isobel company if Michael was working. That evening when Dave came round he was greeted by Mary sobbing her heart out.

'What's wrong love?' he asked putting his arm round her. When she told him the whole story he was horrified.

'There is no way you're living in a pub,' he said. 'My aunt's got a room; we'll see if you can live there.' But when they told Dave's mum, she immediately insisted that Mary move into the spare room until she and Dave were married.

Mum didn't say a word when she heard the news, but I could tell from the set of her lips that the battle was far from over.

19

Mary's Wedding

During the time Mary lived at Dave's parents' house, she would send us little gifts, which her old friend Helen would bring round. At first Mum didn't tell us who they were from, but one day we happened to be there when Helen knocked and heard her say she had brought us some things from Mary. Nothing was very expensive, sometimes a ribbon or a new slide for our hair, but I treasured those things because they were mine and only mine. One day after several months living at Dave's parents' house, Mary and Dave came to visit. It was the first time that we had seen them since the argument. It was a Saturday afternoon, and Pat had been to the shops in Green Lane to get a piece of meat from the butcher there, and had just got back, when there was a knock on the door. It was the family knock: rat-ta-tat-tat tat-tat. Mum was in the scullery getting the meat ready for our Sunday dinner and called out, 'Open the door, can you?'

Pat grumbled as she got up from her chair, which she had just positioned ready for the football results on the television. Margaret and I were playing on the floor with a pile of paper and pencils, Margaret drawing dollies and me drawing horses as usual.

'Oh,' said Pat when she opened the front door.

We heard Mary's voice: 'Hello Pat.'

We ran out into the passage and then stopped suddenly. We weren't sure if we were allowed to hug her or not.

Mum came out of the scullery with that pinched look on her face. 'Oh, what do you want?'

'We want to invite you all to the wedding,' Mary replied trying to smile.

'Wedding? What wedding? You're not twenty-one yet and you need my permission, and you needn't think I'm giving it either,' Mum answered, standing in front of poor Mary.

At this point Dave spoke up. 'Look, we just wanted to know how many of you lot want to come,' he said. 'My mum needs to know how many to cater for.'

Mum swung her stare in Dave's direction.

'Did you hear what I said? She needs permission and I'm not giving it.'

Mary starting to quietly cry and Dave put his arm around her.

'And you can stop that silly nonsense right now,' said Mum with her hands on her hips. I wasn't sure if she meant the crying or the comforting, so I watched Mary and Dave to see what would happen next.

Dave guided Mary back out of the house; they hadn't even got as far as the kitchen. As they left, he turned to Mum and said, 'We're getting married this October whatever happens. If you don't give your permission, we'll just have to ask Mary's dad,' and with that parting shot they walked back down the path to Dave's motorbike with Mary still crying and Mum wearing a look that was a mixture of anger, incredulity and shock. I was puzzled. Didn't Dave know that we didn't have a dad? What did he mean? The air was heavy with the coming storm, but strangely it never arrived.

I don't know what made Mum change her mind about giving Mary permission to get married, but she did.

This entailed a visit to the registrar. We went with Mary and Mum into a big building with shiny polished floors. Mum asked the lady behind a desk something and she pointed to the big swing doors. As we went through Mum turned to Mary: 'You wait outside with these two; I need to talk to the registrar first.' So we duly waited outside. After what seemed like hours, but was probably no more than twenty minutes, the door opened and Mary was called in while we sat outside swinging our legs and waiting. This process was to be repeated every time one of us was to get married, but it would be very many years after that we found out what Mum told those registrars.

A few weeks later, Mum called Margaret and I downstairs. We had been practising rolly pollies on the double bed that Margaret shared with Josie while listening to Dusty Springfield singing 'I Just Don't Know What to Do With Myself' on Josie's tiny transistor radio. I had done so many, so badly, that my neck was wobbling as though my head was going to fall off, so it was quite a relief to have a reason to stop. We ran downstairs to find Mum sitting in her chair by the fireplace with a strange look on her face. She was holding a letter in her hand.

'Do you and Margaret want to be Mary's bridesmaids?' she asked.

'Can we?' I asked. Margaret looked on hopefully.

'Yes of course you can, Mary's your sister! She's coming over on Saturday to take you out to get your dresses.' I was eleven years old and Margaret was almost ten. Of course I had already been a bridesmaid to my cousin Julie when I was seven, all dressed in green satin with a feathery headband and silver sparkling shoes, but Margaret had never been one and was very excited. Even now, almost fifty years later, whenever I hear that Dusty Springfield song I still think of rolly pollies and bridesmaid dresses!

My family were still not going to the wedding. Michael had been forbidden from giving Mary away but Peter had said he would do it despite what Mum had decreed and so that was the arrangement. Then suddenly, just a few weeks before the ceremony, Mum wrote to Mary and told her that the whole family would be going to the wedding after all! This caused all sorts of panic to Dave's mum and dad, who were not only planning the wedding with Mary and Dave but were also paying for much of it, but Mary was still happy that Mum and our sisters and brothers would all be there.

The day before the wedding, Margaret and I were taken to stay at Dave's house, so that we would able to go to the hairdressers early in the morning. Dave's house was a Victorian terraced house in Leytonstone in the East End of London and had no inside toilet, so we had to go through Dave's dad's lean-to if we needed to go. I remember the smell of geraniums and damp earth, and Mary telling us that if we needed the toilet in the night there was a 'pot' under the bed.

When we woke in the morning, Mary was already up.

'Come on, you two,' she said happily, 'we have to be at the hairdressers in half an hour.' We had never been to the hair-dressers before, and were full of excitement at the prospect. I just hoped desperately that my head wouldn't ache. I had devel-oped severe migraine headaches when I was about seven. I remember clearly the first time I had a bad attack. It was on the way back from a day trip to Southend with Aunty, Margaret and Marion. We had gone by train and on the return journey I had vomited all the way home and my head had felt as though it was ready to burst open. I was now constantly afraid of getting a 'bad head', as my Mum would call it. It always seemed to happen when I was excited, afraid, hot or hungry. Today was a potential 'bad head' day and even at eleven years old I feared it.

Once we were dressed, Mary walked us towards the hairdressers.

'What will they do to our hair?' I asked, skipping along beside Margaret, holding her hand.

'What would you like them to do? Do you want it curly?' I started to laugh, Margaret and I both had hair as straight as a poker!

Margaret started jumping up and down, 'Curly yes, curly!' When we arrived we were led into the salon. Mary was whisked off somewhere, and Margaret and I were left to the mercy of a very miserable-looking pair of hair stylists. They plonked us onto a chair next to each other and looked stonily at us.

'I don't know what she expects us to do with these two,' one of them muttered to her colleague. 'Look at this hair! Looks like it's been cut with a knife and fork.'

The other woman smirked in response, 'It looks like they've been dragged through a hedge backwards.'

Our hair was pulled and tugged and roughly fashioned into an upswept style that would have been more suited to a thirty-year-old. These women continued to talk over our heads as though we were invisible; they criticised our hair, the way we were dressed, and muttered and moaned the whole time. We emerged from the hairdressers resembling two miniature astronauts' wives and with all the morning's happiness now replaced with that familiar dread of being different, and not being good enough.

Apart from Peter arriving very late for the wedding – almost too late to give Mary away – the rest of the day went quite smoothly and we managed to have fun. In our yellow nylon flouncy dresses and with our upswept astronaut's wife hair we danced the night away! I have always loved a good family wedding. Even as an adult they remind me of so many happy times throughout my younger life when we would see all of our sisters and brothers together again, even long after they themselves were married and had their own children. Of course the only one who never came, who was never invited, was Sheila. She was the secret sister that I would never meet and never really know, and it was only after my son Sam was born that I found out why.

20

The Sewing Machine

With Mary and my brothers now married, that left only Pat, Josie, Marion and Marge bringing money into the home. Aunty always paid the rent, but food, gas and electric gobbled up the family's income and that was without the added stress of Mum's 'callers' who knocked for their money every week, and who were a persistent drain on Mum's purse. It must have been a constant juggling act for her, deciding who to pay what and when, but she was clever and astute and knew what she could get away with.

Josie was now working in London at an insurance company. She really liked her new job and was very well thought of, especially by the company secretary, Miss Pomfret. She told Josie that she had 'high hopes' for her; that she was a clever young lady and would go far as long as she continued to work hard. Then came the incident of the sewing machine.

Josie was keen on sewing but had to make everything by hand, which took a long time, especially as she didn't have much spare time after she had finished work and travelled home from London. She would go up to her room when she got home and not come down again until quite late in the evening, after everyone else had finished eating. Then she would get her dinner, and sit and eat it before she started her sewing.

She and Mary had started making their clothes some time ago when they realised that it was the only way they could keep themselves neat and tidy for work. Mary had also tried to make Margaret and I a few little things to wear, but now that she was married she wasn't able to do that so often, so the burden fell to Josie.

Mum said that Josie needed a sewing machine.

'I know, but there's no way I will be able to afford one,' said Jo. 'They cost a fortune.'

'I'll ask Mr Blanchflower if he can get us one,' suggested Mum.

Josie shook her head. 'Oh no, no don't. Please Mum, I'll make do.'

But the idea was planted in Mum's head now and within a few weeks an electric sewing machine had arrived. It was a big occasion. Shiny new items like that were not usually part of our life, so everyone was keen to 'play' with it, even though we all knew that it was Josie's. It was put in the front room where Pat slept, and was to be used in there, as there wasn't any space anywhere else to set it up.

Poor Josie was now responsible for the weekly repayments, which no doubt were charged at extortionate interest rates. It was a struggle, but Josie managed to find the extra money each week that Mum needed to pay the sewing machine off. After about six months it became clear that the sewing machine was a white elephant. Josie didn't really have time to use it much, and of course, even fabric was expensive, so slowly the machine became idle. Josie got more and more fed up and must have mentioned it at work.

'Why don't you sell it?' suggested one of the other girls in the office.

'Who to?' asked Josie despondently. 'I don't know anyone who could afford it.'

Miss Pomfret had overheard their conversation.

'If you really want to sell it, Josephine, then I would be very interested,' suggested Miss Pomfret kindly. 'I need to make the curtains for my new home, and have been thinking about getting one.'

That evening when she got home from work Josie told Mum what Miss Pomfret had offered.

'Hmm I think that would be a sensible idea,' said Mum thoughtfully. 'Yes, I think you should go ahead and sell it.'

The sewing machine was duly sold and poor Josie had to carry it into London on the train even though it was quite big and heavy. Josie gave the money from Miss Pomfret to Mum to finish paying for the sewing machine. She was so relieved to have the burden of the debt taken away and gave it no more thought.

A month or two after, Mary sent a dress for me that she had lovingly sewn by hand. Dave's Mum sometimes got off-cuts of a new fabric called 'Crimplene' and Mary had chosen some pale pink to make me a shift dress. It was gorgeous, and I loved it to bits! She hadn't had quite enough of the pink so had sewn a wide band of contrasting purple Crimplene around the hem and the sleeves. I tried it on and it was perfect! Mum made me stand on a chair while she looked on smiling. Then I saw Margaret looking on enviously.

'I'm sure Mary will make you a dress next time,' I said.

Mum looked at Margaret. 'I know,' she said, trying to cheer her up. 'We'll get Josie to make you one.' Then a strange look came over her face, and she was distracted and deep in thought until that evening. Josie was tired out from a long day at work when Mum told her about the dress for Margaret, so she didn't look very keen.

'I don't know, Mum, I haven't got much time at the moment,' she said, knowing that to sew it by hand would take hours of work.

'Well, why don't you ask that nice Miss Pomfret if you can borrow the sewing machine for a week or two? I'm sure she won't mind.'

Josie knew that Miss Pomfret would happily lend her the machine, as she had said so when she had bought it from her.

'Maybe,' she said, 'I'll have a think.'

'Oh please, please, please, Mo Mo,' said Margaret, using the pet name that she had for Josie. Josie couldn't refuse Margaret anything with her big brown eyes and sweet little face.

'Oh all right, I'll see what Miss Pomfret says.'

The sewing machine returned to our house the following week, and Josie took Margaret out on the Saturday morning to

Romford market to choose some material for her dress. She chose a dark purple velvet material, which Josie knew would be a nightmare to sew, but she let her have it anyway. It took a few weeks of the odd hour here and there before the dress was completed. Margaret tried it on.

'You look beautiful!' exclaimed Mum proudly, and indeed she did. Josie had made a good job of it, and the dress, although simple in design, looked really nice.

'I'll take the sewing machine back on Monday,' said Josie, pleased that the dress was finally finished.

'Oh okay, but I know Mary was wondering if she could borrow it to make a couple of bits. She works really fast so it would only be a week or so longer.' Josie agreed to check with Miss Pomfret to see if she minded. Miss Pomfret agreed that she could keep the sewing machine for as long as she wanted.

The next day Mum told Josie that Mary had collected the machine and would bring it back when she had finished with it in a week or so. Three weeks later it still hadn't been returned.

'Mum, can you ask Mary for the sewing machine? Miss Pomfret is taking a week's holiday and wants to make some curtains.'

Mum's face seemed to lose a bit of colour. I watched as she went into the scullery to put the kettle on. Something wasn't right.

'Mum, did you hear me?' called Josie after her.

'Yes, of course. I'll send her a letter and ask her to bring it back straight away.'

'Well, I suppose I could go over there at the end of the week and collect it on my way home,' offered Josie, but Mum came in with the teapot, shaking her head.

'No, no there's no need to do that; Mary can bring it over on Saturday. She wants to see the littluns anyway and Kathleen can show her how nice the dress she made her looks.'

When Saturday came, and Mary didn't arrive, Josie started to get anxious. She was sure Mary wouldn't intentionally let her down, and she began to wonder if Mum had forgotten to write the letter.

'Mum are you sure you wrote to Mary?' she asked.

Mum smiled.

'Oh yes, I forgot to tell you, she wrote back asking if she could keep it for another week, just to finish off some bits.'

Josie was annoyed. 'But I told you Miss Pomfret needs it back. She takes her week off from next Friday.'

Mum promised to go over to Mary's and collect the sewing machine herself on Monday to make sure Josie would have it to take back on Tuesday. Of course on Monday evening it still wasn't there. A dreadful realisation started to dawn on Josie. While she was drinking her tea she kept looking at Mum, who steadfastly refused to meet her eyes. Marion and Marge were washing up and Pat had the television on, but all the time I could feel the tension growing in the room.

Then suddenly Josie said, 'Mary hasn't got it has she?' almost in a whisper. When I looked at Mum I knew that was the truth. She got up and went out into the scullery and Josie followed her. 'You've given it back, haven't you? Mary never had it at all, did she? You've sent it back, back to Blanchflower!' We heard Josie's raised voice, and Mum's calm, quiet replies, but we didn't hear any more words.

Josie didn't go to work the next day, or the day after. She stayed in bed for almost a week, and we hardly saw her. Josie never went back to the job she had loved and to Miss Pomfret, one of the few people who had ever believed in her. Mum rang them to say she was leaving, and she never returned, not even to work out her notice or to say goodbye.

21

Mum's Good Luck

Marge and Ron were getting engaged and were going to have a big party! I was so excited. It meant that all of my sisters and brothers would be there and my aunts and uncles and cousins. Marge had to have a new dress, a special one for the party! The twins went shopping with Mum and when they came home they were carrying two dresses. The dresses were exactly the same except Marge's was white and Marion's was blue. They had a lacy bodice and a full flouncy net skirt, and Margaret and I fell in love with them. When we rushed forward to look, Mum said firmly, 'Don't touch, you'll make them dirty,' so we had to be satisfied with looking at them from a distance.

As the day of the party grew nearer, we got more and more excited. Marge and Ron had hired a hall in Ilford, and our brother Michael, who was now a fully trained chef in the army, was going to do the catering and make the cake.

Then we had some more exciting news. Over the past few weeks Mum had been in a competition. Every week she updated Marge and Ron with her progress.

'Only twenty people left in the draw now,' she said, and the next week: 'Only 10 people left now.'

The first prize was a car, and she was now in the last four. When Ron called round for Marge that evening, she asked him in for a cup of tea.

'You'll never guess what,' she started. 'I've only won that car!'

Margaret and I were amazed.

'Yes,' she continued, 'and I've decided that I am going to give it to you, Ron.' Marge stared ahead with an anxious look on her face.

'After all,' said Mum, 'you've been so good to me taking me and the littluns out; you deserve it.'

Ron didn't look as pleased as I thought he would. Didn't he realise he was going to get a nice brand new car?

Then Mum carried on. 'The only thing is I need to pay the £50 for the prize to be released and to pay the tax and other stuff before I can collect it for you.'

Marge still hadn't said anything, but Ron now replied. 'Where are you going to get that sort of money from?'

But Mum was ready with a solution. 'Well, I thought if you sold your car and gave me the money, I could pay to get the new car released for you,' she said smiling.

Ron didn't answer at first, but I saw him exchange a look with Marge.

'I don't think that's a very good idea,' he said. 'I'll wait until the car arrives before I sell my old one just in case anything goes wrong and then you can have whatever money I get for it.'

Mum looked disappointed, but nodded in agreement. I think something did go wrong because that car never did arrive.

Marge and Ron's engagement party was great fun. We had sausages on sticks, pineapple and cheese on sticks, little vol-au-vents filled with cream cheese, sandwiches and cakes. There was also lots of lemonade and cherryade and the grown-ups had beer and whisky. Aunty got a bit tipsy on the bottle of brandy Michael had brought her and danced with a plate on her head while Mum looked on disapprovingly. On Monday, after it was all over and the girls had gone back to work, Margaret and I crept up to the big bedroom that the twins shared with Aunty and quietly pulled open the cupboard door. There were the dresses! We slipped into them, me in the blue one and Margaret in the white, and then proceeded to bounce on the bed, giggling and laughing until we almost cried with the naughtiness of it.

I was twelve now and my friendship with Anne meant that school continued to be fun.

During our second year at school the headmistress, Sister Joan, told us there was going to be a school trip to Switzerland. It sounded wonderful. The trip would be by rail across Europe and because it would take so long there would be little 'couchettes' to sleep in on board the train. The final destination would by Lake Lugano, which was on the Swiss Italian border.

Anne was excited. 'I think we should go,' she said matter-of-factly as we left assembly. My heart sank. I knew the chances of me being able to go were about zero as the cost would be prohibitive. Several of the girls that we went around with were keen and so the talk from then on was of nothing else. The last date for putting your name down for a place was fast approaching.

Anne was continually on at me. 'Kathleen, will you go and get your name down or all the places will be gone,' she nagged, annoyed that I kept making excuses. The problem was not the 'putting my name down' – it was the £5 deposit that was the issue.

The only member of my family to ever go on a school trip was my sister Josie. She had been sponsored by her school to go to Luxembourg. They had paid all of the cost and even allocated her a small amount of spending money. Josie was always a very good scholar and I think that the school had recognised that she would not be able to take up the opportunity because of financial hardship so had awarded her the trip as a 'prize'. She had absolutely loved every moment of it, and it had sparked a love of travel in her that would last her whole life.

I got home one day after school feeling really fed up. We had been given the deadline of the next day to put our deposit down. Why was it that I couldn't go with my friends? It didn't seem fair. I was resigned to the fact that lack of money meant that I couldn't go horse riding with Anne and Jane on a Saturday, or ice skating, or even to the pictures in the holidays, but I could live with that. This was so much more, something really special that was so out of reach that I had to make myself stop thinking about it. They would all be talking about going all the time, and then when they came back they would be talking about what they had seen and done, and I would be left out of all of it. Different again, just like before, just like in primary school. When Pat and Josie got in from work I thrust the piece of paper with the information about the school trip in front of them. I hadn't bothered to mention it before because I knew it was hopeless.

Josie picked it up. 'What's this then?' she asked scanning the sheet of paper.

'The school trip in May,' I replied almost sullenly. 'The deposit has got to be paid tomorrow.'

'Why didn't you tell us before?' Josie exclaimed.

I shrugged and looked away. I guessed what was coming next. £5 was too much money, and where would they find the rest of the £22 to pay for the trip?

But Josie looked me straight in the eyes. 'Do you want to go?'

I nodded, amazed that she would even need to ask that question.

Then she looked at Pat. 'What do you think?'

Pat shrugged her shoulders.

Then Josie astonished me by saying, 'I'll ring the school from work tomorrow and ask if we can send the deposit next Monday after we get paid. I'm sure it will be fine.'

My mouth dropped open. Could it be true? Was this all it took? Did I just have to ask?

Mum called out from the scullery. 'Ask your Aunt if she wants one or two chops on her dinner.'

'Tell yer mother I'll just 'ave one.'

And then we sat down around the kitchen and ate our dinner, while the whole time I was imagining sleeping on a train that was rushing through snow-topped mountains in a magical country called Switzerland.

22

The Trip to London

Goodness knows what level of hardship poor Pat and Josie had to endure to save the money for my trip, but save it they did. Every week I would take in a little bit more until just a week before we were due to go Josie gave me the final payment. I was ecstatic! Over the past few months Anne and I and the other girls had spent all of our time talking about the trip and I was beside myself with excitement. There were, however, a few blights on my happiness. One of these was the 'what to pack?' issue. Anne had no restrictions financially, so was keen to dictate what we would need.

'We'll have to have a soap bag with a flannel and soap, toothbrush and toothpaste and a nail file,' she announced. There were general nods of agreement, but inside I was beginning to panic. I was pretty sure I could get soap and a flannel but we had never had a toothbrush or toothpaste, although Aunty did soak her false teeth in Steradent. I was pretty sure that this wasn't what Anne meant. As for a nail file, I didn't even know what that was for! This was just the beginning, and just as I would manage to solve one problem, Anne would issue a decree regarding some other essential item that would need to be packed. My head spun. I couldn't ask Pat or Josie for help, as I knew that they were desperately saving any spare pennies to pay for my trip, and Mary was now married. Marge and Marion gave almost all of their wages to Mum and just had enough left over for their fare, and I would never have dared in a million years to ask Aunty for anything, so that just left Mum.

'Mum, I need some long white socks for the school trip,' I asked one day, 'and we can take a home dress to wear in the evenings.' Mum looked over at me while she was ironing on the kitchen table. When we were younger the iron had to be plugged into the light fitting as we didn't have wall sockets, and before that Granny and Mum had an old flat iron. It would have to be heated on the cooking range and then used before it cooled as there was no electricity in the house at that time. This was still out in the garden where Margaret and I had spent many happy hours playing at being grown-ups and 'doing the ironing'.

Now though, we were 'modern'. Not only had electric lighting replaced the old gas mantles which had sputtered and spattered their brightness across the room, filling it with a distinct smell, but we also now had a couple of sockets in the skirting board to plug things like the iron and the television into.

Mum paused from her ironing as though she were thinking things through and then said almost to herself, 'Mmm, you'll need some bits and pieces won't you,' and then carried on ironing. But the seed was sown.

The next day Mum said I wasn't to go to school. I wasn't too bothered, as I knew that Anne was going to a hospital appointment and wouldn't be there anyway. Margaret was off school with a 'cold' so she would be coming out with us. We walked over to the bus stop and caught the 62 to Chadwell Heath station. We got the train to Liverpool Street station which was usually about a half-hour journey, although because we got a slow train that stopped at all of the little stations it took more like an hour. I read the station names inside my head as we stopped, Goodmayes, Seven Kings, Ilford, Manor Park, Stratford, Maryland; on and on we went, seemingly forever. We arrived finally at Liverpool Street, where we got off and walked out into the East End of London. I hadn't been to London very often, although when Pat or Josie had a little spare money they would occasionally take the whole family out, buying each of us a 'Red Rover' bus pass. This pass allowed you to travel anywhere for about 4 shillings each all day, as long as it was 'off peak'. These were brilliant days when we would travel all over London, sometimes with a destination in mind such as Hampton Court or

Kew Gardens, which only cost a penny to get in, or sometimes we'd just jump on a bus and stay on until it reached its final destination and then get off and come back again!

Today though we were in an unfamiliar part of London. We walked around the back of the station towards a large building that looked a bit like a warehouse. When we pushed through the grubby exterior doors into the building it took on a miraculous transformation. It was a massive area that was immaculately clean, the floor shone with polish and there were bright lights illuminating the whole space. All along the walls stood racks of bright new clothes. Hundreds and hundreds of dresses, coats, suits, skirts, knitwear, all presented beautifully. I felt a surge of greed well up inside me. I wanted it all. I wanted to be able to wear lovely things that had never belonged to anyone else, and to look clean and smart and maybe even a little bit pretty. Margaret and I stayed close to Mum. As we walked in I felt eyes upon us, and realised that people were watching. That same old feeling of not being good enough, of Mum being older and fatter than other mums, of having grubby and old clothes, of being different, overwhelmed me and took away the excitement of the clothes, so that I just wished we could go home. Mum had different ideas though. She walked in confidently, approached one of the saleswomen and said, 'I'm one of Mr Blanchflower's customers,' and then proceeded to show the woman a piece of paper and a folded card. The look on the woman's face changed at once, and she nodded and directed Mum to a chair.

'What are you looking for today, madam?' the woman asked, with a smile on her lips but not in her eyes.

Mum answered in her 'special' voice: 'I want a dress each for these two and some shoes for Kathleen.' The lady then asked us to accompany her to the other side of the huge space where there were children's clothes and then left Mum and us alone to look.

I picked out a blue check dress with a white collar and a navy blue shiny ribbon tied in a bow both at the neck and at the sleeves. Margaret chose a plain black velvet dress that would have looked good on someone of thirty, but on a child of ten looked strangely sombre. Then I saw a jacket, it was white with blue trimmings.

'Oh look,' I said, picking it up and fingering it.

'Do you want that as well?' asked Mum.

I nodded enthusiastically. The jacket was duly put with the dresses. Then Mum selected a red skirt with a pretty purple pattern on it.

'What about this?' asked Mum, holding it up to me. Again I nodded, not daring to believe my luck. Mum became almost frenzied. There was a spark of excitement in her eyes, and she had a look about her that we had seen before. The saleswoman finally came back to join us and, seeing the pile of clothes that Mum had collected, went a little pale.

'Do you want to try *all* of these?' she asked, eyeing the assortment of dresses, skirts, jacket, underclothes, shoes and nightdresses. Mum nodded and I was ushered into a corner where the clothes were tried on me. In my eyes they all looked absolutely gorgeous! Margaret wouldn't try her two dresses on as she was too shy, so Mum held them against her and pronounced that they would be fine. The lady began to add up the prices. 'Am I really getting all these things?' I thought incredulously. Then the saleswoman said something too quietly to Mum and they exchanged a few more words that I couldn't hear.

Then the lady said, 'I'll tell you what we'll do. I'll telephone Mr Blanchflower and see what he says.' Mum nodded in agreement and the woman went over to the corner of the space where there was a kind of glass partition with a man sitting behind, head bent, writing with his nose almost on the paper. The saleswoman spoke to him briefly and then he picked up the phone.

It seemed like ages before the lady made her way back across the room smiling. 'Yes that's all fine, Mrs Stevens,' she said using our other special name. I was so happy – we had the best mum in the whole world! The things were then duly parcelled up and Mum had to fill in lots of forms, but luckily didn't have to pay any money. I was puzzled when we left for the station without the clothes.

'Why can't we bring them home with us?' I asked.

'Mr Blanchflower has to bring them because they're too heavy to carry on the train,' answered Mum, starting to get that other faraway look again. I would have been more than happy to have struggled to carry the precious cargo, but I knew there was no point arguing with Mum when she was like this, and anyway, she always made all the rules in our house.

23

A Foreign Adventure

Mr Blanchflower delivered the clothes the following week and he smiled as Mum signed a special piece of paper.

'17/6 Mrs Stevens, starting from next week.'

Mum nodded and smiled back, but after he had gone she told us not to tell Pat or Josie. We never questioned why. We were used to secrets; they were an intrinsic part of our lives. Mum squirrelled the parcels away at the back of the huge wardrobe in the bedroom that she and I shared, until the time came round for me to pack. The clothes suddenly appeared in a large bag that Mum told me to give to Josie. She was packing for me; she was always best at that sort of thing, and had come home from work a bit early to get it done. She lifted the bag that I gave her and my new clothes and the various other items spilled out. I saw the horrified look on her face.

'What's wrong?' I asked. 'Don't you like them? Are they the wrong things to take?' I was worried now, Josie was the only sister to have been on a school trip. If she thought the things were wrong then they must be.

She just shook her head without saying anything and continued to pack. Her lips were drawn tightly together, and when the case was finally packed she said, 'There you are, that's everything now,' without smiling, and put it on the floor of the bedroom and walked downstairs. I could hear her talking to Mum and their voices start to get louder. My stomach churned. I hated conflict, and I could tell by the tone of their voices that they were starting to argue. Josie stomped back upstairs into her bedroom and slammed the door shut, and I went down slowly, worried about the mood Mum would be in. Mum was sitting in her chair by the fireplace and was smoking a cigarette and looking agitated.

'Shall I make you a cup of tea?' I asked trying to cheer her up.

She nodded and then added, 'Pat will be home soon, you can make one for her too,' but she didn't mention Josie.

Josie wasn't talking to Mum. There was an awful atmosphere in the house and we were all walking around on eggshells. Part of me was glad that I was going away on my trip but part of me was terrified that something bad would happen while I was away. I couldn't sleep that night; everything was twirling around inside my head. I knew Margaret was worried, and that I wouldn't be here to look after her, and I knew that Josie was angry about something and that Mum was in one of her downward spirals. Would there be a big argument while I was away? Would Aunty throw things? Would Mum get ill? Would she still be here when I got back? So by the time the morning came and I walked across the road to the bus stop, I carried a heavy weight inside my heart along with the heavy weight of my little case, which I struggled to get on the bus on my own. I was still only twelve years old, but felt as though the world was weighing down on me.

The journey to Switzerland was magical, although parts of it were a bit scary. We had little couchettes to sleep in and I was on the top bunk. I was afraid that I would fall out, but managed to get to sleep in the end, and remember so clearly the smell of the air when I woke up. It was cleaner, fresher, colder and altogether different from the air in Dagenham. Looking out of the windows of the train we watched the scenery change, and saw mountains topped with snow, even though it was late springtime. When we arrived at long last at the hotel our excitement mounted. I shared a room with Anne and little Lizzie M, who was in the first year. We were very protective of her, and felt like the big girls. She would clean her teeth and look in the mirror and say, 'I look like Alfalfa,' and then laugh hysterically at her own joke.

Anne and I were two of the oldest girls on the trip, which was a mixture of first and second year pupils. We assumed the role of protector and guide to the first year's and thought we were very mature. It was probably our fault, however, that we were nearly all killed! Our teachers had told us that we were going for a mountain walk. It sounded like fun, the sun was shining, and we had eaten our continental breakfast of rolls, jam and unsalted butter. The hotel made us packed lunches which we had to carry ourselves, and off we set. For the first couple of hours everyone's spirits were very high. We knew we were going on a boat trip the next day to a place called Isola Bella, which sounded lovely. Then a bank of white cloud obscured the sun and the air turned colder quite suddenly. Anne and I were at the back of the very long and very straggly line of girls, which was beginning to slow more and more as the younger children got tired. The teachers were now a very long way ahead, and were completely out of our sight. We stopped to look at something, I can't remember what, but by the time we tried to join the rest of the group we realised we didn't know which path to take. Some of the younger girls started whining, 'I'm tired, I want to go back,' but of course we didn't know which way back was. Then Anne had her 'good idea'.

'I know,' she said authoritatively, 'I'll climb up on to that ridge and will be able to see over the top of the trees and bushes to where the path is.'

I was less convinced at this but as always I deferred to Anne.

She duly climbed up on to the ridge and declared loudly, 'It's okay – I can see the pathway. It goes down through those bushes,' and she pointed to what seemed to me an unlikely route. But who was I to argue? One of the younger girls had started to cry and there were several others who were threatening to join them.

'Okay,' I replied. 'Let's go,' and I began to usher the group towards the tiny gap in the shrubbery which opened onto a narrow, steep track.

'Down here,' Anne shouted leading the way with confidence. I carried on at the rear of the group, desperately trying to encourage the others to keep up. I took their bags from them and carried them myself, as all the while the bushes got thicker and the track got steeper, until it was obvious that this couldn't possibly be the right way. Many of the younger girls were almost hysterical by now, as they slipped and slid downwards often losing their footing to be hauled back to their feet by Anne or me. Finally Anne called a halt. We sat everyone down and told them to eat their lunch. No one felt much like it but we insisted. We thought it would be good to have a rest and it would also make the bags lighter to carry. Anne then told me to stay with the others while she went to scout out a way back. After what seemed like a very long time she returned.

'Listen,' she whispered to me. 'I don't want to worry the others but we need to go back up. Just the other side of that slight ridge there is a steep drop. There is no way we can carry on this way.'

My heart sunk. It had been hard enough travelling downwards, but to go all the way back uphill was going to be horrendous! But there was no other way, so after picking everything back up we broke the news to the others that we would have to retrace our steps. They were not happy, but they didn't have much choice. They trusted us to keep them safe, and we were determined to do just that. It took us at least two hours to reach the proper pathway again, and it was with much relief and anger that we spied the teachers and the rest of the group standing at the top waiting for us and laughing. No one had been in the least bit worried or showed the slightest concern that we could have fallen off the mountainside!

Our next destination Isola Bella, or 'beautiful island', was just that. It was a tiny Italian island where there were no cars or buses, no traffic of any description apart from the odd donkey and a few cycles. We reached it by ferry and the first thing that struck me as we got off the boat was the silence and the freshness. It was spring and there was blossom everywhere. Beautiful flowers already tumbled out of the window boxes that seemed to hang on every wall. The houses were all painted white, and the Mediterranean light made them sparkle in the sun. The smells were intoxicating and assaulted our senses with a mixture of heady perfumes from the flowers and aromatic herbs and spices that flowed freely from the open windows as the inhabitants cooked their exotic food. Anne considered us to be the sophisticates of the group and suggested we left the main party to wander around. Our teacher had said we were allowed an hour to explore the island and that we would meet back at the ferry. So off we went, my friend Anne and I, walking through narrow cobbled streets that threaded backwards and forwards across the island like looped ribbons. Finally as we climbed down a sloping path that led towards the shore, we saw a tiny local bar. We went in, full of confidence and were directed towards a beautiful balcony that looked out to sea. It was such a clear blue that it hurt my eyes to look at it and made me think it couldn't be real. The sea in England never looked like this. A young waiter came over with a kind smile on his face, probably surprised at the youth of his customers.

I hesitated. 'Um, well . . .'

'Two Pepsis with ice and a slice of lemon please,' Anne ordered confidently.

It was the best drink I had ever tasted.

We left for England the next day and only then did I begin to wonder what I would find on my return, and whether or not all would be calm in the Coates household. When I got back to Barking station with Anne, her sister was waiting to meet her. She ran up, taking her case from her as they walked towards home. I, on the other hand, had no one to meet me. I knew that I would need to get the 62 bus, but didn't have any money. I'm sure that if Anne's sister had realised that I didn't have any way of getting home she would have given me the bus fare, but I was too ashamed to ask.

I stood at the bus stop outside the station and wondered what to do. We didn't have a phone so there was no way of ringing anyone, and I certainly didn't think I would be able to walk all the way home with my suitcase, which was now even heavier than when I left home, filled up now with the little bits and pieces I had bought as gifts for my family. I stood watching several buses come and go, knowing that they could take me home, take me to the family who I had missed desperately for the ten days I had been away. I came to the conclusion that the only way I could get home to them was to try to 'hop' my fare; that is to get on without paying and hope the conductor didn't notice. Sure enough when the next 62 arrived I got on. Luckily there were several people who got on with me, and the bus was already quite crowded. I sat down near the front next to an old lady and looked down at the ground when the conductor shouted, 'Any more fares? Any more fares please?' I felt hot and ashamed and looking down, almost held my breath the whole way home.

As the bus stop outside my house came into view, I started to relax a little and looked towards the platform where you could wait to get off. Again I was lucky, as there were three others getting off at the same stop and one of them rang the bell. On hearing this I quickly jumped up and hopped off the bus as soon as it stopped, without the conductor realising that I hadn't paid my fare, and quickly walked across the road, dragging my suitcase in both hands, feeling as though I were a hardened criminal now and carrying the burden of guilt that all Catholics are born with. I knocked on the front door and heard Pongo barking and Mum coming to open it.

'Hello,' I said, almost shyly. It seemed strange being back home, seeing Mum standing there. I felt as though I had been away forever. Mum stood back smiling; taking my case, she ushered me into the kitchen. She didn't hug or kiss me, and I didn't hug or kiss her. We just didn't do that sort of thing, but I knew she was pleased to see me.

'I'll make you a nice cup of tea,' she said as she bustled out into the scullery to put the kettle on. Margaret was sitting on the settee looking very happy, but everyone else was out at work. I looked around at my home. It was tidy but rather dishevelled and the air was permeated by the heavy smell of cigarettes, dog, and cooking fat that I had never really noticed before. The furniture was old and worn and there was only a threadbare rug on the floor. The walls, ceiling and net curtains that hung at the window were a dirty yellowish colour, stained from the nicotine of three heavy smokers, Mum, Pat and Aunty. At least the damp clothes were hanging on the line in the garden instead of around the walls, as the sun was shining. Pongo was jumping up at me, happy that I was home, and I could hear the kettle whistling as it began to boil. I knew then with a sudden intensity that this was where my family lived, where I belonged. Here was my home, and despite the fear and the secrets and the lies, I was glad to be back.

24

Visiting Mary

Mary had a baby boy! She and Dave had recently moved to a modern house on a new estate in a place called Rainham in Kent. Mum said we could go and visit them. It was coming up to the summer holidays and Margaret, Anne and I were going to spend two weeks with Mary and Dave, and we would be able to help with their new baby Tony. As the day to leave drew closer we started to get more and more excited. Mum packed some groceries in a bag and we put a few items of clothing together and they were loaded into Ron's car. He was going to drive us to Kent with Marge and Mum. We all squeezed into his little car and started off. It wasn't too far, but the difference in what we saw around us was amazing. As we left Dagenham behind us and drove through the tunnel, the houses spread out and the landscape became more and more rural. When we arrived, Mary showed us all around the house. It was very neat and clean but Mum didn't look very impressed.

'It's very small isn't it?' she noted, and I saw Mary's face fall.

'Are you staying for lunch?' Mary asked, but Mum shook her head.

'No, we need to be getting back, we'll have a cup of tea though.'

She seemed keen to be on her way and, after saying goodbye to us, left with Marge and Ron. Mary didn't seem that pleased to see us, although she was kind and showed us where we would sleep in a little bed settee all together like sardines.

It was going to be fun. 'We can have midnight feasts!' suggested Anne.

Of course what we didn't realise was that poor Mary and Dave were finding it hard to feed themselves and the thought of another three mouths to feed was very worrying for them. Mary encouraged us to go out every day, so we wandered along the country lanes, going into the farms to look at the animals. Most people were surprisingly kind and usually didn't mind us. One day we visited a pig farm. The smell clung to us, but then we spied an enclosure with a huge sow lying on her back and a multitude of piglets fighting to suckle from her.

'What are you up to over there?' we heard from the inside of a nearby barn. A heavily built bald-headed man emerged holding a pitchfork in his hand.

'You don't want to be getting too close to 'er,' he advised, 'she's got 'er young uns see, makes um a bit vicious.'

'Can we look round?' asked Anne.

'Yep if you like, but be careful, farms is dangerous places!' he added, smiling now. 'Does you want to hold one of the piglets?'

We all nodded our heads enthusiastically.

He passed us a piglet each to hold. They were so sweet!

'I as to watch 'er in case she rolls on 'em.' He bent to the side and picked up a lifeless purpley blue body. 'See,' he continued, 'this is wot can 'appen. Squashed 'im, poor little thing.'

We looked on in fascinated horror at the poor little stiff-legged piglet.

We would also play in the barns if we could get away with it, and Anne wasn't averse to relieving herself in the corner when necessary, which Margaret and I thought was outrageous!

The sun seemed to shine every day, and the lure of the petrol station on the main road, with its mini doughnut stall, was great, so quite soon the little bit of spending money we had was gone.

Margaret sent Mum a postcard saying: 'Dear Mum We haven't got any money but it doesn't matter Love Margaret X'

Anne decided that we needed to get a job. We walked round the lanes knocking at each house we came across to see if we could get one. One lady had us weeding her garden for the whole day. The sun was hot and we were thirsty, but she didn't even offer us a drink. By the end of the afternoon we were getting excited at the thought of how much we had earned. The lady came out into the garden and gave us a few final jobs to do. Then she pulled her purse from her pocket.

'You've really worked hard girls, and have got most of the weeds out – well done,' and then gave us 6d between us for our efforts! Luckily most people were a little more generous.

Not too long after that we heard that Mary and Dave were going to emigrate to Australia. There was a special offer that meant that they could go all the way to Australia for just £10! Australia – the other side of the world. At that time it was almost the same as saying goodbye to your family forever. The distance was so far and the cost of airfares was so high that the possibility of them coming back home or us going to visit was tiny. Emigration wasn't something new, of course. The potato famine in the 1850s resulted in the slow starvation and collapse of society in rural Ireland. Many families had no choice but to leave the land they loved, to search for work and be able to feed their families. The older people had little chance, but the younger men, and in some cases women, could find an escape. So my great grandfather had joined the British army and been sent to India. In Ireland when family members went away like this they would have a wake as it was thought to be like a death. I think we thought of Mary's going as something equally final, and I felt sad to think I would never see her again. When the time came for her to leave, Mum became quite withdrawn. The rift between them had healed over time. Although there had always been a lack of closeness between them, I think Mum felt the loss keenly.

I was growing up fast, and although life at home was still full of turmoil, my friends were very important to me. The poverty at home should have lessened. Pat, Josie, Marge and Marion were all working now and contributing the majority of their wage to the household budget. Mum still got her family allowance and benefits for Margaret and me and Aunty paid the rent. If Mum had been a manager, life might have been reasonably comfortable, but she wasn't. She had a desperate addiction to the highs of life, times when she would spend money we didn't have on things we didn't need, and couldn't afford. Of course the result of this were the mirror images: the desperate lows, times when there wasn't enough money for food and gas, times when we had to hide from the tally men who knocked on the door with a terrible regularity, week after week after week. It also meant that many necessities of life were absent.

The winter after Mary and Dave left was a particularly harsh one. Snow had begun to fall before Christmas and there was a bitter biting wind that cut through my thin coat as I waited for the bus to school every morning. It was just over a week until school finished for the holiday and as I jumped off the bus at Becontree Station I saw Anne and Jane standing on the other side of the road. I waved and crossed to meet them.

'We're just talking about going carol singing tonight,' said Anne, 'Mrs B's collecting for her son's school.' Mrs B was our needlework teacher, who we really liked. Unlike some of the other staff at the school, she took a genuine interest in us and although we were hopeless sewers she never gave up on us. She encouraged us to persevere and spent time helping us sort out our messes. Her son attended a 'special school' as he had a severe disability, and she often talked to us about the things they did there. Recently she had mentioned that they were collecting money to have a hydrotherapy pool installed.

'Are you coming?' asked Anne. 'We thought if we went round Barking we would get more money.' I knew this made sense, Barking was a much more affluent area than where I lived in Dagenham, but I would need bus fare so I hesitated.

'Oh come on, it'll be great. We can practise at lunchtime.'

I nodded my agreement and we talked about which carols we would sing as we walked to school. That evening I asked Pat if I could have some bus money. She always tried to help if she knew I really needed anything, even though she wouldn't have had much left after paying Mum and her fares. She gave me a handful of coins to cover the cost of my fare. It was freezing as I opened the door to go and meet Anne and the others. I waited for the 62 and shivered in my thin coat and plimsolls. The moisture had been drawn up through the canvas into my socks, almost to my knees, forming a dark grey watermark. I always wore plimsolls – they were the only footwear I had. In the summer this was fine, although my feet sometimes felt hot and sweaty, but in the winter months it was desperate. By the time I got to Barking station where we were meeting it had started to snow again. Anne and the others were already waiting for me outside the Wimpy Bar. Off we went, trailing around the long avenues opposite Barking Park where the posher houses were. We had worked out a routine. We would walk up the path of each house, sing a short carol and then knock. It was my job to speak when the door was opened as I had the nicest speaking voice, and was also the only one of us who could say 'hydrotherapeutic'! People were surprisingly generous, and probably just glad to give us a few coins to get rid of us so that they could close the door on the atrocious weather. Then we had a real stroke of luck. Suddenly we heard the sound of trumpet music. It was the Salvation Army carol singers. At first I thought that this was bad news, as they were much more impressive than our little group, but Anne knew better.

'Look I know what we can do, we can just follow them round and then knock and shake the box. People will think that we are collecting for them!' It was a brilliant scheme and by the end of the evening the collection box Mrs B had provided us with was full to bursting and we hadn't even had to sing!

25

Being Discovered

I think God invented puberty as a form of torture that would make sure we grow up with strength of character!

Mum was sympathetic. 'I've got you some special soap,' she would say and hand me a bar of Neutrogena soap, which all the advertisements said would miraculously cure spots. Of course the spots remained, my body started to change shape, and each month I would have to spend at least a day curled up in a ball with cramping pains in my stomach. Mum would make me a hot-water bottle, give me an aspirin and tuck me up on the settee. Although I was in pain, it was comforting, and oddly became something I almost looked forward to. Being warm, safe and cared for was a luxury and I revelled in it. Margaret was also growing up fast, but still hardly ever went to school. She was quiet and painfully shy, but I had told her as much as I knew about the birds and the bees, which really wasn't much at all.

We had a new teacher at school called Miss Leahy. She taught us maths and PE and was also our form teacher, and she was very different from any of the other teachers we had had before. Miss Leahy was Welsh, and was very athletic. She always wore trainers and leggings and bounced around the school with a calm, firm air of authority. No one dared cheek her or misbehave in any of her classes. No one except Anne, of course. Anne could get away with anything. Perhaps we were such good friends because I saw in her something of my mum. That same charisma, that sense of fun that drew people in and made them want to be near her, and also that same sense of underlying mischief. Anne had an effect on teachers as well as pupils – even on Miss Leahy.

Our popularity in school meant that we were given certain privileges. We didn't deserve them, and pushed the boundaries at any opportunity. I can remember the many tricks we played on unsuspecting teachers, the salt in their cups of tea, the whoopee cushions, the itching powder, but we seemed to survive each attack with a kind of invulnerability. Our reputation grew, and with it an intoxicating sense of power. Then Miss Leahy discovered my brain.

'Kathleen Coates, come out here and finish this problem please,' she'd say, and I would oblige. I had grown quite expert in concealing any signs of academic ability over the years, and had consequently become lazy. Miss Leahy must have spotted something in me, a moment when I let down my guard, a flash of underlying intelligence. And then there was no escape. During maths lessons she would pick me out to solve problems, to explain things to the rest of the class, to do 'special' work which I actually started to enjoy.

'What are you doing in the C class, Kathleen Coates?' she asked me one day. I was taken aback. She was the teacher; how should I know? I just shrugged my shoulders in answer and she raised her eyes. 'You, young lady, are wasting your brain and my time.'

Being noticed for intelligence was exciting and I began to feel that I was special in my own right, and not just as an extension of Anne. It felt strange, and it also felt good, but I knew I was walking a dangerous line. Then came parents' evening.

Miss Leahy asked if my mum was coming. Mum never came to parents' evening. What was the point? I was in the C class. No one came and that suited me fine, because it also meant that there was never any danger of me being moved to a higher stream. I was comfortable in my laziness, and I didn't want to leave Anne behind. But Miss Leahy was determined.

When I got home from school that afternoon, Mum was holding a letter in her hand.

'Your teacher wants to see me,' she said. 'You didn't tell me it was parents' evening next week.' I looked away, pretending my heart wasn't beating double fast.

'Yes, it's on Tuesday,' I answered in what I hoped was a disinterested way.

'I think Pat and I should go.'

My heart plummeted to my knees. *Oh God no*. Everyone would mistake Pat for my mum like they always did; everyone would think Mum was my gran. I would be so embarrassed.

'Oh don't bother,' I said. 'What's the point anyway?'

But Mum was adamant. I never found out exactly what was in that letter, but it must have been powerful stuff!

When Tuesday came around I wanted to die. Mum and Pat got their coats. They didn't have good clothes and they were both very overweight. There was never any money spare for hairdressers so they looked dishevelled and permanently untidy however hard they tried. Both Mum and Pat smoked heavily and the evidence was visible in their nicotine-stained fingers. Teenage years are painful for all sorts of reasons, but one of the most powerful is that need to be the same, to belong, not to be seen as different. Even though at school I had re-invented myself, the spectre of home always lurked, waiting to trip me up and remind me that I could never be quite like the other girls. And now everyone was going to discover my secret.

Parents' evening was held in the school hall and the teachers were positioned at various points around the walls. There were chairs placed nearby so that parents could sit and wait for their turn.

'Where is this Miss Leahy?' Mum asked as she scanned the sea of faces.

'Over there,' I muttered with my head down, dreading what was to come. As we walked across the hall I saw several girls looking at me, but they weren't in my class; in fact hardly any girls from the C classes were there. As we approached, Miss Leahy spotted me and called me over.

'Hello Kathleen, this must be your mum,' she said, extending her hand towards Pat. Mum stepped forward and took it.

'Good evening,' she said in her best voice. 'I'm Mrs Coates.' Mum was never intimidated by authority; she was a very intelligent and articulate woman and could hold her own with anyone.

Miss Leahy composed herself and asked Mum and Pat to take a seat. I stood by mortified. 'Kathleen is in the wrong class,' she began. 'She's a clever girl and has a mathematical brain. I would like her to move to the O-level class next year so that she can take her exams.'

Mum sat nodding, but I couldn't read her face.

Miss Leahy continued: 'I don't know why she's in 3C. She's clearly bright enough to take her GCEs but if she stays where she is she will only be able to take CSEs, which would be a real shame. It will mean lots of hard work, but Mrs Lobbit can give her extra maths lessons over the summer holidays to help get Kathleen ready.'

Mrs Lobbit was a young science and maths teacher who was very trendy and wore modern 60s clothes, short skirts and shift dresses. She had shiny straight hair that was cut at her shoulders in a style that made her look like Sandie Shaw and we all envied her.

Mum hesitated for a few minutes and then smiled at my teacher.

'Kath's not afraid of a little hard work.'

I gulped; this sounded serious.

26

The Halloween Party

Being in the O-level class was a culture shock to me. The girls I was with were focused on their work and the teachers expected homework to be completed on time, and to a high standard. I was halfway between being exhilarating and terrified but I managed to cope. My confidence levels had increased considerably since I was that timid little girl in primary school. By the time I left school I had managed to obtain a clutch of O-levels and was keen to get to work and earn some money.

I needed clothes to go out in and although the discos would usually let girls in for free, we still felt obliged to buy a drink once inside. We usually only ever had to buy that first drink because after that there would be some young man who would be only too happy to supply our drinks in the hope of a good-night kiss on the way home. I had discovered boys!

Mum always encouraged us to have dates. I think she was disappointed and felt a little bit guilty that Pat and Josie had never married, and was keen for the rest of us to find husbands. There had been a period of time when Mum had insisted that I accompany Marion to a series of dances and clubs because now that Marge was 'courting' she didn't have anyone to go with. I had hated it. There was a seven-year age difference between us and the kind of places that we went were beyond my maturity levels. Since Marion had met Geoff and started going steady, I was left to my own devices and the world was full of opportunities. Both Margaret and I had grown into attractive teenagers. Margaret had always been a pretty child but I felt as though I was the ugly duckling turned into a swan as we got more and more attention from the local boys. We both felt so grown up when that Christmas Mum bought us a record each.

Mine was 'Sugar Sugar' by the Archies and Margaret's was 'Tracy' by the Cuff Links and we played them incessantly. I can still remember all the words to both over forty years later.

Halloween was still a fairly low-key celebration, but was starting to gain favour as fashion and trends moved across from America. Margaret loved all things witchy.

'Shall we ask Mum if we can have a Halloween party?' she suggested.

I gave this some thought. 'Do you think she'll let us?' I was sceptical. We had never even had birthday parties when we were younger. In fact the only party in our house that I could remember was when Josie was twenty-one. Mum had invited all our aunties and uncles over, apart from those in Birmingham. We never saw much of Uncle John's family, and they were rarely mentioned in our house by Mum, although Aunty would sometimes say, 'It's a shame the Birmingham lot can't come,' and Mum would turn away without meeting Aunty's eyes.

Michael had made a cake for Josie with '21' written on it and as my birthday fell two days before Josie's, Mum told me the party was for me as well. Of course even though I was only nine I knew that this wasn't really true but I went along with it anyway. The overriding memory of that day was not the disappointment that Josie was the only one who got any presents, or that the cake only had her name on it, but the utter embarrassment of having Julie, my godmother, calling upstairs for me.

'Kathleen,' she called. 'Come on down so we can say Happy Birthday.'

I could see her standing at the bottom of the stairs looking up to where I was crouched behind the banisters. I think she thought I was upset because I was feeling left out, but the truth was that I couldn't find any clean clothes to wear.

'I'll come down in a minute,' I replied, panicking at the thought. Eventually I managed to find a heavy tartan kilt that someone must have donated to us. As it was the middle of a warm August it wasn't particularly comfortable, and I still remember that awful hot scratchy feeling of the rough wool on my bare legs.

So when Margaret made her suggestion about Halloween I was unconvinced.

'We can ask if you like,' I said and she nodded enthusiastically.

'You ask,' she said. 'You're the oldest.' I was just seventeen and we both worked in London in offices. Jobs were plentiful at that time, especially if you could speak nicely, were attractive, and could read and write well. We fulfilled all of these criteria, so had been in work since we left school – Margaret as soon as she was fifteen and me at sixteen. Just like our siblings before us, most of our wages went to Mum, who still had her tally men, or 'callers' as Aunty called them, who continued to bleed our family dry.

'All right, I'll ask, but if she says no I'm not asking again.'

To our complete shock and surprise Mum agreed at once.

'Oh yes, that's a good idea,' she said, her blue eyes twinkling, 'we can decorate the kitchen with witches and make some party food.' On the rare occasions when Mum had hosted family parties in the past, all of the furniture from the kitchen, including the television and settee, had been piled into the front room that Pat used as her bedroom, so that was what was arranged. We rolled up the rug in case people spilt drinks, and cleared a space in the middle of the room for dancing. There was also a table of party food, and all this in a room measuring about 14ft by 12ft!

'The boys can bring the drinks,' Mum said, 'otherwise it will cost too much.' We knew this wouldn't be a problem. I had met a boy called Patrick who was four years older than me, and he was bringing his friends. It was customary for boys to bring drinks to parties. It would usually be huge 7-pint cans of beer called 'Party Sevens' that had to be opened with a can opener and would often spray their contents all over the room and anyone standing close by. Occasionally they would bring a bottle of spirit or two, and there would sometimes be a few bottles of Babycham for the girls.

Margaret and I went over to the phone box to contact our friends, who all had phones in their homes by this time, and so it was arranged.

We bought black sugar paper from the shop across the road and cut out witchy shapes and stuck them on the walls with Sellotape. Mum helped us push the pineapple cubes and cheese onto the cocktail sticks.

'Look, we can stick them in the grapefruit to make hedge-hogs,' she suggested, really getting into the spirit of things now. Josie made vol-au-vents filled with cheese spread and fish paste, and we made some cheese sandwiches.

Aunty went around sniffing loudly. 'All this fuss,' she mumbled. 'Tell your Mother I'm going over to Aunty Mags's.'

I breathed a sigh of relief as she headed out the door. I always felt on edge when Aunty was around; she was still volatile, even in her sixties.

It was on that evening that Margaret met her future husband Tony.

The party was a huge success. We played records really loudly, and Mum came and knocked on the door to tell us to turn it down a bit.

'Oh don't worry about it,' Tony said, 'we can just make out we've done it.' He was always very confident and jokey.

Mum came back a few minutes later and knocked again. Tony pulled her into the room. 'Now then, let's have a dance.'

Across the other side of the room, I braced for an explosion.

'Oh you cheeky monkey!' Mum said, but to my utter amazement she was laughing as she did so.

By the time the party ended Tony had won her over, and Mum was on his side, encouraging Margaret to go out with him the following night.

Although she was only fifteen, Tony was obsessed by her. He was tall and dark and a real 'Jack the Lad' from Plaistow, East London, and most exciting of all he drove a Mini Cooper! He took her out almost every night, although Mum always insisted that we were home by 10.30 in the week and 11 p.m. at the weekend. Wednesday night we had to spend at home and tell our boyfriends that we were 'washing our hair'. They were the rules and woe betide us if we dared to break them, so Margaret never did. I, on the other hand, was a rebel. Perhaps it was Anne's influence, or just because I was the older sister, but I was always pushing the boundaries. Not long after Halloween I wanted to go to an 'all-night party' in London with Patrick. These were very trendy and most of my friends had been to one or more. It was considered a very grown-up thing to do.

Mum was adamant.

'No, definitely not,' she said, arms folded, when I asked her.

'But it's a Saturday night, and I don't have work in the morning,' I wheedled. 'Patrick will bring me home in the car, and I can lay in on Sunday.'

But there was no budging her. Mum had made up her mind.

'What if Margaret and Tony come?' I tried, thinking this might give me a chance.

Mum didn't answer for a few minutes. She went out into the scullery and put the kettle on. When she came back into the kitchen she made a suggestion. 'If Patrick and Tony dig up the front garden for Aunty and weed outside the front door, then you can go,' she announced. I couldn't believe my luck and went over to phone Patrick straight away. Of course he and Tony kept their side of the bargain and so did Mum, but it set a precedent. From then on our lives were all about bargaining. She used us as a kind of currency to get things done by the boys, which was rather inconvenient at times, but at least it meant that we got to do the things we wanted most of the time.

Marion and Marge were outraged.

'How come you're allowed to go out till past twelve? We had to be in at half nine at your age,' they complained, even though they were both married by this time. I just shrugged my shoulders and smirked.

Things didn't always work out so smoothly though. The one thing Mum didn't ever budge on was having one night in a week for supposed 'hair washing'.

'But I wash my hair every night!' I argued. I thought it was a stupid rule, more about Mum holding onto her control over us than anything else.

'I don't care what you do,' Mum shouted back. 'You're staying in tonight, and that's that!' and she stomped upstairs with a pile of dry washing. Normally I would have given in, but tonight Patrick wanted to take me out with his friend Jim and his girlfriend Sheena, who was one of my friends from school.

I phoned Patrick.

'I can't come tonight.'

'Why not?' he asked, with an edge to his voice. He was getting more and more fed up with having to placate Mum all the time just to be allowed to take me out.

'You know what she's like; she'll go mad if I don't stay in.'

He went quiet at the other end of the phone.

'Look, Jim and Sheena have taken a night off from their bar job to come to that new disco tonight. It will look really bad if we don't go.'

I loved dancing and in the 70s it was big business; every pub seemed to have a discotheque. They were all flashing lights, loud music and hormones.

I made a decision. 'Okay, I'll come. I don't know how, but just pick me up at eight. I'll be ready.'

Patrick was from an Irish Catholic family who also lived in Dagenham, although on another part of the Becontree estate. He was four years older than me and an apprentice printer. We had been going out for almost a year now. He was twenty-one and was quite tall, stocky and broad, with blue eyes and floppy brown hair. He was very ambitious, a real hard worker, and looking forward to completing his training. 'That's when I'll start earning really big money,' he would say, 'and I can buy you things like Tony buys Margaret.' The truth was, I didn't care at all about that, but Mum did.

'Have you seen that lovely gate bracelet that Tony bought Margaret?' she asked. 'Its 18-carat gold, you know.'

I knew all right, just like I knew about the ring, pendant, charm bracelet, watch and numerous other gifts that Tony could afford to shower on her.

'Tony's already finished his apprenticeship, Mum,' I would point out.

Still, Patrick felt it, and would say, 'One day, you'll see; one day soon I'll give you everything you ever wanted.'

Poor Patrick, he couldn't have got it more wrong.

After I'd rowed with Mum, Margaret would always ask: 'Why do you do it? Why don't you just get home on time / stay in one night a week / not wear your skirts so short? I don't get it.' Well, I didn't really know why either; I just felt that I was old enough to make up my own mind. I was almost eighteen so, as far as I was concerned, I could do what I liked.

That Wednesday I snuck upstairs to put on my make-up and get changed, while everyone was eating their dinner in front of the telly as usual. I put on my new white silky trouser suit. Margaret and I had a favourite shop near Barking Station that sold trendy clothes quite cheaply, and we also shopped in Petticoat Lane Market, so managed to stay fashionable on a very tight budget. I thought I was magnificent! I watched out of the bedroom window, and saw Patrick's little blue Ford Anglia pull up outside at 8 p.m. sharp. Flying downstairs, I burst out of the front door and shouted behind me, 'Bye Mum,' and I was gone. I knew I would have to pay but would worry about that later.

As I jumped in the car Patrick turned and said, 'Wow, you look gorgeous.' I was very slim now and I had lightened my long hair from mousey brown to a coppery blonde. Being attractive to boys was as intoxicating as having friends. In fact it made me feel even more powerful, and I loved to feel boys gazing after me when I walked into the room, even though I was still very innocent.

'What are you doing?' he laughed, as I wriggled out of my trousers. I pulled on my long white platform boots so that I could wear the tunic as an extremely short mini dress. I knew Mum would have gone ballistic if she had caught me!

'You can't go out like that,' he said, suddenly looking concerned.

'Why not? I wear hot pants!'

'That's different,' he said, looking more and more uncomfortable. 'Everyone will be looking at you.'

I smiled. That was exactly my intention.

27

My Secret Sister

We had the phone connected when I was about seventeen and it had been a revelation. No more going to the phone box! Aunty was wary of it at first but was getting more confident about using it to call Aunty Maggie and her other siblings. Mum loved it! She was always keen on gadgets of any kind and buying them on the 'never never' had contributed to the huge debts that she still carried around with her in that big black bag. Like a millstone around her neck it dragged her down and she never let it out of her sight.

Aunty was now retired from Plessey but had gone out and got herself a part-time job in Ilford in the café at Clark's bakery. Margaret and I would sometimes get the bus there on a Saturday to look at the shops.

'Come into me for your lunch,' Aunty would offer, and if we did she would always say, 'what do yer want? Welsh Rarebit?' and would scurry around and present it to us proudly.

'I don't want yer money,' she would say, waving us away, which was just as well as we never had any.

One day Josie and Pat were home from work, as they had both taken a few days holiday, and my brother Michael's middle daughter Sheila was staying at our house. She was only about eight, and loved her Nanny desperately, as did Michael's other two daughters, Vicky and Tricia. They would frequently argue about whose turn it was to come and stay, and the result was often that they all came. I dreaded those times. It wasn't because I didn't love them, just that our house was so crowded already that an additional three bodies made it almost unbearable, especially as they were lively young children. They had all inherited their mum and dad's good looks; they had Michael's colouring so their hair was blonde, but they had Isobel's huge eyes surrounded by dark thick lashes, although where hers were dark Spanish brown, theirs were a bright blue. It was Sheila who had won the fight this time and Pat and Josie were going to take her and Pongo to Valentines Park on the bus to feed the squirrels.

Just as they were getting ready to go, the phone started ringing. I was getting ready to go out with Patrick later that evening and Mum was in the middle of making tea, so Aunty, who had arrived home after her lunchtime shift, wandered out into the hall where the phone was perched on a little table and answered it. I ran down the stairs assuming it would be for me, and stopped short as I heard Aunty shouting into the receiver.

'Hello,' she said, putting on her posh voice. 'Who?' She was going quite deaf now and struggled to hear people on the telephone. 'Who is it? Oh my God!' A shocked smile sprang to her lips. 'Wait . . . Pat, it's your sister Sheila! Florrie, it's Sheila!'

Time stood still. No one moved. No one went towards Aunty in the hallway.

'Pat,' Aunty called again. 'It's your sister Sheila.' I caught sight of Josie and Pat who had been almost on the point of leaving, holding little Sheila's hand. She looked mystified, confused that there was another Sheila on the other end of the phone, and struggling to understand why everyone had suddenly stopped in their tracks.

Pat finally responded. 'I'm not talking to her.' She made to continue towards the door, but then Mum appeared from the scullery.

'It's Sheila,' repeated Aunty again, looking from one to the other, getting more and more agitated. Still no one moved to take the phone from Aunty; Mum bustled back into the scullery, so finally Aunty thrust the phone at Pat who listened for a while, occasionally making a mumbled response.

'I couldn't care less,' she said, 'we're not interested.' After another few minutes she hung the phone up and grabbed little Sheila's hand, muttering, 'Ron Coates is dead.'

With that they left, leaving Aunty, Mum and me lost for words until Mum said, 'Ask your Aunt if she wants a cup of tea.'

Aunty just sniffed, shook her head and, mumbling under her breath, turned away.

No one ever discussed that phone call. No one went to Ron Coates' funeral, no flowers were sent, no card of sympathy to Sheila, daughter, niece, sister, half-sister, was written. The hatred that his former wife and other children felt was still as raw as the day he had deserted them decades before.

It did stir Aunty's memories though. She started letting things slip out. Maybe it was because she was getting older and sometimes forgot the unwritten rules of secrecy, maybe she was being her mischievous self, or maybe she was starting to realise that we all had a right to know about our past. At first there were just occasional comments made when Mum was at the shops or had gone to see Michael.

'He was a terrible womaniser, yer know,' she would suddenly announce completely out of the blue. We would sit in silence. We knew that if we tried to pull any information from her she would shut up like a clam, but if we didn't respond it was almost as if she were talking to herself.

'She was big with Josie when 'e was messing around; 'e said Josie wasn't his,' she continued tutting. 'Wicked thing to say,' and then nothing. Margaret looked at me quizzically; we knew a little about our Mum's marriage to Ron Coates. We had even seen a faded sepia photo of their wedding day, Mum looking beautiful, young and happy, Ron Coates tall and thin and equally youthful, seemingly happy too. Their first three children, Sheila, Michael and Pat, had been born in quick succession with barely a year to eighteen months between them, and then she had got pregnant with Josie when Pat was just over a year old. They were still in their twenties and were soon going to have four children under six years old! Ron Coates left before Josie was born and that was when things for Mum must have started to spiral out of control.

The one thing Aunty would be drawn on was our sister Sheila. If Mum was out we would sometimes dare to broach the subject.

'Aunty, have you read any of Sheila's books?' we would ask, attempting innocence. We knew that she had because we had seen them in her bedroom, and we also knew that she was extremely proud that Sheila was a successful writer.

'Yes I 'ave,' she answered. 'They're a bit lovey-dovey for me, but she's a very clever girl, yer know.'

We chanced our luck. 'Why did she go and live with her dad?' Aunty sniffed loudly. 'Make a cup of tea.'

I leapt up; perhaps she was in a talkative mood. I made the tea, and as Margaret and I sat with her in the kitchen we tried a bit more probing.

'Why don't Pat and Josie talk about Sheila?'

'Your mother was very good-looking, you know.' Aunty carried on sipping her tea. 'All the boys were after her. She could have had anyone, anyone, but she chose 'im.'

We stayed quiet.

'She should have ditched him as soon as 'e started mucking around. It was wicked what he did.' Sip, sip. 'Your poor sisters and little Michael, all of them crying they were, and hanging on to me and your Granny.' Sip sip. 'I still don't know why he did it.' Sip sip. 'Wicked.' There was a loud sniff and then silence.

We waited with baited breath.

'It wasn't her fault; she was only a child. Your mother went mad when she found out.' Sip, sip, sip.

What was she talking about? Who was only a child? Mum? Sheila?

'Who do you mean, Aunty?' I asked.

This was a mistake. Immediately she got up. 'I've got to do me garden,' she said, putting her tea down and picking up her little spade from the hallway as she went.

'Yer mother will be 'ome soon,' Aunty threw over her shoulder.

Margaret looked at me. 'What was she talking about?'

'I don't know, but I'm going to find out.'

'Oh yes, and just how are you going to do that?' Margaret asked.

'I don't know yet, but I am.'

I was sick of secrets, sick of mystery and sick of being treated as though I were still a child. I was eighteen now. It was my right to know, wasn't it?

28

Going to Work

I had been at work for over three years and had been employed in a variety of roles. I had been a receptionist, a telephonist, had worked in a typing pool, been a kind of secretary, and generally had a great time working to live rather than living to work. I had learnt early on that underachieving was a safe option. If you always took on jobs that were easy you could concentrate on the more important things in life like dancing, dating, wearing nice clothes and having fun with your friends. Margaret and I were still very close, and often went out in a foursome with our boyfriends, Tony and Patrick, and sometimes with bigger crowds as well. There always seemed to be someone who was having a party. It was the done thing to have a 'steady boyfriend' and it was also the done thing to get engaged and married young, so when Margaret told me that Tony wanted to get married I wasn't surprised.

'What do you think?' she asked me as we walked to the station, swishing her long black hair. We were both slim and pretty and loved fashionable clothes. We never had any difficulty attracting boys so were quite used to being called out to by any likely young man who fancied his chances.

'Do you like him?' I asked. I knew Margaret would listen to me, she always did, and I felt it was quite a responsibility.

'Yes I do like him; he's really kind and is always buying me presents.'

'Well if you want to get engaged, why don't you? You don't have to get married for a while.'

She nodded and smiled. I knew I had given her the answer she wanted, but wasn't sure if I had given her the answer she

needed as a sixteen-year-old girl with her head in the clouds.
They started saving for the wedding straight away, or rather
Tony did. Margaret didn't earn enough to save and what spare
cash she had went on clothes. Mum hadn't put up any objec-
tions to their marriage; in fact she seemed to be all in favour of
it. They had saved up about £50, which at that time was quite a
lot of money, in order to put a deposit down so that they could
rent a flat of their own. Mum thought she might be able to help.

'I know this friend of Aunty Maggie's,' she told them one day.
'She wants to rent out the top floor of her house but she hasn't
got the money to convert it.'

Tony's ears pricked up; he always liked the idea of a bargain.

'If you could give her the £50 she can put it towards having
the building work done, and the money will act as your deposit.'

Margaret and Tony agreed and Tony went and withdrew the
money and gave it to Mum. Three months later there was still
no news of the flat. Tony asked Margaret about it.

'Has your Mum sorted that flat yet?' he asked.

She shook her head. 'No I don't think so.'

'Can you ask 'er about it then?' Tony suggested. After all, that
£50 represented all of their savings.

But Margaret shook her head again emphatically. 'No, just be
quiet and stop going on about it will you?'

Of course the flat never materialised and neither did the
money. Tony complained to Margaret. 'I don't understand;
where has the money gone then?'

Mum explained that the builder who was supposed to be
doing the conversion had gone broke and had run off with this
poor lady's life savings, including the £50 of theirs. Tony was
angry and wanted to go round there to sort it out, but Margaret
told him that it couldn't be helped, and so they started saving for
the second time.

Margaret and I had never been short of male attention. One
Christmas when I was working on the Thamesview Estate in an
office attached to a small factory, I remember going to the local

pub, the Volunteer, for an office party. The lads from the factory were all there as well, and by the end of the first hour I had a long row of drinks that had been bought for me lined up waiting for me to drink them. By the end of the afternoon I was so drunk I could hardly find my coat. I went back to the office and found my boss, Mrs Lovell, a kindly lady who was tall and elegant and had a beautiful speaking voice. I can still picture her amused look when I asked in a slurred voice, 'Ish it okay for me to go home now Mrs Lovel?' That was probably the sickest I have ever been!

Tony was a very jealous boyfriend, and wasn't happy that Margaret was also popular at work. She worked quite near to me at that time, and was the receptionist at a local firm. Her boss was considerably older than her, though probably still only about thirty, and was besotted by her. He was always asking her to go out with him, even though she told him she had a boyfriend. She was still only sixteen at the time and didn't have the sense not to tell Tony. Once she did, he went mad. 'What?' he roared. 'I'll kill him!'

Margaret realised she should have kept quiet, but it was too late. The next day when she got to work there was a note on her desk. She had been fired. Tony had got there first and had shared a few words with her boss!

Margaret and Tony were married when she was just seventeen and he was twenty-two. It seems insanely young now, but it wasn't particularly unusual for working-class families at that time. Mum and I went with Margaret to arrange for the registrar to attend the wedding. At that time Catholic priests were not allowed to conduct the legal side of weddings so the registrar had to be booked and would attend the church to complete the formalities in the side room.

As we arrived at the offices, Mum turned and said, 'You two wait there while I go in first and I'll call you when we're ready for you to come in.' Margaret duly sat and waited for the call and the process was concluded. This was a scene that was repeated prior to each of our weddings and it wasn't until after she'd died that we discovered what happened. Unbeknownst to us, she'd go in and claim that the bride's father died in Canada – a fairy-tale designed to explain our multiple names.

Margaret and Tony had a big Catholic white wedding but soon after she started to slip into a deep depression. It was this that prompted her to apply to become a trainee State Enrolled Nurse at Southend Hospital, which was to have a profound effect on the rest of her life, transforming her from a timid, compliant, shy young girl into a highly skilled and qualified nurse and a confident young woman.

29

New Opportunities

At the same time that Margaret was applying to become a nurse, I was getting restless and dissatisfied with my office job. I had lots of friends, a steady boyfriend, and a bit more money now, but I was bored. I decided I wanted to be a teacher without the slightest idea of what it would entail. I suppose I had always been the big sister to Margaret, always felt responsible for her, for calming things, keeping situations under control, but now that she was married it was as though a burden had been lifted and I wanted to spread my own wings. I had a friend at work that I often confided in and when I shared my thoughts she encouraged me.

'I think it's a great idea,' she said enthusiastically. 'You'd be a great teacher, I reckon.' I felt buoyed up by her confidence in me and when she came in to work a few days later with the name and address of a teacher training college that her cousin had gone to, I decided to take the plunge. It was called Digby Stuart and was in Roehampton, West London. It had the added advantage that it was only for women, as although I liked male attention I had gone to an all-girls convent school, so wasn't used to co-ed.

Patrick was sceptical. 'Why do you want to go all the way over there?' he asked. 'It'll take you at least an hour to get there each day.'

'I'm not going to live at home,' I told him. 'I'm going to stay at the college in the week.' That was not met with any enthusiasm from him, so when I found out shortly after applying that I was an O-level short of the admission requirements, he couldn't hide his pleasure.

'Oh well,' he said, 'it's probably for the best.' I was so angry inside – it might be best for him but it wasn't best for me! I decided then and there that whatever it took I was going to get into that college one day.

The following spring I applied to take my O-level Art as an external candidate at a local secondary school. It felt strange to be walking back into a school after all this time. When I arrived to sit the first paper, I had done no preparation whatsoever. It was art, wasn't it? And I had always been good at art. The lady in the office pointed me in the right direction and I walked into a big classroom with tables set up. I was wearing my white cheesecloth tunic top over my jeans and my blonde-streaked hair was hanging loose, so I walked in feeling nervous but suitably arty. There were examples of the pupils' work everywhere, paint pots laying around and a general buzz of creativity, and in the middle of it all stood a young man probably no more than four or five years older than me. He had long dark hair, kind eyes and stubble on his chin. To my surprise he was wearing a T-shirt and jeans. The teachers that I knew from my school days had been mostly nuns, and those that weren't were usually mature and sensibly dressed older women. We certainly were never taught by men, let alone attractive young men!

His eyes lit up when he saw me. 'Hi,' he said hurrying over to where I stood. 'Can I help?'

'I'm here to take the exam.'

With a broad smile he led me over to a vacant table. He was kindness itself and by the end of that first day I was beginning to feel more confident. There were three 'papers' to sit in all, arranged over three days. At the end of the third day, as I was about to leave, the young art teacher handed me a letter.

'Please read this when you get home,' he asked, smiling into my eyes. My heart gave a little skip and I smiled back. But as I walked out, I was painfully aware that I was wearing the solitaire diamond ring that Patrick had bought me when we had got engaged a few months before. It had been very expensive, but now that he had finished his apprenticeship money was more plentiful. We'd had a big party and my sister Pat had kissed me on the cheek for the first time ever. Patrick had been insistent that we got engaged when I told him I was determined to go to college. I suppose it was a kind of label saying 'Don't touch, already spoken for' but I didn't really mind too much. Usually I loved my ring, although it made my hand feel heavy. I liked all the gifts we had been given and being the centre of attention at the party; I even quite liked Patrick. We had got used to each other; he was kind and considerate and had accepted and been accepted by my family. His mum was a lovely, funny Irish lady, who I liked to believe was as fond of me as I was of her. Anyway Margaret had said it was about time we got engaged; after all she and Tony had already been married for over a year.

When I got back from that last exam I opened the letter.

'Dear Kathy,' it began. 'When I saw you for the first time a few weeks ago, I thought an angel had walked into my classroom.' I gulped as I continued to read. 'You looked so beautiful standing there, so scared and vulnerable, I just wanted to pick you up and run away with you, and look after you for ever. Please meet me so that we can talk. I promise nothing too heavy, just a chance to speak to you without a class full of kids watching us. Here is my phone number – please, please, please ring me . . .'

'What's that?' asked Mum, seeing me standing in the hallway with the letter in my hand.

I jumped. 'Oh nothing,' I said, looking guilty.

'Let me see then,' she continued. I held the letter downwards so she couldn't read it.

'No, it's nothing. Just embarrassing.'

'Don't be silly, let me have a look.' She held her hand out and I passed it to her reluctantly. She scanned the pages.

'Hmm, what are you going to do?'

'What do you mean? Nothing of course.'

'Why not? Don't you like him?' she asked.

'I'm engaged!' I retorted, shocked at her attitude.

'Yes, but you're not married are you?' she added, looking at me closer than she normally did.

I felt myself blushing; Mum never talked to us about this kind of thing. It felt uncomfortable and wrong but I didn't know why. I took the letter back and ran upstairs. I re-read it a few times that night before throwing it away, but I often thought of that young man and his kind eyes and wondered what might have happened if I had rung that number.

'I've got in!' I shouted, waving the official looking letter from West London. 'I've got a place for this September!' I was so excited. Mum looked over at me, and Pat smiled.

'That's good,' she said.

Mum added, 'You'd better ring your cousin Julie and tell her; she will be so pleased.'

When I had passed my Art O-level and re-applied for a place at the college I hadn't really thought through the implications if I was offered a place. Yes it was exciting, but the enormity of it suddenly dawned on me with a thud. I would be living away from home; I wouldn't be earning any money; I wouldn't know anyone; Patrick would be annoyed; but above all of these concerns was that same old doubt, that familiar feeling that I wouldn't be the same as the other girls, that I wouldn't be good enough.

Mum said we would need to apply for a grant, so we went together to Dagenham Town Hall at the Fiddlers to see about me getting one.

'Tie your hair back,' Mum said, when I came downstairs ready to go. 'You need to look smart and tidy.' I pulled my long blonde hair into a tight ponytail.

'Is this okay?' I asked, standing on my tiptoes trying to see in the mirror that hung on the kitchen wall. When Margaret and I were little, Mum, determined that we wouldn't be vain, would tell us, 'Don't look in the mirror, or you'll see the devil pop up behind you.'

It was years before I had the courage to look at my reflection, and even now, at nearly twenty, I almost expected to see horns, a hairy face and red eyes peering at me over my shoulder!

'Yes, that's better,' she said as we hurried out of the front door.

Aunty was in the garden as usual, fork in hand. The flowers that grew across the front of our house were magnificent now. There were several rose bushes that tumbled their way towards the privet hedge, and a mixture of colourful perennials that gave the impression of a cottage garden. Aunty had cultivated this completely on her own, and over the years it had become a solace for her when she needed to escape. She had gathered the plants together over time, not by buying them, but by bartering with friends and neighbours. When we were younger we would be embarrassed when she stopped outside a garden that she noticed looked particularly pretty and called out to ask if she could have a cutting. I don't believe anyone ever refused; in fact they would more often than not get into a deep, long-winded conversation about plants. She waved us off and turned back to her pruning.

The Town Hall was an imposing 1930s building – austere and forbidding. Mum wasn't daunted though; she knew how to handle authority. I, on the other hand, was feeling increasingly anxious. As we approached the reception desk, Mum handed the grant application to the man behind the desk.

'Oh yes,' he said, hardly looking up, 'you need to go down that corridor and take the first right through the double doors, then up the stairs and it's first door on the left.' He had lost me after the double doors, but Mum was sharp and led the way. When we got to the door marked 'Maintenance Grants', Mum turned to me.

'Now you wait out here while I go in and I'll call you if you need to come in.' I was more than happy to oblige and sat on a chair near the wall. Mum was in the room for about half an hour when the door opened.

'Come in for a moment please, Kathleen,' a kind-looking man asked.

'So, you are going to college to become a teacher?' he asked as he continued to write on the form in front of him. 'We just need you to sign this and then we can start the application process.'

As I bent to sign I noticed that the name on the form was Kathleen Stevens. I hesitated and glanced at Mum. 'What name should I sign?' I whispered to her. The man looked at me over the top of his glasses with his eyebrows raised.

'Your own name of course,' he said suspiciously.

I hesitated again, should I write Kathleen Coates or Kathleen Stevens? Mum just calmly indicated the place on the form and said quietly, 'There, that's where you sign, K Coates, on that line there.' I did as I was told and we handed the man the form and left for home, buzzing with anticipation.

30

The First Step

The day I was due to start college, Patrick drove me to Barking Station to get the District Line to Hammersmith. I had packed a small suitcase that Josie had lent to me; it was covered with stickers of all the exotic places she had visited. Josie had worked her way up over the years and now had an exciting job as the manager of the Travel Office at Plessey. It was an important position that carried with it power and influence, and her salary had increased to reflect the responsibility of her role. She got flown all over the world by airlines that were keen to secure business from such a big company, and stayed in hotels that had similar motives. It must have been bizarre for her to pack her bags and leave our increasingly dilapidated and dowdy council house in Dagenham and fly off to strange and unfamiliar destinations, often travelling business or first class, and all free of charge!

When Patrick kissed me goodbye, I noticed an unfamiliar look in his eyes. 'Are you sure you want to go?' he asked, holding on to me tightly.

'Yes – I think so,' I said, but actually I was starting to think that this wasn't such a good idea after all. I wanted to be a student, it felt like a trendy, modern thing to be, and I liked the excitement of the unknown, but as usual this was tempered with anxiety. As the train pulled out of the station I waved to Patrick, and watched as everything that was familiar and safe faded out of sight. I realised with a jolt that for the first time in my life I was going into the unknown alone.

The instructions for where to go were very easy to follow and I found my way to the bus garage in Hammersmith where I had to catch the 72 bus to Roehampton. I saw the buildings of the college and rang the bell to stop the bus, my stomach turning somersaults.

In the entrance hall of the college there were lots of young students, both male and female, milling about.

A lively young woman bustled up to me. 'Hello there,' she greeted me, smiling down at my case, 'and where have you flown in from?'

I looked at her, puzzled. 'Dagenham.'

'Oh,' she said, and I watched the interest leave her face. 'You have to sign in over there.' Pointing me in the direction of a wide table, she disappeared into the throng.

The registration process seemed endless. There were numerous queues to join, and a multitude of forms to fill in, and during that time I got chatting to some of the students around me.

'I thought this was an all-girls college,' I said to a girl called Gerry.

'It was, but this year they opened it up to boys as well. Great, isn't it?' She smiled mischievously. She was small and pretty with tightly curled blonde hair, and was from North London. We soon found that we had things in common. We both had steady boyfriends, and we were both slightly older than most of the other students as we had worked before coming to college. In a college that was predominantly full of affluent middle-class students, Gerry and I stuck out as coming from working-class backgrounds.

'What's your main subject?' she asked. Although we were training to be teachers we had to choose a main subject to study.

'Art,' I said confidently; it was the only thing that I felt I was any good at.

'Oh I'm geography, but we will be in lots of education lectures together.' So we palled up.

The college had found me approved lodgings in East Sheen, which was a short bus ride or long walk from the college. Most of the students that came from London or the surrounding areas were lodgers, as the campus rooms were reserved for those who came from further afield.

The first six weeks of college were set aside for an 'approach course', which was time given over to visiting each of the main subject departments to ensure that we had made the right choice. One of the first departments we went to was the drama department. The leading lecturer was a very old, very posh lady called Mrs Dalgliesh who terrified everyone. When Gerry and I bundled into the drama theatre we sat ourselves down towards the back. Neither of us were planning to do drama as a main subject so we thought we might be able to slide out before the end of the session. Mrs Dalgliesh stood up gracefully and with elegance.

'Good morning,' she enunciated perfectly with her rich deep voice. 'I know that you are all keen to hear about the endless possibilities that choosing drama can bring to you, but *what* . . . can you bring to drama?' She paused and looked around her dramatically, scanning our faces with her hooded eyes.

'You will all be familiar with our old friends Chekhov and Ibsen. The Greeks will no doubt conjure the ancient world for you, and some of you may even know Beckett and Pinter. Ah yes, I can see heads nodding.'

I didn't have a clue what or who she was talking about, so kept my eyes down. Being small had its advantages, I thought, as I slunk further into my chair.

Another lecturer stood up. He was a tall thin man with a smiling open face and a bright red cravat tied round his neck.

'Welcome,' he bellowed at us, throwing his voice at the walls so that it echoed back at us and extending his arms as though to enclose us in an embrace. 'Welcome my friends!' He introduced himself as Ted. 'Be prepared for a morning of exhilaration and creativity, my dear ones.'

He then proceeded to give us a tour of the drama department facilities including the green room, the stage, the lighting and sound box, the dressing rooms, and last but not least the room where the props were made. This was the place that I wanted to be! I was swept away by the electricity in the air, the sheer variety of experiences and the excitement of performance! Then I came back to earth with a bump. Mrs Dalgliesh was now addressing us again.

'You have tasted the intoxicating nectar that is drama and all that it could be for you but first . . .' (long pause) 'first we must see what you can offer the dramatic arts!'

We were handed out a copy of a play I had never heard of, 'A Doll's House' by Ibsen. We were given a few minutes to acquaint ourselves with the play and were then to read from it.

I felt prickles of sweat forming on the back of my neck, and my hands became clammy. Although I used to love reading aloud to Margaret, I hated public speaking. My eyes swam over the words as I desperately tried to make sense of them, and I listened with torment as one after the other we were asked to read Nora or Torvald.

Before long it was my turn. I stood as the others had done and took a deep breath. Pushing aside my nerves, I thought about Nora. Nora the wife, the doll, the caged songbird, the little squirrel. Nora the deceiver, the forger, the desperate and suicidal woman, and all I could think of was Mum and I read like I had never read before, with all of my emotion, all of my passion, and all of my suppressed anger stinging my lips.

When I stopped and looked up from the text all eyes were riveted on me and there was a hushed silence. I saw Liz sitting with her mouth open, and Gerry looking at me as though I were a stranger as Mrs Dalgliesh walked towards me, a look of rapture on her face.

'Oh my dear,' she whispered, 'that was wonderful,' and she reached over to hug me. I signed up for drama as my main subject there and then, leaving the safety of the art department to others.

Throughout my first year, every Friday afternoon I would leave college and my new life behind, get the 72 bus to Hammersmith station and travel back to Dagenham. It was a strange kind of dual existence. Patrick and I were engaged and planning a wedding while I was in Dagenham, and in Roehampton I was the young education and drama student, seduced by the theatre in all its guises. I loved it all, acting, producing, make-up, choreography, set design, lighting and sound, everything! I was also fascinated to be learning about learning, how children's minds and bodies develop, and what I as a teacher could do to help them. I walked around in a bright haze while I was away, only to return to the grim reality of 1970s Dagenham on my return. Mum was still desperately in debt despite Josie and Pat repeatedly giving her money to pay her 'callers' off. Within a few months more new things would surreptitiously appear and have to be paid for.

It was towards the end of my first year at college that things came to a head.

31

A Clean Slate

Josie made a decision. She wanted to help Mum, but first she needed to know how much was owed. She took a morning off work to try to get to the bottom of it.

'Mum, we have got to sort out this money,' she started. 'I'm going to pay off your callers. I'm sick of this constant worry and pressure.'

Mum turned to her and a nervous look swept across her face as though she knew what was coming next.

'But I need to know exactly how much you owe and who to.'

Mum looked away. 'Well, I'm not sure really,' she mumbled, busying herself by tidying around. 'Not much now.'

'Okay, if you give me all of your cards I'll work it out,' Josie offered.

'No no, that's okay. I think it's about £100.'

Although that was a considerable amount of money Josie wasn't stupid and wasn't going to be fobbed off. She knew Mum well and also knew not to believe her where money was concerned.

'I'm going to do this, Mum,' she insisted, 'and I'm going to do it once and for all, so you might as well hand over the cards to me now.'

Mum looked at her for a moment or two and then turned to me. 'You go and tidy upstairs while I talk to your sister.'

I did as I was asked and left them to it. There were no raised voices, and so I guessed that Mum had acquiesced. Josie was as stubborn as Mum was, and almost as scary when she wanted to be! She never told us how much she had to pay, but I know it took her over a year, using every spare penny she had, to finish them all completely. The relief when the last payment was handed over was enormous. Josie sent me over to the bakers to get half a dozen Belgian buns that day, delicious doughy concoctions filled with dried fruit and topped with a snowy white swirl of icing.

'Here's to the end of the tally men!' she said, raising her cup of tea and smiling. It was a celebration of determined endeavour, and Josie was justifiably proud of herself! As we ate the buns with steaming mugs of tea, there was a sense of a new era beginning.

Shortly after that momentous day, Mum got a letter from Marge and Ron who were now living in Australia close to Mary and Dave. 'Oh Marge is going to have another baby,' she read out to us. 'It's due in September.' Mum got a wistful look on her face. It was many years now since Mary had emigrated, and now that Marge had joined her it must have been sad for Mum, losing them both like that. Josie had joined Mum up to a special club for families of people who had emigrated as '£10 Poms', designed to help them save enough money to plan a visit. The cost seemed prohibitive to us, but we knew that Mum still dreamed about going to see her Australian grandchildren.

'I think I'll send her something for the baby,' Mum said, starting to smile. I didn't really give it much thought, but shortly after a large parcel appeared wrapped in brown paper.

'Oh. What's this?' I asked Mum. It had been pushed into my side of the dressing table in the bedroom she and I still shared when I was home from college.

'It's just something for Marge's new baby,' Mum answered casually, not meeting my eyes.

A niggling thought crept into my head. 'Mum, where did you get it from?'

She bustled out of the room. 'Oh I got it in Ilford. In Bodgers, I think it was.'

I was distracted at that moment by the phone ringing. It was my school friend Anne. She was off this weekend and wanted to know if Patrick and I would like to come over for a meal at her flat at Gants Hill. Like Margaret, Anne had just finished her nurse training at Barking Hospital. She had been going out with Tony V for a while now. He was such a sunny person, and seemed to suit Anne perfectly. He had been a merchant sailor when they first met, but Anne had encouraged him to become a fireman and that was what he did now. He was a handsome lad and had a great sense of humour. We always had fun when we went out in a foursome, so I readily agreed. By the time Pat and Josie got home that evening from work I had completely forgotten about the parcel.

At 5.25 p.m. exactly Mum put the kettle on, with the usual words, 'Oh nearly time for the girls to come home,' and bustled around in the scullery, preparing dinner. Aunty was sitting in the opposite corner to Mum where she always sat, and was reading *Bleak House*. She loved Dickens, and had a full set upstairs in her room, and would read them in rotation. I couldn't tell you how many times she'd read each book.

'Ask your aunt if she wants peas,' Mum called into the kitchen where we sat. Aunty was quite deaf now and hadn't heard, so I went and stood in front of her.

'Aunty, do you want peas?' I asked.

She looked up. 'What?'

'Do you want peas?' I tried again, louder this time.

'Aye? Peas? Oh yes, I'll 'ave a few.'

As I went to tell Mum Aunty's reply, I heard Pat and Josie arrive at the front door. Mum seemed agitated; it was quite warm in the scullery, and she seemed flustered, spilling some gravy.

'Oh damn!' she muttered crossly.

The girls took off their coats and made their way into the kitchen and Mum asked me to take the tea in.

There was a loud knock at the door.

Mum hurried to answer it, shouting out, 'It's just the man for the football money.' She still did the pools every week and a man collected the money every fortnight.

Pat and Josie were drinking their tea when Aunty put her book down and sniffed. 'It ain't football week; 'e came last Monday.'

Pat and Josie exchanged looks, and Josie got up and went towards the door. Mum was still talking to the man who stood there. We heard raised voices, the loudest of which was Josie's. I moved nearer the door so that I could hear what was going on and heard Mum saying, 'But it isn't much, only 10 shillings a week, and I can easily afford that,' and then Josie's reply, deep, clear, firm and menacing.

'I am telling you now, once and for all, that if you sell my mother one more thing you will never be paid for it. I have spent the last year clearing her debts and I don't intend to do it again. How much does she owe for it?'

A man's voice mumbled a reply and I jumped out of the way as Josie barged into the room, went to her handbag and took out a cheque book. She went back out into the hallway and shortly after we heard the door slam shut with a bang. Josie came back into the kitchen, her face red with anger and Mum turned back to the dinner. No one mentioned the incident, but Mum never got into debt again.

32

Mum's Job

I was luckier than many of my fellow students because I had office skills and experience that enabled me to get a holiday job in the city. This was a stroke of luck as despite having a full grant, money was still tight. Pat and Jo gave me £5 a month between them, which helped tremendously, but there always seemed to be another book to buy or play to see. Patrick always paid for me to go out when I was home, and even occasionally came up to East Sheen and took me out there, but my fare back to Dagenham every weekend made a hole in my finances, as did the teaching resources we needed to buy.

I managed to get temping work through an agency and was earning a reasonable amount of money. At the end of my first week I offered Mum some 'keep' money.

'No, I don't need it now,' she said proudly.

I was puzzled. 'Are you sure?'

'Definitely – I'm going to get a job.'

I thought I had misheard. 'Pardon? You're getting a job?' Mum hadn't worked outside the home since I was born, to my knowledge.

'Yes, I've applied for a job as a cook,' she offered settling herself down in her chair and lighting her cigarette. She inhaled deeply.

'Mum, no one is going to give you a job as a cook. You've never had a job before.' Mum was going to be sixty at the end of July but I didn't mention that.

'Don't be daft,' she said crossly, 'I worked for years before you were born. I was a silver-service waitress in London, you know.'

I did know, as it happened, because throughout our childhood she had conjured up an exciting life of restaurants and clubs in London, which Margaret and I would always try to persuade her to talk more about.

'But that was years ago,' I said more gently now, realising that I had upset her.

'All right, we'll see then.'

The conversation was closed.

When Pat and Josie arrived home later that evening they looked tired. I knew even then that they had given up their lives to make sure that we younger ones were safe, and to try to make sure that we had the chances that they had missed out on.

The next day I found another piece of the puzzle, although the jigsaw of my life was still far from complete.

It was Tuesday morning and my sisters had all left for work. Margaret was coming over to see me later that morning as she had a couple of days off. I knew she was really enjoying her nurses' training, but I also knew that she had to work long hours and that it was very hard work, so wasn't surprised to see her arrive with her pale skin looking even whiter than normal and her big brown eyes red with tiredness.

'What's wrong?' I asked as I opened the door to her.

'Something really embarrassing happened yesterday,' she whispered as she came in to the kitchen and sat herself down. 'Where's Mum?'

'You're not going to believe this,' I replied. 'She's got an interview!'

'What?'

'She's got an interview!' I repeated. 'In London – she's applied to be a cook for London Transport.'

Margaret just looked at me incredulously. 'But she's not a cook.'

'I know,' I said, 'but you know what she's like – she'll be able to convince them, I bet.'

Margaret shook her head in disbelief. 'But how will she manage it? All that travelling?'

'Do you want a cup of tea?' I went out to the scullery to put the kettle on. Margaret followed me, and stood playing with her long black hair as I switched on the gas.

'It was awful yesterday,' she started, chewing her lip. 'All of us new trainees had to go the classroom together for registration; there must have been about twenty-five of us, all sitting there, when our tutor came in.'

I listened as I poured the boiling water into the old stained tin teapot that we seemed to have had forever.

'She was going through our documents, and when she came to me she called out in a really loud voice "Margaret Butler?" And as I raised my hand she looked at me and said, "Oh yes, Margaret, can you please just explain why it is that you have two different maiden names?" Well I nearly died! I didn't know what to say, and just stammered that I wasn't sure – and then everyone was looking at me as if I were an idiot or something. It was so embarrassing!'

As we took our tea back into the kitchen, I was thinking hard. This was madness. We were both adults. Margaret was a married woman, for goodness' sake! And still we didn't know why we had different names, who our father was, and why no one ever mentioned our secret sister!

'Right, I think it's about time that we started asking some questions,' I said, sounding more confident than I really felt.

'You're not going to ask Mum?' said Margaret fearfully.

'No of course not, but perhaps we can try to find out from someone else.'

'But who?'

I paused. There had to be someone who would talk to us as adults; someone who would know the secrets. We sometimes snatched at nuggets of information from Aunty when she was in the mood, but she always stopped short of giving us complete answers. Even when we had directly asked her what she knew about our father, she had just sniffed loudly and said, 'I can't tell yer about your father without telling you about yer mother,' and then walked out of the room leaving us as ignorant as before.

But as I sat sipping my tea with Margaret I suddenly realised there was someone. It was so obvious now; there was someone who might be persuaded to tell us about our past, someone whose own mum, our dear Aunty Maggie, would have certainly been in our Mum's confidence – my godmother and cousin, Julie.

33

The Children's Home

Mum was going to be out for the whole day because she had to go to Baker Street for her interview, so I phoned up Marion and begged her to drive us over for a visit. As usual Julie was incredibly welcoming, and made a wonderful spread for our lunch. We managed to eat, although inside my stomach was flipping around. Sitting listening to Marion and Julie catching up, I knew that if I didn't take the plunge soon, I'd run out of time to accomplish my mission.

Julie asked me how college was.

'Oh it's really good. But, hard work.'

'And are you managing okay with money?'

'Oh yes – there's the grant, and Pat and Jo are so kind, helping out with everything.' I paused and then launched in. 'I wish Pat and Jo had been able to go to college or something; they're both miles cleverer than I am. Why do you think they didn't? Was it just the money?'

Julie looked at me and then at Marion. 'No, not only that,' she replied cautiously.

'What then?'

Julie paused, and was obviously considering whether or not she should continue, so I prompted her. 'We really want to know about what happened when they were little. Aunty has told us some things about their dad, Coates, and how wicked he was, but we'd like to hear what you know.'

Julie looked down. 'Hmmm, well I don't know whether he was wicked – not really. I was only the same age as Pat so I don't remember him much at all. But I do know what my mum told me.'

I sat still, almost afraid to move in case I broke the spell.

'They were only little. I think Pat was about six so that would make Michael seven, Sheila eight and poor little Josie only about four.'

I watched Marion and Margaret. We were all three of us sitting on the edge of our seats. Three grown women waiting to hear about the past, hoping desperately that it would help us to understand more about ourselves.

Julie went on. 'It was winter but probably wasn't very late, because Mum remembers that Dad wasn't home from work, but it was dark when the phone rang. I remember Mum talking to Dad about it once he got in. Aunty Edie had called from the phone box. She was really upset, almost hysterical.'

I was almost holding my breath. Marion lent nearer to me and put her hand on my shoulder. Margaret was sitting quite still but her big eyes were tightly fixed on Julie.

'There were two of them apparently. One was a policeman the other was a woman, probably from the social, I suppose. The children didn't want to go with them.'

'Go with them where?' I interjected and immediately regretted my interruption. I had learnt by now that the best way to get information was to wait for it to tumble from a person's mouth rather than trying to pull it out forcibly.

But this wasn't Aunty talking now, or Pat or Josie, and this wasn't Valence Avenue, so Julie continued.

'To the children's home.'

'Children's home? But why? Where was Mum?'

'I don't know the answer to that. I'm sorry but all I know is what my mum told me. She just kept saying to my dad, "I should have taken them; I should have taken them," over and over as he was trying to comfort her.

'They were all crying – the children were all crying and clinging on to Edie,' Mum told him. Apparently Aunty Edie swore at the policeman and at the woman. She shouted at them and tried to hang on to the children but the policeman held her arms down and kept apologising, but they were adamant that they had no choice. It was the law, they said, it was the law, as if that made it all right.

'The policeman got upset, but it wasn't really his fault. He couldn't have let them stay there, you see.'

'But why not?' asked Marion.

'Because their father had told them, told the social, that your mum wasn't there, and that Aunty Edie was out at work all day and that Granny was an old woman in her seventies. She was struggling to look after them you see, five little children all under eight, it was just too much.'

She stopped and looked round at the three of us. 'You didn't know any of this did you?' she asked, already guessing the answer.

We shook our heads and Marion said, 'No – we didn't know.'

'Julie,' I started warily. 'Do you know anything about our dad?'

Julie swivelled round to meet my eyes. Did I see pity there? Or was it just kindness? She paused before answering slowly, 'Whose dad?'

I looked at Marion and then at Margaret. 'Our dad,' I repeated.

'Do you mean yours or Marion's?'

'Stevens,' I replied, feeling more and more confused. Julie looked away towards the window. She had always been so close to Pat that I wonder if she felt maybe she was betraying too many secrets. She waited for a moment and then went on.

'Well Reg Stevens was a good man according to my mum; that's all I know. He was good to your mum, but just whose dad he was, I really can't say.'

'Can't say because you don't know or can't say because you don't want to tell us?' I asked, starting to muster some courage.

'Mum and Dad will be home any minute,' Julie murmured. Walking into her little kitchen she put on the kettle, and we knew it was time to go. Marion had to get back for the children anyway and Julie was determined to say no more.

On the way home there was a deep silence at first as we all tried to come to terms with what we had heard. It had been a strange day and we were left with more unanswered questions than before.

By the time we got home Mum was already back from London.

'Well, aren't you going to ask how I got on?'

With all that had happened today, Mum's first interview for at least twenty years had gone completely out of my mind. My hand flew to my mouth. 'Oh yes, yes, of course I am. What happened?'

'I am now the head cook at the Baker Street depot of London Transport,' she said proudly, sitting herself down in her worn old chair and kicking off her shoes. Margaret and I looked at each other in disbelief.

After all these years our mum could still manage to completely shock and surprise us! And then we both started laughing, almost hysterically, as Mum looked on completely bemused.

34

The Runaway Train

I would be having a big Catholic wedding as had all my siblings before me. The church and the hall for the wedding breakfast and regulation disco in the evening were booked for July at the end of my second year at teacher training college; I would be just twenty-one. For my final year I would continue my course as a married woman and have to commute into college daily by train and bus, which would probably take at least an hour and a half each way.

When I was at college it was as though I changed into a different person, and the two halves of my life were kept firmly apart. I still went home to Dagenham almost every weekend, and would resume my role as fiancée, daughter and sister, while at college I was a producer, actor, make-up artist and most importantly of all, soon-to-be teacher. The more I learnt about children, and the impact of external forces during their most formative years, the more I started to compare this with my own childhood. I wanted to know more. I started to have trouble sleeping and began to have vivid dreams that I didn't under-stand, and would wake up in a sweat, shivering.

Since our visit to Julie we'd got stuck, and hadn't been able to find anything else out about our past. Margaret was living in Canvey Island with Tony and was concentrating on her final exams, and my life was pulled between studying and wedding preparations. I was still desperate to know more about my child-hood, but just didn't seem to have the energy or time to continue to ask the questions. Some of the memories Margaret and I shared we never spoke about and they got buried in the baggage of day-to-day living. I tried to convince myself that it was easier that way, but inside I had a gnawing hunger to know more.

As the end of my second year approached the reality of the wedding started to dawn on me. I couldn't talk to anyone really. Margaret was desperate for me to be married like her, Anne's boyfriend Tony was great friends with Patrick, my friends at college all thought it was terribly grown-up and exciting, and Patrick's family were over the moon. It was only me that knew about my growing dread of being trapped. I kept remembering the first play I had read at college: Ibsen's 'A Doll's House', and how Nora's husband treated her, the heroine, almost as a pet. I couldn't help comparing the relationship I had with Patrick to theirs. He even had a pet name for me, 'Boo Boo', that made me cringe, but I tried desperately to be the girl he wanted me to be.

There was one girl called Rachael who was in the drama department too. She was slightly older than me and was considered to be very mature and intellectual. We happened to be travelling on the bus to Hammersmith station one Friday, and she started to ask me about the wedding.

'Are you all ready now?' she asked, making small talk. I guessed that weddings weren't on Rachael's agenda really, but she was a pleasant, friendly girl.

'Yes, everything is sorted out, I think,' I responded drearily.

'Well you don't sound very happy about it.' She smiled. 'Wedding nerves?'

'Mmm, I guess so.' I looked out of the window as the sun shone down hotly. 1976 had been the hottest summer on record so far, and the bus was very stuffy.

'Are you going on honeymoon?' she asked. I just wanted her to stop talking, or at least I wanted her to stop talking about the wedding. I could feel tears beginning to sting my eyes and didn't want to embarrass both of us on a crowded number 72 bus!

'Yes, we've booked two weeks in the Canary Islands.'

She started to laugh. 'The Canary Islands! That's going to be even hotter than here!'

I returned a watery smile. 'Mmm, I know.'

What I wanted to tell her was that I had a recurring dream that I would wake up in the sunshine and realise that I was married and that my life was over. I wanted to tell her I was terrified of being trapped, that I didn't know what love was, who Patrick was and most importantly I didn't know yet who I was! But I didn't know Rachael well enough to say those things to her. She fumbled with her bag and then looked at me directly in the eyes. I don't know what she saw there but it prompted her to say in a slow and serious voice, 'You're really not happy about all of this are you?'

I shook my head, and then the tears did begin to slide down my cheeks. I left them there unchecked and looked away.

'Kath, you've got to do something!' she said, putting her arm around my shoulder.

I was aware that other people on the bus were beginning to look, so I quickly brushed my tears away and tried to smile. 'But don't you see, I can't do anything? I'm trapped.'

'You're not trapped! No one can make you get married if you don't want to.'

I tried to explain. 'It's like I'm on a train speeding out of control, and the passengers are on board. The reception is booked, dresses are bought, honeymoon booked and, worst of all, everyone is really looking forward to a big Irish wedding – everyone but me! And if I derail the train to stop it there will be a massive crash, it will just leave too many casualties – don't you see?'

She shrugged her shoulders. 'You're insane. Don't be bullied into this.'

I knew she thought I was weak and probably stupid as well, and I suppose I was, but I was used to looking after people, calming conflicts not making them, and the last thing I wanted to do at that moment was to cause an almighty explosion. No, there was no choice. I would be getting married at the end of July.

When I got home Mum was in the scullery washing up. We had a fridge now and although it was very old it worked beautifully. Aunty Maggie had donated it to us when they moved to Bishop's Stortford. It was a 1930s design so took up a lot of space but the benefits it brought far outweighed the disadvantages. I was desperate for a cold drink so went straight into the tiny scullery to see if the new addition could provide one.

Mum looked up. 'Oh, you're earlier than I expected,' she said, smiling.

'So are you,' I answered, surprised to see her home from her cook's job in London.

'Oh Friday is POETS day.'

'What's that then?'

'POETS day!' she repeated, pleased that she had learnt a new saying from her colleagues. 'Push Off Early, Tomorrow's Saturday!'

She seemed really happy in this new job and had surprised the whole family, firstly by actually getting the job , and secondly by going to work three days a week, leaving home at about 5 a.m. and not usually returning until about 6.30 p.m. She was earning lots of money as well, and for the first time that I could remember she looked really, genuinely happy. How could I spoil that new state of happiness by turning everything on its head? No, I would just have to stick it out. I had got myself into this mess and now I would just have to put up with it. It wasn't that I didn't like Patrick or that he wasn't a really nice young man, but I just wasn't ready to be the person he needed me to be, and I wasn't sure that I ever would be.

'I've got my new hat for the wedding,' she said proudly. 'Josie got it for me in Ilford. It's a really good one – not cheap.' She dried her hands on her apron and led me into the kitchen. 'Look, here it is.' She plucked out a pretty blue hat covered with tight fabric flowers, and pulled it on to her head. 'What do you think?'

She looked so sweet. Although she was quite overweight and her hair was silvery white and rather thin, she still had a rosy bloom to her complexion, and bright twinkling eyes. She had kept her lovely soft skin and there were very few wrinkles on her face. She had some gentle laughter lines, but they suited her and she was sixty-one after all.

'Mum, you look gorgeous,' I smiled, and she smiled back and put the hat away in its bag, humming 'I'll Be Loving You Always' to herself. I walked upstairs to the bedroom we shared, and saw my dress hanging on the wardrobe door covered in plastic. My heart gave a lurch. At college I loved dressing up, I loved acting and becoming a different person from the real me, loved hiding behind the mask of theatre. On my wedding day in just a few weeks' time, I was going to have to give the best performance of my life.

35

My Wedding

The end of term and my second year at college arrived. We had a party to say goodbye to Mrs Dalgliesh, who was retiring. Typically of the drama department it was to be a 'Chekhovian moment' by the lake in the grounds of the college. The sun had shone brilliantly all day, and although it was 6 p.m. by the time we gathered together, it was a magnificent evening of soft breezes skimming off the lake, dragging the aroma of the musk roses and honeysuckle towards us as the bees droned soothingly. The trees were shaking their leaves gently, offering some welcome shade. I closed my eyes for a moment and imagined I was far away on my own and could do whatever I wanted, with no wedding, no honeymoon and no life mapped out in front of me. Then one of the other girls called out and the spell was broken. I came back to reality with a jolt.

I should have been happy, I reminded myself. My end of term production piece had been really successful. Our task had been to stage an excerpt from one of the plays we had read. We not only had to produce it but also had to cast it, set the scenes and make the props, light it and rehearse it. It was a tough challenge, but we had all relished it. I had decided on a scene from 'Waiting for Godot' by Samuel Beckett. There was something about the bizarre nature of the play, the strange conversations that the characters trapped themselves into, the hopelessness of their condition, that appealed to me. I decided to cast the characters of Vladimir and Estragon as clowns, and two of my fellow drama students consented to play them. They were brilliant; they listened to my every instruction, discussed it all with me and basically did a fantastic job. It was mainly down to their amazing interpretation that I was awarded an A–. *Why can't life just go on like this?* I thought. *Why does it have to change?*

As the term ended I collected my things together, packed my case and returned home to Dagenham, where preparations for the wedding were at full throttle.

'Aunty will press your dress,' Mum said. This had become a tradition in the family. 'Your aunt used to iron for the Prince of Wales,' Mum would tell us time and time again. 'The collars were terrible to press; she had to dip them in starch to make them stand up stiffly.' So Aunty would always be given the chore of pressing our wedding dresses before the big day. It was strange really because it was just about the only household job she ever did. When I was a child I remember Aunty always being placated, always being served dinner first, and having to walk round on tiptoe when she was home in case we disturbed or upset her. As she went to work every day, she was never expected to do any housework or cooking. As a matter of fact she was a terrible cook, although she did sometimes have a go. Bacon sandwiches were her speciality, and she would fry the bacon up, swimming in melted lard, until it was crispy and then slap it into the middle of two doorsteps of white bread and say, 'There you are. Yum yum, piggy's bum.' She had been known to try to cook a suet pudding but although we had eaten it because we were so hungry it had lain in our stomachs for ages, sitting there like a lead weight.

Apart from 'cooking', Aunty would occasionally have a bleaching frenzy. She would come home from work carrying bottles of the stuff, and then proceed to slosh it everywhere until the whole house smelt like a swimming pool.

'This place is filthy,' she would shout, bustling round with her bottles and cloths. 'We'll all be down with the fever!'

We came to dread the stinging smell that choked our throats and burned our nostrils which followed in her wake.

Now Aunty was nearing seventy and starting to slow down. She could still have an outburst of temper if provoked, but was more mellow now, so much so that Margaret and I thought she might just respond to a little probing. The week before the wedding, Mum had gone to work and so Tony agreed to drop Margaret off at our house in the morning. Aunty was already out in the garden even though it was early, and waved to Margaret as she got out of the little Mini.

"Ello Margaret,' she called affectionately, 'I'll make you a cup of tea.' She put down her spade and followed Margaret into the house. 'Kathleen, your sister's here,' she called out, and I came downstairs, trying to formulate a plan.

'I'll make the tea, Aunty,' I offered. Aunty made awful tea, and anyway I wanted to get her in a good mood. She sat down with Margaret in the kitchen and I could hear them chatting.

'Do you want some bacon? I'll make you a bacon sandwich,' she offered. 'No? What about some toast and jam then? Nothing? Look at you, all skin and bone; no wonder if you don't eat.'

I brought the tea in.

'Just like when you were little, an 'am bone with a frill on, that's what you are,' she joked. Margaret and I sat with Aunty as she drank her tea. Sip sip.

'Do you want to go and get a cake from the baker's?' she continued. 'Here, take some money.' She rummaged in her bag.

'No, it's okay Aunty. We don't want any cake, thank you.'

'I can leave me money around now, you know,' she continued. 'If I put this five pounds on the mantelpiece it would still be there tomorrow,' she continued, apparently amazed at this fact. Poor Aunty – we could only guess at the things she had put up with from Mum over the years.

'Your mother's got plenty of money now. Ah, but she's had an 'ard life, yer know.' She carried on drinking her tea: sip sip. We didn't answer; we knew the rules well.

'You might fink she's bad, but she only ever did what she did for you children.'

Aunty lapsed into silence, deep in thought. Margaret and I sat waiting when suddenly she continued. 'Your Uncle John loved 'er, you know. She was wrong to take advantage like that, and he never really forgave her.' Aunty sniffed loudly and continued. 'Ah well, it's a long time ago now and I suppose she didn't know what else to do.' We exchanged glances – what was all this about?

'Aunty Betty is coming to the wedding you know, and she's bringing Dot and George.' Aunty Betty was our Uncle John's widow, and we hadn't seen her since the last wedding. They had lived in Birmingham for the whole of my life, and had brought up their children there, but both Dot and George, our cousins, had visited on occasions. George was a lovely, funny young man, who had bought me a toy sewing machine once when he had arrived unexpectedly and found that it was my birthday.

Aunty now sat without saying another word and finished her tea. Sensing that she was about to go back to her garden I decided to take a chance.

'Aunty, what did she do to Uncle John?'

Aunty got up without meeting our eyes, sniffed loudly and said, 'The Lord makes work for idle hands.' Putting her cup down loudly on the table, she went back out of the front door to her precious garden.

On the morning of my wedding day I got up and went over to the hairdressers to have my hair styled with my sister Margaret. We were both going to wear our long hair loose. I had a little 'Juliet' cap with a beautiful lace veil, and my dress was a simple Empire line with scalloped, almost medieval, sleeves that draped gracefully. It was a delicate dress that suited my tiny frame, and I felt very special as I walked down the stairs out into the sunlight on my brother Michael's arm. It was the tradition at that time for all the neighbours to come out to their gates and see the bride off, and I felt a bit shy as we made our way to the shiny black car. I didn't say anything on the short journey to church, but my insides were twisted in knots. The sun was hot and the church felt cool and calming as I walked down the aisle to become a married woman. The church was full to bursting, and every head turned as I made my way towards the altar, clutching a bouquet of Madonna lilies, just like my mum had many years before me in this very same church. A shiver ran down my spine, despite the heat, and I looked to where Patrick waited, with his smart new suit and freshly cut hair, little knowing that the vows we were about to make would last for such a short time.

36

The First Cracks Appearing

After we got back from honeymoon, we set up home in Rainham. It was a sweet little house that was built at the turn of the century, with a long strip of garden at the back. Unfortunately it was perched right on the side of the A13, a busy dirty road running through Dagenham towards Ford's, and lorries thundered past relentlessly night and day.

Mum had been over before we got back, and had made sure that it was clean and dust free, even putting a bunch of flowers on the table. It was a lovely thought, and brightened my mood considerably. The weather in the Canary Islands had been intolerably hot, and I was keen to get back to England.

At that moment the phone rang. It was my school friend Anne, calling to tell me that she and her boyfriend had split up.

'Oh no! When did that happen?'

I could hear her hesitate. 'Actually, just before the wedding. We didn't want to tell you because we didn't want to spoil your day. So we just played along.'

As I tried my best to cheer her up, it was difficult to ignore the sick feeling of foreboding in my stomach.

My last year at college was the hardest. Being married was difficult in so many unexpected ways. Patrick didn't seem to realise that college was tough, especially in the final year. As a drama student, I was often working into the night and sometimes had to sleep on a friend's floor as it was too late to travel back to Rainham. Patrick was working nights for much of the time, and his job was very demanding, so he came home exhausted, slept and then got up expecting a cooked meal and a sympathetic ear.

What he got for much of the time was either a solitary evening or a distracted young wife whose thoughts were still in Roehampton, either in the drama theatre or in the education classes. I knew I was being unfair, but I also knew that this was important to me. I had my final exams soon and I was determined to pass.

Things struggled along, but we started to argue over trivial things. What we had both failed to realise was that we had grown in different directions. Just seeing each other at weekends for the last two years also meant that we didn't really know each other any more and now that we were in each other's company for much of the time, the cracks began to show.

My third year finally ended, and my exams were over. As I headed back to Rainham, having said goodbye to my college friends and a different way of life, I thought how strange it would be to be one person again instead of two.

'I've passed,' I announced as soon as Patrick arrived home from work. He looked tired and worn out, but still managed a broad smile.

'That's great news,' he said, giving me a hug. 'I'm starving, is there any breakfast?'

I turned away and went to cook some sausages, feeling hurt. I had worked for this moment for three years. I was a qualified teacher not just a housewife. But rather than picking a fight I served up the meal and chewed on a piece of toast, telling myself I was just being silly.

37

My First Teaching Job

It wasn't easy to get a teaching job the year I qualified, as there had been a review of teacher's pay scales the year before that had awarded a huge increase. This had prompted many teachers who had opted to leave the profession to return, and consequently there were very few jobs around. One of the girls from college, Maggie, had managed to get a job at an all-boys comprehensive in Stratford.

'I can put in a word for you if you like,' she offered kindly.

'But I'm middle-school trained, not secondary, and I'm planning on working in a primary school,' I replied. But then I started to think. It would be easy to travel to, I would have a ready-made friend, and at least I would be teaching.

'Okay,' I said. 'If you could, that would be great; thanks Maggie.'

The following week I was called for an interview at the school.

I knew that it was a boys' school and I also knew that I didn't want to look too young or attractive, so I pulled my long hair into a tight ponytail and twisted it into a bun at the back of my head. In a plain beige shirt dress, a touch of make-up and flat shoes I made my way to my first interview as a teacher.

The headmaster was a huge Scot with a broad body and a broader accent. He must have been about six foot tall and as he came to meet me at the door he extended his hand.

'Well halloo there, young lady. I hear that you would like a job in ma school?'

I looked at him as he stood there smiling down at me, and felt myself shrink even smaller than my five foot.

'Yes please,' I responded, smiling back even though I was quivering inside.

'Take a seat,' he said, but as I went to sit he stopped me and said, 'No, wait now, why doncha come and meet the lads first?' and he took my arm and guided me out of his office and into the dimly lit corridor that led to the rest of the school. He showed me round, and introduced me to some of the teachers. They all seemed very friendly, but the classrooms looked untidy and rather neglected. Then he took me into the sixth form common room. I looked about me; there was graffiti scrawled on one wall and half-full paper cups clustered on every surface, surrounded by discarded crisp packets. Several teenagers – some White, some Afro-Caribbean, all considerably taller than me – were lounging on the chairs eating crisps. They all stopped as we came in and looked at us with a smirk on their faces.

'Helloo boys,' the head said and turning to me continued, 'This young lady wants ta come and be a teacher here – whaddya think?'

They looked me up and down and one of them sucked his teeth and said, 'Na – I don't fink so!'

They all laughed and continued to chat amongst themselves. I wanted to die, but the head just grinned and led me back to his office where he promptly offered me the job!

When I rushed back to Dagenham to tell Mum, Pat and Josie were already home from work. Josie had eaten her dinner and gone up to her room as she usually did, so it was just Mum, Pat and Aunty sitting in front of the television. I bounced into the kitchen. 'I've got a job!' I announced, standing in front of the telly. 'It's a proper teaching job! And I'll be earning over £3,000 a year!'

Mum gave a watery smile but Pat just said, 'Mind out of the way, I'm watching this.'

I went into the scullery and put the kettle on.

I started at my new school in September and loved working there. The kids were great fun, and although it was extremely hard, the rewards were incredible. There was also a great sense of comradeship among the staff and we gave each other mutual support. When you needed someone to moan to, laugh with, or simply to talk to we were there for each other. As many of us were young teachers in our first jobs we had loads of energy and enthusiasm and working in a boys' comprehensive in East London at that time, we needed it!

It was here that I met two of the most important people in my life: my dear friend Sherry, and the man who would become pivotal to my future – Colin, remedial teacher, political animal, brave champion of the underdog, known as Mr Softy by the children and Superhero by the staff. The man who would change my life forever and turn it upside down.

That first term went by like lightning. I was learning so much, and often getting things wrong, but it was an incredible place to be. One day in mid-December, Maggie came over to me in the staffroom, and plonked herself down beside me.

'Are you coming to the cooks' Christmas party?' she asked, as she got out her sandwich.

'Oh I don't know. When is it?'

She munched through her lunch quickly; we always seemed to be in a hurry.

'It's on the last day of term after the kids have gone. Go on, it'll be a laugh,' she promised. 'Everyone is going.'

I couldn't think of a good reason to refuse, so I smiled. 'Oh okay then, if you insist.'

As I called the register the day before we broke up for the holiday, I noticed that there was some disturbance at the back of the classroom.

'What are you up to, Michael?' I asked, looking in the direction of the laughing.

'Nuffin Madam,' replied the little short blond boy who was always at the centre of any trouble. He was surrounded by Devon and the twins Melvin and Kelvin, big West Indian boys who liked a good joke.

I peered towards them. 'Come on, what are you doing? It's not Christmas yet you know.' I had grown very fond of my tutor group, even though it was made up of some of the most challenging boys in the school.

Michael came out to the front of the class. 'I've 'urt myself, Miss.' As he thrust his hand towards me I looked down and saw that his thumb was covered in blood.

'Oh no! What on earth have you done to yourself?' I asked, reaching out for his hand, at which he started to giggle. On closer inspection I realised the hurt thumb was a fake, and not a very good one at that.

'Oh, very funny,' I said, dropping my hand and sending him back to his seat. Then I had an idea. 'Tell you what, boys, shall we play a joke on Miss B?'

They were very keen! My friend Maggie had her classroom next door and it just so happened that she had a strong aversion to anything to do with blood. We made our plan. Kelvin would run into Maggie's room and ask her to help as there had been an accident. Meanwhile I would be holding Michael's wounded hand, getting hysterical.

Off he went; the rest of the class was silent, craning their necks to get a better view.

Maggie came rushing through the door. 'What's the matter? What's happened?

'It's his thumb!' I wailed. 'He caught it in the window.' I put on my most pathetic and desperate look.

Maggie took charge. 'It's all right boys,' she said firmly, 'go back to your seats.' She ushered the boys away and moved towards Michael and I. 'Let me see, Michael,' she said tentatively, moving towards the 'injured' hand.

Michael thrust his hand at her, moaning in mock pain, and as she went to look at it the 'severed' thumb flew off, at which she let out an almighty scream and the whole class erupted into uproarious laughter. Before we had a chance to recover, I glanced up to see the face of the headmaster looking through the window of the door. He came in.

'Is there something the matter, ladies?' he asked with a broad Scottish growl. 'Are these boys misbehaving?'

'Oh no, thank you,' I insisted, 'everything's just fine.' The head didn't say anything else but he must have known that we had been up to mischief, and I think I caught a sly smile cross his face as he turned and left the room.

We had a great time regaling our colleagues with the story during the party the next day, and it sounded even funnier after we had drunk copious quantities of alcohol! The party was great fun and I danced with lots of the other young teachers, all of us feeling the relief of finishing our first term without any major mishaps. By the time I went to catch the bus back to Rainham though my mood had changed. I didn't want to go back there, it didn't feel like home, and I didn't feel that I belonged in that house with my husband. I stood waiting for the bus, and realised that, unlike my colleagues, I wasn't glad it was the end of term. In fact I couldn't wait to get back to my boys and my friends in January.

38

Making a Decision

As the new term started, I decided to try to be more positive about my situation. It had been hard to pretend to everyone, including Patrick, that everything was fine, and that I was settling in to married life, but I had done my best.

Maggie was waiting for me when I arrived early on the first day back.

'Stuart is organising a skiing trip to Aviemore at the end of February,' she told me. 'Do you want to go? It will work out really cheap if we go as teachers with the kids, and we won't have to look after them during the day because they'll be having their skiing lessons.'

'Oh I don't know, Mags,' I replied. 'I'm not sure Patrick would like me going.'

'Oh come on – he doesn't own you, does he? It'll be fun.'

'Okay, I'll think about it,' I said, and went up to my classroom to get ready for the boys to arrive. What I hadn't told her was that I thought I might be pregnant. I was really depressed about it and hadn't told anyone, but I didn't think that skiing would be a good idea if I was. I made a deal with myself – if I was expecting then I wouldn't go, but if I wasn't then I would! The next week I found out that it was a false alarm, and so went straight away and put my name down for the trip. I wasn't ready to be pinned down just yet.

The trip was great fun, and the boys had a whale of a time. I learnt how exhilarating slicing through the snow can be, even though I was a complete beginner. On the first day all of us adult beginners were standing in a line on the nursery slopes.

'Now,' said our very patient instructor, 'I have taught you how to snowplough to stop, so we're going to have a go one at a time.'

Off we went. Debbie was first; around she went, heading back to the end of the line. Then it was Maggie's turn. She pushed off and we watched her go.

'No, no!' shouted the instructor. 'Turn! Turn!'

But Maggie wasn't able to turn, so she headed towards us at some speed and then proceeded to knock us down like skittles! Luckily no one was hurt and eventually we all got the hang of it and managed to negotiate the nursery slopes with some expertise by the time we had to go home.

Coming back to Rainham felt like a big anti-climax, and I realised with a jolt that I'd been dreading it.

Back at school, time flew by and before we knew it Easter was approaching. Things at home were not getting any better. It wasn't that we were constantly arguing, it was just that we wanted different things from our lives, and were beginning to resent each other for not being able to be the person we needed. I was getting so desperate that I confided in my friend Anne. I was shocked at her response.

'Kathleen, you two were never suited,' she said after I had tried to tell her how I felt.

'What do you mean?'

'You were never right for each other. I could have told you that years ago.'

'But I don't understand; why didn't you?' I returned angrily. The thought that it had been so obvious to someone else shook me to the core, especially as this person was my closest friend.

'Kathleen, it wasn't for me to tell you what you should do. I knew that you'd tell me to mind my own business.' She was right of course; although we were very close we had always respected each other's decisions.

I looked closely at Anne for the first time in ages, and noticed that she had worry lines beginning to appear on her smooth freckled skin, and that her eyes had lost their old sparkle.

'Do you still miss Tony?' I asked gently now, conscious of how caught up I'd been in my own problems.

'No,' she answered quietly, 'not really. We just weren't right for each other either. But I'm more worried about you now. What are you going to do?'

'Oh Anne, I don't want to hurt anyone, but I can't stand pretending to be happy anymore.'

'Then don't,' she said matter-of-factly. 'Just leave.'

'How can I leave? We're married!'

'So? Just because you're married doesn't mean that you have to put up with being miserable. Just get out and blow everyone else.'

I wiped my eyes and started to think that maybe Anne was right. Maybe I could just leave. What was the worst that could happen? We couldn't be any more unhappy than we were now, could we? What about my family; what would they think? And most of all, how could I tell Patrick? What would I say?

I made my mind up – I wouldn't tell him, I would write him a note!

My mind feverish with the thought of escape, I made plans. The first day of the half-term holiday was a Monday, and Patrick was back on day shifts for the next three months. After my conversation with Anne, I had decided that it would be best to leave as soon as possible even though I felt sick inside at the thought of it. I had packed a suitcase of clothes and belongings and had a couple of big bags full of my college books and other paraphernalia. As I was getting my things together, I couldn't help thinking what a terrible person I was, and how everyone would think I was crazy, cruel or both. I didn't cry; inside I was excited at the thought of freedom, even though this was tainted by the knowledge of the hurt I would be causing to Patrick by not having the courage to tell him to his face, and also what our families and friends would think of me and what I was doing. I tried to push these thoughts out of my mind and concentrate on the task in hand. I had written the note and kept it very short. I wasn't sure how to explain how I felt, so in the end I just told

Patrick that I had to leave because I knew we were both unhappy and it wasn't fair to carry on like this.

Propping the envelope on the mantelpiece I looked at my watch and saw that the minicab would be arriving any minute now. There was a sound of hooting outside and as I looked out I saw the car waiting for me. Grabbing my things, I stopped and looked round one last time, and in that split second I knew without a shadow of a doubt that I was doing the right thing, and with that I turned and walked out, shutting the door firmly behind me.

When the minicab driver saw me, he opened the car door and got out to take my bags. 'Blimey love,' he joked, 'wot you doing? Leavin yer 'usband?'

39

Telling Everyone

I arrived at Valence Avenue just before Pat and Josie were due home. I knew Mum would be there and I wanted the chance to talk to her before they arrived. When she opened the door to me she looked taken aback but just said, 'Oh,' and opened the door wider for me to come in. I dumped my things in the hallway and followed her into the kitchen.

'I've left Patrick.' I said it with defiance, expecting her to be angry.

'I thought so,' she replied coolly.

'I'm going to stay with Marion, but would like to stay here tonight if that's okay?'

'Yes, that's fine.' She lit her cigarette and inhaled deeply. 'Why are you going to Marion's?'

I hesitated before answering, not sure how to explain. 'Because he'll come here looking for me.' As I looked around me I couldn't help noticing the yellow nicotine stains that covered the walls and ceiling, the scratched paintwork and the worn, tired furnishings. There was no way I could ever come back here to live. Besides I couldn't cope with my family's endless disapproving looks.

Once Pat and Josie returned from work, their reaction was entirely as I had predicted. Pat said angrily, 'Why have you left? What's he done?'

'It's not like that,' I tried to explain. 'He hasn't *done* anything. We just don't get on, that's all.'

She looked away. 'Well I think you're terrible. You can't just leave. What will poor Patrick do?'

Josie walked into the scullery and banged around for a while before storming back in. 'Kathleen, I don't know what's going on, but it's not right you know – you're married now.'

'I know,' I responded, 'that's the trouble. I don't want to be married.'

'Well you should have thought of that before – it's a bit late now,' added Pat. 'You can't just change your mind.'

Suddenly and unexpectedly, Mum leapt to my defence.

'Keep your nose out of it, both of you,' she said sharply. 'It's none of your business.'

All three of us were taken aback and looked at Mum, who carried on as though nothing had happened.

'Now then, I thought we would have fish and chips tonight because I haven't cooked any dinner,' and with that she rummaged in her purse and thrust a pile of money on the table 'I'll have cod and chips, but wait until Aunty gets home and we'll see what she wants.' Then she went into the scullery to put the kettle on without a backward glance.

When Aunty arrived a few minutes later, the tea was on the table ready. 'Ask your Aunt what fish she wants,' Mum said.

Aunty looked up as she took off her jacket. 'Oh now, what shall I 'ave? A bit of cod roe? No, I'll have a nice wing of skate,' she said licking her lips exaggeratedly, 'and a wally.'

'I'll go over,' I volunteered, jumping up, glad of an excuse to escape the charged atmosphere.

'Ain't you going home to cook Patrick's dinner?' asked Aunty in all innocence.

We all looked anywhere but at each other until Mum said firmly, 'She's left him.'

Aunty tutted loudly. 'Well I don't know, bloody kids. You're just like your mother.' She sniffed loudly as I left for the chip shop, feeling like a naughty child.

Later that evening there was a loud knock at the door. We all stopped what we were doing and Mum got up. 'I'll go.'

My heart was beating fast as I sat rigid with anxiety.

From the kitchen we could hear muffled voices, but no one sounded angry. Then the door closed and Mum came back in.

'He said he didn't know where you were,' she announced.

'I left a note. He must have seen it.'

'Well, he said he didn't. Anyway, I told him you had left him, but that you weren't here.'

I could have kissed her. I knew I was being cowardly, but it had taken all the courage I could muster to get out of that house.

'Did he seem upset?' I asked quietly.

'Well he didn't look that pleased, but he wasn't angry. It almost seemed like he wasn't surprised.'

I nodded. That made sense. Patrick must have realised that it wasn't working between us, but maybe he was just too kind, or maybe too cowardly, to do anything about it. Maybe it was me that had been brave after all. That was a strange notion, one that I hadn't considered.

For now though I needed some time to gather my thoughts, and decide what I was going to do after I left Marion's. I didn't intend staying there for more than a few days, because I didn't think it would be fair. I had started to look for a little flat of my own, somewhere not too far from school that I could live in all by myself. It would be the first time that I had ever done that. All of my life I had shared a room with someone. Even at college there were other girls close by, and of course once I was married I had lived with Patrick. Although I was twenty-three now and an adult, I was still such a child. I wanted to know how I would cope on my own and whether or not I would be able to survive in the big world, standing on my own two feet. One thing was for sure – I was certainly going to try.

That night, as I crept into the bed that I had shared with my Mum for so many years, I stared up at the ceiling and the flaking paint and thought about the mess that I had got myself into. I glanced over at Mum and wondered about how she had felt all those years ago when her marriage to Ron Coates had ended. Had she left him or he her? I had never been sure. Aunty had said I was just like her.

I shivered. Maybe I was.

40

A New Flat and a New Romance

It wasn't long until I found myself a little bedsitter in Leytonstone, which was only a short bus ride from my school. I felt more grown-up now than I had ever done before, a real independent young woman. When I first lived there it felt strange to be on my own. I did have a phone, which was brilliant, and meant that if I felt lonely or nervous I would at least be able to phone someone for a chat, so was pleased when it rang about a week after I moved in.

'Kath?'

'Hello Mum,' I answered cheerfully, determined to be upbeat. 'Are you all okay?'

'Yes, we're fine. Aunty's gone over to see your Aunt Mag so she'll be gone all day.' Then she hesitated. 'Kathleen, you know that I have been through the same things as you; I know what it's like. You do know that don't you?' she said quietly.

It didn't sound like Mum at all really. All at once I felt her sadness, as though she were somehow able to transmit all her regrets, the disappointment her life had been, without saying very much at all.

'Mum, can I come over for a talk?' I almost whispered. I wanted to seize this moment. At last, this could be when it would end, a whole lifetime of secrets and mysteries. I could feel my heartbeat quicken, my hands go clammy and my head spin with possibilities. Mum wanted to tell me something, wanted to explain, I could sense it.

'Of course,' Mum said, speaking almost as quietly as I had. After I hung up I immediately phoned Margaret and told her what Mum had said.

'I'm going over there straight away,' I told her. 'If you want to come I'll see you there.'

I was in Valence Avenue within forty minutes, knocking on the door of my childhood home.

Mum answered, and looked almost shocked to see me.

'Oh, I didn't expect you to get here this quickly.'

'I know; I was lucky with the buses,' I answered, trying to keep my voice calm.

As we sat down with the tea Mum had made, I looked up at her.

'Mum,' I started, 'you know what you said on the phone . . .'

She looked away. That familiar faraway look came over her, a look that I hadn't seen for a while now, covering her face like a shroud.

'That was all a long time ago,' she said without meeting my eyes.

'But I just wanted to know . . .'

'It doesn't matter now; it's all too long ago. And anyway,' she said, picking up the clock from the mantelpiece and peering at it, 'Aunty will be home soon.' With those words her face closed up like the shutter of a camera and I knew that was all. There would be no talk. When Margaret arrived, about half an hour later, I caught her eye when Mum wasn't looking and gently shook my head. She knew what that meant without me needing to say a word. She knew that today would not be the day we would find any answers.

One of the problems with my new bedsit was the rent, which was very expensive, so that with bills, food, fares and other bits and pieces I was really struggling. By this point I'd made friends with one of the other teachers at the school. Her name was Sherry, short for Sheherazad, which better reflected her exotic looks. She was tall, slim and olive skinned, with a crown of raven curls, and she taught modern foreign languages. We were unlikely friends when I think about it and our backgrounds couldn't have been more different, but something drew us together. Years later I discovered that although her childhood was very different from mine we shared many things – among them a fear of desertion and a commitment to improving the lives of the children we taught.

Sherry shared a flat with an art teacher, Penny. It was a special teachers' flat. These were designated council properties put aside for teachers, to encourage them to take up positions in more challenging school districts.

Sherry approached me one morning. 'Penny's moving out of the flat at the end of term. Are you interested in taking over her room?'

'Oh yes please!' I responded with enthusiasm. 'But what's the rent?' When Sherry told me the cost, including all bills, I was even happier. In total I would be paying less than half what I was paying for the bedsit, and it was a lovely modern flat in a purpose-built block in Upton Park. It even had a rubbish chute!

I booked a date to move in and Colin – 'Mr Softy' – offered to help. He was about five years older than me, and very skinny with a crop of reddish blond hair and a small beard, both of which were badly cut, but I really liked him. He was funny and clever and kind, and was always ready to help out any of us newer teachers. Colin taught most of the remedial groups, which were the children that we would these days refer to as having a Special Educational Need (SEN), and he was always keen to try to find innovative ways to engage and motivate the boys and help them to see that education could help them to change their lives for the better. At that time many people had given up on these children, which infuriated Colin, and we teachers would often have discussions about the intolerable unfairness of the system, and what we could do to change things.

I arranged to move in with Sherry on the first day of the summer holidays and so Colin agreed to pick me and my belongings up in his car as I didn't drive.

He usually cycled to work from his teacher's flat in a tall tower block in Stratford, so I was surprised to see him arrive in an old Sunbeam Talbot car that he was in the process of renovating.

'This is a funny old car,' I said laughing as he pulled up and swung open the door. 'How old is it?'

'It was made in 1955, I think,' he answered, proudly stroking its aged paintwork.

'That's only a year younger than me,' I smiled, and Colin began to put my bags and boxes into the little boot. The car was painted British Racing Green, and had lovely curved bumpers and leather seats. Although it was quite rough around the edges I loved it! We loaded up the car and set off for my new flat share.

We started to chat about things and then he asked tentatively, 'Are you separated from your husband now?' I was a bit taken aback, as although it wasn't a secret, I hadn't broadcast the fact.

'Well, yes I am actually,' I stuttered. 'How did you know?'

'This is our school we're talking about here. Everyone knows everything – you should know that by now.'

'Hmm well, I didn't think it was such a big deal really,' I answered irritated. I didn't like the idea of being the topic of people's conversations.

'It is to me,' he said softly. I wasn't sure I had heard him correctly, so didn't comment.

'What I mean is,' he continued, 'that it's a big deal to me, because if you are separated from your husband, I for one am very glad. I mean very, very glad.'

I looked at him as he stared fixedly ahead at the road. I hadn't really thought of him like that. Although we had been good friends since I started at the school, our friendship hadn't had any romantic connotations.

My heart was starting to somersault, and I felt awkward suddenly. This was a sensation I hadn't expected. Once we had unloaded the car and I had sorted a few things away, Sherry asked if we would like to go out with her and her boyfriend, who confusingly was also called Colin, and also taught at the same school as us. There was a Labour Party Social being held that evening in East Ham.

Colin looked at me. 'I'd love to go. What about you?'

I nodded.

The evening was great fun and included a fish and chip supper that I couldn't eat because I felt funny inside and strangely confused. Many of the teachers from school were there, and I was very conscious of being smiled at and whispered about. It was all very good-natured but still very embarrassing! As Colin walked me back to the car he put his arm around my shoulder for the first time and I felt a warm, unexpected glow of happiness.

From that night on Colin and I started to 'go out'. He turned my life upside down and inside out and I felt as though he had given me back my wings and I could fly wherever I wanted to. We talked endlessly – about school, the children, politics, our families, books we had read, plays we had seen. We just seemed to slot together, as though we had always known each other, and every time I saw him my stomach did flip-flops! One day, later in the holiday, Colin came round to see me full of excitement.

'I've seen an advert for a holiday cottage in Devon,' he said with a big smile on his face. 'It's for hire next week because they've had a cancellation – shall we go?' It sounded perfect so I agreed, and during that holiday in that tiny cob cottage deep in the Devon countryside, I think we both realised that we had fallen in love.

Colin and Sherry became great friends with my Colin and I, and although we didn't know it at that time, they went on to help us survive the most traumatic time of our lives.

41

Babies and Other Mysteries

Sherry was desperate to have a baby. She and her Colin had been trying for quite some time, but so far they had not been successful. They bought a beautiful old four-storey Georgian house in Hackney to renovate ready for their longed for family and kept themselves busy between that and teaching. At about the same time Colin and I bought a house in Ilford. It was a very smart little Edwardian house that had been 'done up' really well by the previous owners, so it was extremely comfortable to live in if a little boring. I was almost twenty-six and Colin thirty-one when we decided that the time was right for us to also think about babies.

I had a real dread of marriage though, and was quite hung up about it. My first marriage had been a big mistake, and I now associated weddings with deceit and hypocrisy. My family had taken ages to come to terms with what I had done. Margaret and Tony hardly spoke to me for a while, and Pat and Josie were extremely disapproving, although since Mum had told them to mind their own business they didn't say much. Aunty had made her feelings known right from the start, and whenever I visited the house and she was there, she felt it her duty to point out my shortcomings.

'Where you livin' now?' she would ask, knowing full well the answer.

Mum would say, 'She's just living with Colin, because he's got a nice house with plenty of rooms,' as though anyone really believed that fiction.

I had taken Colin to meet Mum with a real sense of anxiety, but she had been fine, although I could see she was watching us like a hawk. She had told everyone in the family that I had left Patrick because he beat me, which couldn't have been further from the truth, but I suppose she felt she had to justify my actions.

The idea of having a baby before you got married at that time was still a little unconventional, especially for a Catholic family in Dagenham, so when I eventually became pregnant we had a problem.

I was adamant at first.

'No, I really don't think it's a good idea,' I said when Colin broached the subject of weddings. 'There's no point. We're happy as we are, aren't we?'

'Yes we are, but it just feels strange.'

'What feels strange?' I asked.

'Well, when I introduce you to someone, or talk to someone about you, I don't know how to describe you. I say "my girl-friend" – but you're so much more than that, it just doesn't sound right.' He hesitated. 'And also we won't know what to call the baby. Whose name will the poor little thing have, eh?'

I laughed, and gave in. 'As long as it's just us,' I said. 'No big wedding, and no white dress!'

'Definitely!' he agreed. He wasn't the sort of person who liked a lot of fuss.

We booked the register office for 2 January without telling anyone at first but we knew we would need witnesses. 'Do you want to ask your sister Margaret?' Colin suggested.

'No, I don't think that's a good idea. She won't want to do it anyway. I think we should ask Sherry and Colin.'

So it was decided.

Colin and Sherry agreed at once, congratulating us heartily. I felt sad for Sherry because she was still not pregnant, and had dreaded telling her about our baby, but she had been really lovely and happy for us.

In the end I decided I would ask Margaret and her husband Tony if they would like to come to the wedding. When I told her about it, Margaret went quiet for a while and then said, 'Oh I'm sorry but we can't make it that day. We'll be at Tony's mum and dad's.'

I tried to hide my disappointment. 'Don't worry, we just thought you might like to come – it's no big deal really. It will be just a little wedding.' I asked her not to tell anyone else about it and hung up, trying hard not to be hurt.

The day of our wedding was bitterly cold and windy. It was the middle of winter and the landscape looked bleak. We'd moved house recently, and were now living in a modern house on a small estate in Frindsbury, Kent. It was very rural, which was why we liked it. Colin had grown up in Balham, South London, and we had both spent our lives dreaming of an escape to the countryside. This was our first stab at it. As we both still worked in East London it was quite a commute, and being in the early stages of pregnancy didn't make it any easier.

We hadn't told anyone about the wedding except for Margaret, not even Colin's widowed mum. He was an only child and, looking back, I can't believe we kept it from her. She had been so kind and accepting of me, even though she hadn't liked the fact that we were living 'in sin'. Still, I was afraid. I couldn't bear the thought of this wedding being anything like my first, with all the relatives and uncomfortable associations. So in the end just the four of us drove to Chatham Register Office on that cold January day.

When I went over to Mum's the next week I told her our news.

'Oh,' she said, 'I knew you'd get married again.'

Margaret now had a little girl called Emma, who was the sweetest little thing I had ever seen, and was pregnant with her second baby. I hoped that now I was expecting too we would be able to regain some of the closeness that seemed to have diminished over the last couple of years, so I wanted to tell her before the rest of the family.

Margaret was ecstatic. 'That's great! What date are you due?'

When I told her the end of June we laughed, realising that our babies would be born just two months apart.

We made an arrangement to meet at Mum's the following Saturday so that we could go shopping in Ilford. We both wanted a Moses basket and Margaret had seen one in Boots that was really pretty. When we got to Mum's she was in a happy mood. She had retired from her job about six months before, but still had plenty of spending money. Pat, Josie and Aunty paid for everything between them so Mum had her pension to spend in any way she liked.

Pat came in with a plate piled high with bacon sandwiches.

'Here you are,' she said plonking the plate down on the table. 'You must be hungry.'

'Oooh thanks,' I said and as I helped myself the phone rang.

'Who's that?' Mum asked. Both she and Aunty would always say that whenever anyone phoned, as though the other people in the room had some kind of sixth sense and could tell without answering it!

Pat walked out into the hallway and then called out to Mum. 'It's Mary, quick!'

Mum pulled herself out of the chair and hurried to the phone.

Phone calls to and from Australia were very expensive at that time. I tried to listen as I munched my way through the tasty food, but couldn't really hear what was going on. When Mum finally came back into the room she was beaming. 'Mary's coming over!' she announced happily. We were all so excited. It was about seven years since we had seen her and now she was coming home.

Mary's first visit home was joyfully anticipated by all of us. Of course over the years we had kept in touch by letter and the rare phone call, but it wasn't the same as being able to see and talk to her. It was almost like old times again, with nearly all of us together again. When it was my turn to have Mary to stay with me, I was over the moon with excitement.

'Where do you want me to put my case?' she asked, bundling through the door.

'Just chuck it down anywhere,' I answered, ushering her in, and giving her a whistle-stop tour of our little home.

'It's funny you live in Kent now,' she said, looking out of the window over the playing fields of the school next door. 'It's where me and Dave started out.'

Over the next few days we talked endlessly about everything, but inevitably it wasn't long before we got to talking about Mum and her secrets. When Mary had left for Australia I had still been a young teenager, but now I was an adult and I wanted to hear what Mary knew.

'I know some things,' she offered, 'mostly from cousin Dot; although Julie will talk about stuff if you get her in the right mood.'

'Yes I know,' I said. 'We got her talking one day, and she told us about Pat, Michael and Josie going into the children's home.'

'Hmm, yes, well, that was about the time I was born, I think; but do you know why Mum wasn't there?'

'No. Do you?'

'Yes, I do. Well, I think I do – you see Josie and I have talked, but she was only little so she doesn't remember everything that clearly.'

I was on the edge of my seat when Colin came in with tea. 'There you are,' he said, placing the hot mugs of tea in front of us. 'Shall I put some dinner on?'

'Yes please, anything will do,' I said hurriedly, and thankfully he left us to continue our conversation.

'Well,' said Mary, 'the thing is . . .' She stopped and looked at me for a minute. 'The thing is . . . did you know that I was born in prison?'

'What? What do you mean?'

'What I said,' she repeated. 'I was born in prison – well not literally in prison, but Mum was in prison when I was born.'

'In prison for what?' I asked incredulously. 'What had she done?'

'She had committed bigamy. She was in prison because she had married Reg Stevens, my dad, while she was still married to Ron Coates.'

'Oh God,' I said, 'poor Mum! But why did she do it?'

'Who knows? Things were different then. Remember it wasn't long after the end of the war; everything was still muddled up and confused.'

'What? You mean she didn't know she was still married?'

'No – of course she knew, but she didn't care, I suppose. Perhaps she just thought she deserved a bit of happiness.'

I was taken aback by this revelation, but I was totally unprepared for the next.

'That was the first time,' Mary continued slowly, her eyes sliding away from my face now, as though she wasn't sure whether to continue or not.

'First time what?' I asked, frightened that she was going to stop, just as all of the other people I had asked did.

'The first time she was in prison,' she continued, still averting her eyes. 'Do you think we should help Colin with the dinner?'

'No! Blow the dinner – tell me what you mean!'

'Okay,' she said quietly. 'If you want to know, I'll tell you all I can, but I don't know everything.'

I waited while she sipped her tea, and then, swallowing hard, she carried on.

42

More Secrets Revealed

'I think Mum must have met Reg Stevens when she was working as a waitress in London. At least that's what Dot was told,' Mary said, thoughtfully. 'Apparently he adored her, fell head over heels for her, but he never knew she was already married.'

'But how did she hide it? What about the children? Where were they? Sheila must only have been about eight, and the others were younger. Who was looking after them?' I asked, my head starting to ache with that old familiar pain.

'Well Granny was still alive, and Aunty lived there as well, so I suppose it must have been them.'

'But Granny would have been in her seventies . . . Wait, that's when they were taken into the children's home, wasn't it? How could Coates do that to his own children?'

'I don't know, but of course we only know one side of the story.'

'What about Peter? Who was his dad?' I asked. 'Ron Coates or Reg Stevens?'

'I don't think it was either of them. I'm not sure anyone knows the truth about that, apart from Mum.'

'But you said she was in prison again. What was that for?' I asked, greedy for more information now, despite the throbbing in my head and sick feeling in my stomach.

'Well, it was when you were about two and a half, not long after Margaret was born,' Mary said, watching me closely for a reaction. I tried to hide my shock, but then distant memories began to surface.

'The big building,' I said suddenly interrupting her. 'The

big building where I went to visit her – I thought it was a hospital!'

Mary shook her head. 'No – it wasn't a hospital,' she said sadly.

'Oh God, poor Mum. How did she bear it? But what was she in prison for that time? I don't understand.'

'Slow down! We have to go back a few years,' Mary said, twisting her hands in her lap. 'So I was a little baby when she got out the first time, and Mum took me with her to stay with Uncle John in Birmingham.'

'Oh yes.' Again a memory flashed in my head. 'Aunty said something about that, but she wouldn't tell us any details, just that Mum did something bad to Uncle John.'

'Yes it was something bad all right. She went up to stay with Uncle John and Aunty Betty. Dot was only young, about eight I think, the same age as Pat.' Mary stopped speaking, and looked at the floor.

'Go on,' I encouraged, 'I'm a big girl now.'

'Okay, well Uncle John had his own painting and decorating company, so Mum offered to do his accounts for him. She's very clever, you know.'

I nodded.

'After a while, Uncle John started getting some complaints about overdue bills, payments that went missing, invoices that were returned as unpaid, that kind of thing.'

'Oh God no,' I said slapping my hand over my mouth, I could guess where this was heading.

'Well, she was basically cooking the books.'

'Not her own brother's business!' I said, knowing that I wasn't as surprised as I should have been.

'Yep that's right. He ended up so much in debt that he had to be declared bankrupt; he lost everything, and basically had to start all over again.'

'Oh poor Uncle John. No wonder we hardly ever saw him.'

'Yep, Aunty Betty found it very hard to forgive Mum, but that's not all.' She hesitated.

'Go on!'

'After she had swindled him out of his money, Uncle John told her to go back to London, but the money was all spent, so he even had to pay her fare.'

'No . . .'

'But apparently before she left, Reg Stevens arrived in his navy uniform, desperately looking for her, and persuaded her to go back with him.'

'So is he definitely your dad then?' I asked.

'Well yes, I'm pretty sure he is, and Marion and Marge's.'

'But not mine and Margaret's?' I asked, already knowing the answer.

'No, I don't think so.'

'Even though his name is on our birth certificates?'

Mary nodded.

'So who is our dad?' I asked. 'And what about the second prison sentence? What was it for?'

Mary shrugged her shoulders, 'I'm really sorry, but that is something that I'm afraid I don't have the answers to.'

43

Scary Situations

By the time we heard Mum had been taken into hospital, Margaret and I were both quite heavily pregnant.

'It's nothing to worry about,' said Pat when she phoned me. 'They're just taking her in for some tests, but she's fine.'

'Well she can't be fine if she's having tests,' I replied. I was feeling really tired now and work was becoming more and more of a strain.

Pat reassured me that Mum was soon going to be discharged and that I shouldn't worry, and it was easy to be convinced, as things were quite hectic in my life at that moment.

Colin and I had both moved on from the school where we had met. Colin was working at a Special School and I was now working at an IT centre. It had nothing to do with information technology though! The IT stood for Intermediate Treatment and it was run jointly by Education and Social Services for young offenders, as a last stop before borstal. It was set up in a big old Victorian house in East London where there were a group of us – some teachers, some social workers – trying to keep about fifteen youngsters out of trouble, and hopefully teach them something as well! They were a good bunch, but could be very challenging. Many of them had been through a traumatic childhood, and had been offending for many years: TDA (taking and driving away), theft, burglary etc. We all grew very fond of them, although their behaviour could be exasperating, inconsistent and frighteningly volatile.

When they found out I was expecting a baby they became very protective. We would often take them for outings into the countryside and they would be so kind and caring, helping me down the steps of the minibus with such tenderness.

Then there were the other times.

I was almost at the point of going on maternity leave and the Easter holiday was fast approaching. It was hot that year, although it was only March, and my 'bump' seemed enormous! So much so that the hospital had sent me for an ultrasound scan to see if I was having twins. I was feeling very uncomfortable and clumsy, and so when Rob, the head of the centre, suggested taking the kids swimming, I opted to stay behind in the house with anyone that wasn't going. Although we were fond of our charges, we were also realistic. Experience had taught us that if any of the kids opted to stay at the house it was usually in the hope of stealing some of the contents.

Freddy was fifteen. Despite his skinhead hair and bovver boots he could be the sweetest boy going. He was the apple of his mum's eye, and she would always iron a sharp crease in his jeans in an effort to make him look presentable.

He wasn't pleased when he realised I was still there after the others had left.

'Why ain't you f***ing gone, Kath?'

Using strong language was commonplace among the kids there – it wasn't meant to be an insult – and they always called us by our first names. We tried to make the centre as much like a home from home as possible. These youngsters had pushed against authority most of their lives, and if we were going to get anywhere with them we had to take a different approach.

'I don't feel up to it, Fred.'

'You don't f***ing trust us, do ya?' he said petulantly, pushing a chair out of his way.

'That's got nothing to do with it, Fred. You know we can't leave you in the house on your own.'

Steve and Tommy were there as well. Steve was a tall, broad boy, and was usually quite sensible, but Tommy had a history of aggressive behaviour and I was obviously thwarting some plan the three of them had hatched.

'F***ing 'ell, Kath,' Freddie started to shout, getting into a temper now. 'You lot, yer aw the f***ing same; yer say ya f***ing trust us but ya f***ing don't, not really.'

I could see that the situation was starting to get out of hand and was very aware that I was on my own, heavily pregnant and facing three very angry young offenders. I tried to think how I could defuse the situation,

'Look, why don't we just have a cup of tea? Then we can cook some dinner for when the others get back. They'll be starving.'

I started to turn towards the kitchen area, when suddenly Freddie said, 'I don't f***ing believe it. This is a load of bollocks!' and pulling his hand from behind his back I watched, almost in slow motion, as a sledgehammer hurtled towards me. It clattered in front of me, hitting the table with an almighty bang, and the three boys, including Freddie who had thrown it, stared with a shocked look on their faces as I stood motionless in front of them.

Tommy broke the silence. 'That's f***ing out of order Fred; totally f***ing out of order.'

Fred turned and slammed upstairs, shouting, 'Oh f*** off, why don't ya? Bollocks to the lot of ya.'

Steve and Tommy came over to me.

'You awright, Kath?' Steve asked quietly.

'Yes I'm fine, thanks both of you.' I eased myself down into one of the room's comfortable armchairs.

'He didn't mean to hurt ya, yer know Kath,' Steve continued. 'He's jus' annoyed cos ya didn't go and leave us 'ere.'

'I know, I know Steve, but he could have really hurt someone,' I said, feeling quite shaken now it was over.

'I'w make ya a cup of tea Kath, awright?' offered Tommy, and I nodded my thanks, glad that I only had a few more weeks to go before I would be at home waiting for the arrival of my baby.

44

A Bittersweet Birth

When Mum came out of hospital she seemed more subdued than usual. Margaret began to wonder if there was something serious wrong, but Pat reassured us that although Mum had been diagnosed with type 2 diabetes, there was nothing to worry about. She had been to the diabetic clinic and seen the nurse, and now knew how to adjust her diet to deal with it.

Mary had gone back to Australia a few months ago and we all missed her, but we kept both of our 'Australian' sisters updated regarding Mum's health problems. I suppose when you have a family as big as ours there's always someone missing, but we felt the loss of Marge and Mary all the time, even though it had been many years since they had emigrated.

Margaret had her baby, another beautiful little girl they named Rebecca. She was the model of Margaret as a baby – a shock of very dark black hair and enormous eyes fringed with curling black lashes.

I waited impatiently for the arrival of our baby. It had been a hot spring and was now becoming an even hotter summer.

'I wish this baby would hurry up and arrive. I feel like a lump in this heat,' I moaned to poor Colin as he kissed me goodbye before leaving for work.

The summer holidays were approaching when my due date, 21 June, came and went.

Colin suggested calling the baby Titania if it was a girl, after the fairy in 'Midsummer Night's Dream'.

'I hope you're joking,' I said laughing. I wanted a little boy and I already had a name in mind . . . .

On Monday night as I was trying my best to relax and stay

cool, I felt a twinge. Within a few minutes my waters had broken and I was in the first stages of labour. We travelled to the hospital in Chatham by ambulance, as it was quite a long distance, and our baby boy was born at 10.45 the next morning. He had a head full of wispy red-blond hair that glinted in the light and eyes the colour of bluebells. He was beautiful, and we called him Sam, just as I'd planned.

When I was offered a postpartum cup of tea, I drank it thankfully, smiling and still fuzzy-headed from the Pethidine and the gas and air I had taken. I didn't really take much notice when the midwife took the baby, and used a suction tube on him. I knew that babies often swallow mucus during the birth. I still wasn't alarmed when she took him out of the room saying, 'I'm just going to get baby checked by the paediatrician. Nothing to worry about.' This was my first baby after all, and I assumed that this was all perfectly routine.

When she returned a while later without Sam I began to feel anxious.

'Is he all right?' I asked, expecting to be reassured.

'I'm afraid that he might have a little problem,' the midwife answered kindly, not meeting my eyes. 'Doctor just needs to do a few tests, and then he'll come and talk to you.'

My head sprang up from the bed, 'What do you mean a little problem?' I whispered, not wanting to hear the answer. Colin held my hand tightly, a look of real concern crossing his face.

'Let's just wait for the doctor, shall we? Then he can explain,' and with that she left us clinging on to each other, terrified that the tiny bundle we had held and stroked a moment ago wasn't coming back.

After what seemed like an age, the doctor arrived with a nurse who we hadn't seen before. They came in, and as I looked at their faces I knew that this wasn't going to be good news.

'Mr and Mrs Hardy, good afternoon,' the doctor began. 'Now I'm afraid that your baby has a few problems.'

My mind was going into overdrive now. A minute ago it had been a little problem; now it was 'a few' problems.

'Let me explain,' he continued. 'Baby's windpipe and food tube are joined, and that needs sorting out.'

Colin and I exchanged looks and I saw my fear reflected in his eyes.

'How?' Colin asked. 'How can it be sorted out?'

'Well, Baby will need to have an operation to separate the two. The condition is called tracheoesophageal fistula or TOF for short,' the doctor said, speaking slowly as though we were stupid and wouldn't understand. I sat and stared at him, trying to make my muddled head focus.

'When?' Colin asked.

'As soon as possible,' the doctor replied. 'We will need to transfer him to London today. The ambulance has been ordered, and the operation will be done either tonight or very early tomorrow morning.'

I knew I was going to cry then, and sniffed back the tears as Colin put his arm around me.

'Can we go with him?' he asked.

The doctor gave me a pitying look 'You can,' he indicated to Colin, 'but I'm afraid your wife will need to stay here until the midwife signs her off. We need to look after Mum too, don't we?'

I felt patronised by the doctor but I knew that he was trying to be kind.

'But I want to go too,' I said, the tears becoming heavier as I spoke.

The nurse then came forward and took both my hands.

'Look now, you have had a rough labour and you're exhausted. You need to get your strength back for when Baby comes home from hospital.'

'He's *not* Baby,' I almost shouted. 'He's called Sam!'

'All right then,' continued the nurse calmly, 'then Sam will need you to be fit and well when he comes home. We'll get the midwife to get you stitched up and then she can assess when she thinks you will be well enough to travel to London.'

I gave in and then hated myself for doing so. I was weak from a long labour, and had been torn badly so needed a lot of stitches.

I felt nauseous from the drugs, and from the news that we had just been given, and there was a familiar dull ache beginning behind my eyes. The doctor arranged for me to be wheeled down to Special Baby Care to see my Sam one more time before he left. He was in an incubator now and there were tubes everywhere. He was too fragile for a last cuddle.

Then he went off to London in an ambulance with his daddy, leaving me behind.

45

The Terrible Fear

I was put in a side room. When Colin came back to see me after Sam had been operated on we sat and cried together, our arms around each other, clinging on desperately but not saying a word.

No one else came near me except for the occasional midwife. I had been stitched and cleaned up, and they had offered me food that I couldn't eat, conversation I couldn't take part in, and kindness I wasn't interested in; then I was left alone. The other mums probably assumed that my baby had died, so they would creep past my door, and sneak a pitying glance, but never come in to talk to me. Colin was back and forwards between Chatham and London to see Sam, and my family stayed away. I felt abandoned. No one sent me a baby card, there were no excited congratulations, and the doctors still refused to let me out of hospital.

Then Mum arrived. She came bustling into the ward looking dishevelled and determined, and I've never been so glad to see her. She brought me grapes. I probably would have laughed any other time, but instead I only just managed not to cry. Mum never liked overt expressions of emotion, and crying was always referred to as 'being silly', so I kept my tears in check.

'Hello love,' she said. 'Where's Colin?'

'He's gone up to the hospital to see Sam,' I answered. Saying our baby's name was still hard. It didn't sound real; it was as though I was talking about a stranger, someone I didn't know.

'When will you go up there with him?' Mum asked, moving the things around on my bedside cupboard, keeping busy.

'Well, I haven't seen the midwife today yet. She should be round any minute now; hopefully she'll be able to tell me.'

Mum shuffled her feet and fidgeted about. I could tell she felt awkward, didn't know what to say.

'How did you get here?' I asked, as though I really cared.

'Bus and train and then another bus.' She had always been resourceful, and she was comfortable travelling on public transport even though Pat had passed her driving test many years before and had a nice car now.

We continued to talk about other unimportant things, until she suddenly said, 'You won't lose him, you know.' She looked at me directly and I believed her; despite all of my fears, I believed what she was saying. At that moment the midwife arrived and Mum said her goodbyes and shuffled out of the room back to Dagenham without a backwards glance.

It was two weeks before I was able to join Sam at the hospital in London. Although I was allowed a tiny room of my own that I shared with him and his little incubator, the walls were glass and the lights were on all night. I was desperately trying to feed him myself. It was difficult, as my milk had almost dried up by then, but somehow we managed. It was the neonatal ward for very sick babies, many of whom died while we were there, so it was not a very happy place.

By the time we were discharged, and allowed to take our baby home, I was terrified. I didn't feel like he belonged to me at all, and I was also afraid that I wouldn't know how to care for him, that I would get it wrong. The truth was that I was still afraid he was going to die.

It was on the day of the royal wedding of Charles and Diana that we had our first outing as a family. Colin wanted to take Sam to see his mum, who still lived in their family home in Balham. It was a Victorian terraced house, old-fashioned and dilapidated, with flaking paint outside. Inside was always neat and tidy though, with a huge aspidistra taking pride of place in the middle of the front room. Throughout the journey I'd been on edge. When we arrived we found that Colin's mum had, as usual, put on an enormous spread.

'I've just made a few things,' she said, indicating the vast array of sandwiches, pastries and cakes that were laid out on the ironing board. The table itself was already heaving with two places set for a huge roast dinner.

'I've had mine already,' she said. She always ate before we arrived. I think she was either shy, or wanted to free herself up to run around after us, despite our protests. Colin's mum Beat (short for Beatrice) was now in her late seventies, but she was very active and independent. She ushered us in but didn't attempt to take the baby. I think she was probably a bit scared, as were most people.

'How are you, Kathy?' she asked, busying herself with the preparations.

'I'm fine,' I lied, smiling back.

'Let's have a look at the little chap then.' She pulled back the shawl that the baby was wrapped in. 'Oh, he's a lovely little fellow, aren't you?' she said, stroking his face gently.

Sam opened his big blue eyes, and gazed at her earnestly. He was beginning to squirm around looking for food, so I decamped into the front room and sat in the armchair to feed him. For the first couple of minutes he was fine, drinking greedily, then suddenly he stopped and pulled back with a jerk. As I looked down I realised with horror that he was motionless and didn't appear to be breathing. Shaking him, I shouted for Colin, who was still in the other room chatting to his mum.

'Quick, he's stopped breathing! He's stopped breathing!' I screamed in panic. They both appeared at the door and rushed in, Colin grabbed the baby and banged his back, while all the while Sam was getting bluer and bluer. I was in a state of complete breakdown at this point, shivering and crying, with Colin's mum desperately trying to calm me down and phone for the ambulance at the same time. Finally Colin turned Sam on to his front and gently gave mouth-to-nose/mouth resuscitation. It worked. Sam gave a few short gasps, and then began to breathe normally again, so that by the time the ambulance arrived just a few minutes later he was calm and so were we. It had seemed as though hours had passed, but in fact it had all happened in a few short minutes. We were taken to hospital so that the doctors could check Sam, and were kept in overnight. It didn't happen again and the doctors assured us that it was probably just a normal choking accident that could happen to any baby.

I knew better.

Over the next few weeks the same thing happened again and again. The pattern was set. I would be feeding him, he would gasp, stop breathing, turn blue and then come round after resuscitation and be fine by the time the ambulance arrived. Thank God that Colin was on school holidays. I could never have coped alone, and worst of all I knew the doctors didn't believe us.

'They think we're making it up,' I complained to Colin, as once again the ambulance had arrived to find Sam breathing normally. 'They think I'm paranoid, I know they do.' I was so upset and frustrated the tears slid down my cheeks. 'I can't bear it. If he's going to die then I just wish he would; I can't go on like this.' I dropped my head into my hands crying, ashamed that I could say those words. But I meant them. The misery of holding my baby in my arms only to have his life threatened time and time again, with no one taking any notice . . . it was intolerable.

Then it happened in hospital.

Sam's consultant had finally admitted him to Great Ormond Street to do some checks. For the first day he was fine, and then they put a special tube through his nose and asked me to feed him as usual. As soon as I began to feed him, he made the now familiar gasp, stopped breathing and began to turn blue. I rushed out of our little room with him still in my arms and called for help. The nurse took one look at him and shouted to her colleague, 'Press for the crash team!' and then everything burst into life around me, Sam was whisked away and I was ushered out of the room and restrained by a nurse, all the while knowing what was happening to my baby.

I was almost glad. At last they believed me.

46

Finding Sam

Sam had a second operation, which thankfully solved the problem of his breathing. It was a new beginning for us as a family, but as I brought him home, he still felt like someone else's baby. I was afraid to love him.

My friend Sherry had got pregnant about six months after me and had now had a baby boy of her own called Tom. Colin and I were desperately trying to sell our house in Kent so that we could move nearer to our friends and family. We needed their support so badly. Finally our house sold and we were faced with the problem of finding a new home fast.

My sister Margaret had seen a little cottage for sale in a village about twenty minutes from where she and Tony now lived. The problem was it was a wreck and in need of total refurbishment. Our friends Sherry and Colin came up with an answer.

'Come and live here with us, lass, while you do up the cottage,' suggested Colin B in his broad Geordie accent. 'That way you and Sherry can help each other with the bairns, and the hospital is only about twenty minutes away. It's a win win.'

We agreed before they had time to change their minds!

One morning we had just put the babies down for their morning nap and were looking forward to a coffee.

'I'll put the kettle on,' Sherry offered, and I settled myself down at the big wooden kitchen table with a pile of post. As I flicked through the letters I picked out one addressed to me that was postmarked from the Isle of Man. My heart beat fast as I held it tightly in my hand.

'What's wrong, Kathy?' Sherry asked, and I suddenly realised I had frozen and was staring at the envelope.

'I've got a letter. I think it might be from my sister.'

'Oh, which one?' asked Sherry, pouring the hot water into the percolator. She wiped her slim hands on the front of her dungarees, and sat on the chair opposite mine.

I swallowed heavily. 'Sheila.'

'Sheila? I don't remember you mentioning Sheila. Which one is she again?'

I wanted to rip open the letter and devour its contents, but I was almost scared to read it.

'Well, it's kind of a long story,' I said, 'but if you're interested . . .?'

Sherry nodded slowly. 'Only if you want to tell it.'

I closed my eyes for a minute, took a drink of my coffee and began to fill her in. About the split. About Sheila choosing to live with her father and blanking Pat in the playground when they were both at the Ursuline. About the others being sent to children's homes.

'Poor little things!' murmured Sherry.

'They never talk about what happened there . . . but they were very unhappy. Anyway, Margaret and I wanted to know about Sheila, so we wrote to her publishers to get her address. She writes romances, you know.'

'Look, why don't you take it upstairs to read?' Sherry suggested. 'I need to go and get a few bits of shopping anyway. Do you mind listening out for Tom?'

I agreed readily, relieved that I was being given the chance to be on my own. I wasn't sure what the envelope contained, but whatever it was I wanted to have some time to think about it.

Once Sherry had left, I plucked up the courage to slide my finger under the flap of the envelope and open it up. I held the sheets of paper in my hand and began to read.

The letter told of Sheila's life, as a journalist, author and mother of five. She asked about us, what we did, whether or not we had children, a kind of easy-going letter that you might write to a long-lost acquaintance, not a sister – not even a secret one.

I sighed, and sat down to reply. This time I would dig a little deeper.

I tried again and again, but every letter I got back was the same: friendly and interesting, but giving nothing away.

During the months that we stayed at Sherry and Colin's, I still felt removed from Sam. It was a strange feeling, a detached, arm's length kind of relationship that I had with him. I would hold him, I played with him, I kissed and cuddled him, but it wasn't quite right, and I'm sure he sensed it too. Then not long before we moved into our little cottage things changed. We had taken Sam to hospital for an overnight stay as the consultant was worried that he had seen something that might mean yet another operation. Colin and I had been so worried, but we had got the phone call early that morning to say that there was nothing to worry about; it must just have been a shadow on the X-ray. When we arrived to pick Sam up, weak with relief, something strange happened.

Colin and I walked into the ward just as the children were being given breakfast. Sam was sitting on a tiny chair, still with a drip in his arm, tucking into a mashed up bowl of Weetabix with a serious yet determined look on his tiny round face. I looked at him, his big blue eyes, his red-blond hair, and suddenly my heart gave a lurch. All the love that I had kept in check, all the tenderness, swam over me and I almost drowned in the warmth of it. I felt such a surge of powerful love that I had to hug him. As I bent down I stroked his soft little face, I breathed in the sweet smell of him, and whispered in his ear, 'Mummy's here now.' He turned towards me and gave me a huge smile. It was as though he knew that his mummy was really here now, that things were going to be different from now on, and indeed they were. Sam was mine now and I was his; we had found each other at last.

47

Talking to Aunty

Margaret had not long had her third baby, and everyone had come for the baptism. They called her Elizabeth Edith, which seems like fate now because she would be the last baby that Aunty Edie would hold.

Aunty was becoming more and more fragile, although she still retained her sense of fun. 'Come out, Jimmy Green!' she would say with a mischievous smile when she accidentally passed wind. Her hair was quite grey now, but still thick and curly. She had never been as overweight as Mum, but more recently she appeared to have shrunk into herself.

The day after the baptism Aunty and I were invited to lunch at Margaret's house. As it was an unusually warm day for April, Margaret suggested we sit in the garden.

She placed baby Lizzie in Aunty's arms for a cuddle.

'Ooh, she's the model of yer mother,' Aunty said, rocking the baby back and forth. 'Hello my darling,' she cooed gently.

Lizzie gazed up at Aunty, spellbound.

'*Little girl you're crying, I know why you're blue,*' sung Aunty, softly rocking the baby in her arms.

The sun was shining, and the smell of lilacs was heavy in the air. Feeling warm and lazy like a cat, I felt myself starting to drift off to sleep.

Margaret broke the silence suddenly. 'Aunty, can I ask you something? Do you know who our dad is?'

I jerked awake with a start. Surely I must have dreamt that?

Aunty carried on singing:

Better go to sleep, now, little girl you've had a busy day.
You've been playing soldiers, the battle has been won,
The enemy is out of sight
Come now, little soldier,
Put away your gun, the war is over for tonight.

'Aunty,' she repeated, louder this time, in case the old lady hadn't heard, 'if you know, please tell us.'

Aunty stopped and looked down at Lizzie. 'You'd better put 'er to bed; she's gone fast asleep.'

Margaret took the baby gently and laid her on her lap.

'Did you hear me Aunty?' she continued, refusing to let it go.

'Yes I 'eard yer,' Aunty answered, irritated, 'I've told yer before, I can't tell yer about yer father without telling yer about yer mother.'

'Please Aunty,' I joined in now, 'we really have a right to know,' but Aunty just looked away towards where the other children were playing at the end of the garden.

'Be careful now,' she called out to them as a clod of mud flew up in the air. 'Mind yer 'eads.'

Margaret and I exchanged an exasperated look, when suddenly Aunty continued. 'He was good to 'er, 'e was,' she said, refusing to meet our eyes. 'He would 'ave stuck to 'er like shit to a blanket, if she adn't dun wot she did.'

We sat bolt upright now, hardly daring to move, knowing from experience that the slightest distraction could stop the conversation dead.

'Jewish 'e was, so kind, always 'elped 'er out, money, flowers, whatever she wanted. But then when it all stopped, she couldn't manage, you see, that's why she 'ad to do it, and they took 'er away again.

'I said to your Granny more than once, "I can't stand no more; either she goes or I go," and do yer know what yer Gran used to say? She said "She's going nowhere." I knew then, see, that she couldn't turn 'er out, not with all you children, so I just 'ad to put up with it.

'Anyway,' she added, 'yer mother was always 'er favourite. It was always Florrie that she wanted.'

Aunty gazed into the space around her, seemingly gathering her thoughts and then continued. 'She was determined not to die till yer mother got out, yer see, but as soon as she came back home, your Gran gave up. You must 'ave been about the same age as Becky and Sam are now, maybe a bit older.

'Anyway, where's me cup of tea? I feel like me throat's been cut,' and with that Lizzie woke, and Margaret fed her out there in the garden, with the children playing, the sun shining, and one more little piece of the jigsaw falling into place.

48

A Sudden Death

Later that summer we went with Pat, Josie and Mum to Crewkerne in Somerset for a week's holiday during the May half-term.

We were staying in a lovely old stone cottage, complete with leaded windows, and exposed beams, surrounded by the most beautiful cottage garden, spilling over with flowers. 'Aunty would love it here,' I said to Colin, while we watched Sam playing with Mr Lion, his favourite plastic ride-on toy.

'Perhaps we should try to take her some cuttings?'

We decided to take Sam for a walk in the nearby woods, and set off promising to be back by dinner time, leaving Mum and my sisters to enjoy the garden in peace. The trees were almost in full leaf, and when the sun shone through their branches it sent dappled drops of light sweeping across the forest floor.

As we walked, we talked about Mum. I had always shared everything with Colin, and he knew as much as I did about my past; we didn't believe in secrets. He also knew that there was a deep, burning need in me to know who my father was, to understand my Mum and make sense of my muddled memories.

'I really find it hard to understand why you can't just ask her outright,' he said, not for the first time.

'You know what she's like; she wouldn't answer me, or she would pretend she hadn't heard, like she did to Mary when she plucked up the courage to ask.'

My sisters and I had laughed when Mary had told us that Mum had just said, 'Yes, I will have another cup of tea,' when she had asked about her dad. We all knew the rules, and what to expect if we tried to flout them.

'There's just no point,' I continued, watching Sam weave in and out of the trees.

'Mummy, can we have a dog like Aunty Pat's?' he asked.

Pat and Sam were best friends and adored each other. She spoilt him terribly. He could do no wrong in her eyes, and the feeling was mutual.

'One day maybe,' I said absentmindedly.

'But surely if you tell her how important it is to you to know, surely then she would have to tell you?'

'I don't want to upset her.' I knew how hard it must be for Colin to understand the complexities of the relationships in our family. Nothing was as straightforward as it seemed.

'Well then, what about Pat or Josie? You're not telling me that they don't know more than they're saying.'

I just shrugged. It was like an itch that I couldn't scratch; every now and then the ignorance, the secrets, became intolerable.

We carried on walking in silence, both lost in thought, with Sam running up every now and then to show us an interesting stone, or a bug that he had spied crawling through the undergrowth.

When we approached the cottage, Mum was standing outside smoking a cigarette and leaning on the door frame. She looked strangely distracted.

Sam ran up to her. 'Nanny, I got you some flowers!' He thrust a handful of daisies towards her.

She bent down and took them and patted his head. 'Go in and find Aunty Pat.' When he was out of earshot she drew deeply on her cigarette and said in a flat, unemotional voice, 'Aunty's dead.'

The breath was sucked out of my body as I tried to comprehend what she was saying. 'What?'

I hadn't realised how much I had loved Aunty until that moment. I had been so preoccupied with myself and my own little family, that I had failed to notice her continued decline, had ignored the way she had looked when Geoff had picked her up to go and stay with Marion just a few days ago.

'She knew she was never going to come home again,' I cried bitterly to Colin later that night. 'I saw her looking around, like she was trying to fix it all in her head, take it with her: her chair in the corner, the old photos on the wall, her precious garden . . . all of her memories . . . and all I could think about was that I wished she would hurry up and go so she wouldn't wake Sam up as she left!'

Colin held me close and tried to comfort me but it was no good. I pulled away and curled up on the bed in a tight ball. Aunty was gone and I was inconsolable. I had never once told her that I loved her.

I cried myself quietly to sleep that night, and dreamed of an old lady with a mischievous smile and a sparkle in her blue eyes, who swore more than she should, had a fiery temper, threw teapots, liked a drop of brandy, sang and danced, loved her garden and our children who sometimes played in it, but most of all a woman who gave up her own life so that she could keep us all together and safe. She had been loyal to Mum to the end, never betraying her secrets.

They say that you go through stages of grief. At first comes the overwhelming desolation, then the next stage: anger.

'I don't understand,' I said through tightly drawn lips. 'Why didn't the doctor resuscitate her?'

Me, Margaret and Marion had met up at Mum's to help arrange the funeral, and had taken the children for a walk to Goodmayes Park.

It was worse for Marion. Aunty had been staying with her when she was taken ill.

'She knew she was dying,' she explained. 'She just kept saying, "Let me go, let me go." She was ready; she knew it was her time.'

The three of us watched the children run towards the lake where the swans were gliding across the sparkling water. How could the sun shine so brightly amid so much grief? Aunty loved the park, and she would sometimes walk through there on her way home from Mass on Sundays. For all the swearing she had been a devout woman, never missing a service.

I turned away and called to the children, 'Don't go too near the water.'

'Do you remember Aunty telling us that a swan would break your arm if you went near its babies?' Marion asked smiling.

It felt strange to be walking in the park that had been such a big part of our childhood. The memories of happier visits crowded in. The cricket matches we had all played, the races we had run.

We stopped to admire the beds of flowers, and then Marion said, 'All she had was her old rosary beads and a little miraculous medal that she always pinned to her vest.'

'Oh poor Aunty,' Margaret said starting to cry again.

'The ambulance man gave them to me. He shouldn't really have taken her from my house, you know, she was already dead, but when he realised that Cathy and David were upstairs asleep he took pity on us, I suppose.

'Mum must be upset,' I said, to reassure myself as much as anything. 'Aunty has been part of her life for so long. I mean, I know they argued, but I think they loved each other, don't you?'

'I think Mum finds it hard to feel sadness; in fact I think she finds it hard to show love,' said Marion.

'But she must realise what Aunty gave up because of her?' I said. 'That must mean something?'

'Of course it must!' Margaret added with conviction.

'Well, I suppose she loved Aunty in her own way, but she didn't exactly show it did she?'

'I don't know, I never really thought about it,' I admitted.

'Well,' Marion said, 'I certainly don't think she has ever loved me.'

It was Margaret who broke the silence.

'Of course Mum loves us,' she said. 'She's the best mum in the world.'

Marion looked at us carefully. 'Yes, I think you're probably right. She does love you two, but I don't think she has ever loved me, or Marge and Mary.' Her eyes slid away from ours as she continued. 'What you two still don't understand is that she was never there when we were small. In fact I remember her coming to see us in Valence Avenue once, and we didn't even know who she was. Aunty said to us, "Come and give your mother a cuddle," and we just looked at this stranger standing there. We didn't know her at all.'

'Where was she then?' I asked. 'Not prison again?' Margaret gave me a look. It felt a little disloyal to say the words aloud, but we both needed to find out the truth.

'No, not that time. Who knows? It might have been London or Southend or anywhere. I don't suppose we will ever know now Aunty is gone. Mum had another life, a secret life wherever she was, and it didn't include us, her ever-expanding brood of children, that's for sure.' Marion hesitated, and then went on, 'And when she finally did come back to Valence Ave to live, she used to send us to bed you know, we had to be upstairs by half six even when we were older, just to get us out of the way. You never had that, you and Margaret; you were always the favourites, the babies. We just got sent to bed without any dinner, just bread and jam for our tea. How do you think that made us feel? Loved? No, I don't think so.'

As we walked back to the house in silence, my mind was in turmoil. If Margaret and I could find out where Mum used to disappear to and with who, we might just be able to solve the questions that eternally tormented us: the identity of our father, and why we had never known him. Then I remembered Aunty and the loss hit me again like a slap. What did any of it matter anyway? The person who had stood up for us, who had been beside Mum through all of it, that person was dead, and then I remembered a saying my friend Anne had often used: 'You never miss the water till the well runs dry,' and I smiled. Aunty would have appreciated that.

49

Josephine

By the time Sam was three and a half, Colin and I had plucked up the courage to try for another baby. I was frightened. I knew that Sam's condition wasn't thought to be hereditary, but that didn't completely reassure me. Margaret was expecting her fourth baby and I knew that if I didn't have one soon, I never would. I wanted desperately to know what it would be like to have a 'normal' baby with no problems. I wanted to be able to enjoy the excitement and happiness that other women felt after they gave birth, without the crushing terror that had accompanied my experience and followed me throughout the first year of Sam's life. Within a couple of months I was expecting. When I told Margaret she was overjoyed.

'That's great,' she said, 'they'll be born about the same time apart as Becky and Sam.'

I was devastated when I miscarried my baby at twelve weeks. There didn't appear to be any cause; I was just told to try again in a few months. Depression began to overwhelm me. I couldn't believe I would ever have a healthy baby. When Margaret gave birth to her fourth daughter she called her Faye, the name that I had picked out for our baby. The name suited her completely. She was tiny and fragile, with fine wisps of black hair, and enormous blue eyes. When I visited Margaret in hospital I looked down at the baby enviously.

'She's beautiful,' I murmured, stroking her pale skin.

Within a month of Faye being born I found out that I was pregnant again.

The doctor was very cautious. 'Bed rest!' he advised sternly. 'Bed rest and lots of good food!' The hospital had now identified that I had a fibroid, and it was that which they thought may have caused my previous miscarriage. Colin was very strict with me, but I put my foot down when he suggested that I might use a bedpan!

'I hope you're joking?' I said, 'Because that is not going to happen!' But I did rest. I wanted this baby desperately and I wasn't taking any chances this time.

About six weeks before my baby was due, I was watching a new comedy series, *Blackadder*, which I thought was hilarious. As I watched I felt a few minor contractions. When I told Colin, he was worried.

'Why don't you ring Margaret and ask what she thinks?' he suggested.

'Oh for goodness sake, it is just practice contractions, I think they're called "Braxton Hicks",' I said, but I rang Margaret anyway just to be sure.

'How bad are they?' she asked.

'Well, I suppose they're quite painful,' I replied as I paced up and down our tiny living room.

'And how frequent are they?'

'About every five minutes or so, I suppose.'

'I think you should ring the hospital,' she advised, 'just to make sure.'

Luckily our cottage was immediately opposite the hospital that I was booked in to have the baby, because when I rang they insisted that I come in immediately.

'Okay,' I said, 'I'll walk over with my husband.'

I couldn't believe it when they insisted that he drove me. It was literally as far to our driveway as it was to the hospital, but Colin insisted we do as we were told, so I climbed into the car for the thirty-second journey!

After chauffeuring me, Colin drove Sam to my mum's. By the time he arrived home later that night the phone was ringing to tell him that if he wanted to see his baby born he had better get over there quickly. Our baby girl was born as Colin walked into the delivery room. I heard the midwife say to her assistant,

'Thank goodness, her airways are clear,' and I knew that my baby was going to be all right even though she had been in such a hurry to get here. She had arrived six weeks early and was the most beautiful baby ever. She was tiny, weighing just 4lb 10oz, but was perfect, with the same red-gold hair as her brother and the same enormous blue eyes. She was like a baby doll and I fell in love with her immediately. Unlike my previous delivery, I felt really well and was out of bed by the time Colin arrived the next morning with Sam.

'Be careful,' he said. 'Do you think you should be out of bed already?'

I laughed. 'I'm fine. Look Sam,' I said, calling him over, 'here's your baby sister.'

Sam peered into the cot. 'What's her name, Mummy?'

I looked at Colin over our two little ones' heads. We hadn't had a chance to decide yet, but in my heart I knew what kind of little girl my baby would be. She would be strong, fiery and creative, just like my favourite heroine in *Little Women*, and just like her Aunty Josie.

'Shall we call her Josephine?' I suggested to Sam and Colin. They nodded their agreement. 'What second name shall we give her?' I asked Sam, 'You can choose if you like.'

Sam gave it no more than a couple of seconds thought and then suggested firmly, 'Jet Plane – I think we should call her Josephine Jet Plane.'

Colin and I exchanged a smile; we might have to persuade Sam to think of a slightly more conventional name. Later that morning we agreed on Kate – Josephine Kate, our perfect baby daughter!

Jo, as we called her, was indeed a perfect, contented baby. She was easy to feed, slept well, and was a peach of a baby, always smiling and happy. Those early days as a family of four were some of the happiest of my life.

50

Trying to Hold On

By this point, Margaret and Marion lived with their families just around the corner, so we saw lots of each other.

Marion had decided to train to be a teacher and was now attending a local teacher training college.

Mum had not been very encouraging to poor Marion.

'You'll make a terrible teacher,' she said when Marion told her. 'You don't even like children.'

Marion was hurt and upset. 'I don't understand why she's always so horrible to me,' she said later that evening when she popped in for a cup of tea. 'It's as though she always has to put me down, make me feel useless.'

'I'm sure she doesn't mean to be hurtful,' I assured her. Mum had been just as dismissive of Marge when she had decided to go into nursing, telling her that she wouldn't be any good because she was afraid of blood. 'Perhaps she's just trying to protect you, in case it doesn't work out.'

Marion took a gulp of tea. 'Yes, maybe, though I think we both know that's not the real reason,' and with that she left for home.

I knew that Mum was funny about some things. She liked to be able to boast about us to other people, but she would always remind us, 'Don't tell the devil too much of your mind,' as though she was always expecting the worst to happen. It is strange how you retain an irrational fear for your whole life, and the worry that something bad was waiting just around the corner was something that we all still carried with us.

I had another miscarriage shortly after Jo's first birthday, and had been very upset, but we knew we were lucky to have two lovely children, and so were able to put it behind us the best that we could.

By the time Jo was three, we had decided we would definitely like another baby. I had always wanted a big family, and was envious of Margaret's growing brood. I needed to catch up! I was feeling very tired, and Margaret persuaded me to go to the doctors to get checked out first.

The doctor's surgery was small, and the doctor that I saw was the only member of the practice. He was a kind man, but unfortunately had a rather insensitive bedside manner. When he examined me he smiled. 'Ah Mrs Hardy, you are pregnant! About three months at least I should think.'

'I can't be,' I replied. I knew that I wasn't expecting a baby, I wasn't an idiot.

'Well I'm afraid you can be, and I think you are,' he stated matter-of-factly. 'What makes you so sure that you're not?'

'Because I have been having periods, heavy ones,' I told him, 'and anyway, I don't feel pregnant.'

The doctor looked perplexed, and then called his nurse into the consulting room.

'Feel this,' he indicated to her.

She felt around. 'Mmm yes,' she said nodding.

'Do you feel the lump?' he asked her. I felt my insides turning to water. A lump? A hot prickly sweat broke out on my neck and hands.

'Yes, yes I can,' she murmured, palpating my abdomen.

'It's enormous,' the doctor continued, talking to the nurse over me, as though I was invisible, 'the size of a melon!'

'Well Mrs Hardy,' he said, as though he had just noticed that I was there, 'you have a very large lump in your womb, and we need to get it checked out as soon as possible. I'll get you referred to the hospital immediately.'

'So this is it,' I thought to myself. 'I knew things were too good to be true. I've got cancer and I'm going to die.' The faces of my two children came into my mind. How could I leave them? How would Colin cope on his own with two young children? The negative thoughts swam around inside my head, panic spiralling out of control. As I drove down the country lane close to our cottage, I considered driving into a ditch. For a few seconds, in my mind that was an actual possibility. I just didn't want to have to face up to it.

Then I remembered the doctors speculating about me having fibroids. I desperately clung on to the possibility that the lump was something like that – something fixable.

I shuddered to myself as I turned my key in the door and heard Sam and Jo calling out, 'Mummy's home! Daddy – Mummy's home!' My heart did a somersault as I thought, 'Yes, but for how long?'

I went into a downward spiral of depression, worse even than the months after Sam was born. I suppose that I had never really fully recovered. People didn't expect me to be depressed. I wasn't 'that sort' of person, whatever that means. When the social worker used to wander round the neonatal ward that Sam was in as a baby, she would often go up to the other mothers and ask them if they were OK. I knew that many of them were given counselling and other types of support, but she would look at me reading my book as I sat next to Sam's cot, and say 'You're fine aren't you, Mrs Hardy,' as a statement, not a question, and every time she said it I would smile at her and nod my head.

'Yes thank you.' I would say. 'Absolutely fine,' when inside I was falling apart. Oh the lies we learn to tell to protect ourselves from ourselves. My drama training came in handy, here. I was still a good actress;, no one knew how shattered and damaged I was inside.

It was the same now. I hid my terrors from almost everyone, but Colin knew. I cried myself to sleep some nights while I was waiting to go into hospital.

The consultant had been kind.

'Mrs Hardy, without opening you up and having a good old poke around, we can't be sure whether it is a fibroid or something a bit more troublesome,' he told me. Then he hesitated before going on. 'You have two children, don't you?'

I nodded fearfully.

'Well I want you to have a good think about whether your family is complete,' he went on. He was a tall slim man with kind eyes, and he was looking at me now questioningly. 'Because that will help us to decide what to do next'.

I wasn't sure what he meant.

'I don't understand,' I said. 'Can you explain please?'

'Of course,' he said obligingly. He lent forward and took my hand. 'I am almost certain this is just a fibroid,' he started by saying, 'but there is a small chance that it is something more sinister that we will have to deal with promptly.' I knew what he meant now.

'If it is just a fibroid, I can do a myomectomy, which means that you will keep your womb, and can continue to have more babies if you want – although I have to tell you that the fibroid will probably grow back and you will have to go through the operation again at some stage in the future. If your family is complete, then I can just whip out your womb once and for all, and "Bob's your uncle," no more problems.' He smiled. It sounded so easy. He patted my hand, 'You have a chat to your husband outside and let me know before you leave,' and with that he ushered me to the door.

Colin was waiting patiently outside. I wasn't crying when I joined him, but my hands were trembling. He put his arm around me.

'Are you OK?' he asked. 'What did he say?'

I told him that I had a choice: have a myomectomy, which would leave my womb intact but meant that I might have similar problems in the future, or undergo a full hysterectomy. Of course, if the lump turned out to be malignant my choices would be narrowed even further.

'I think you should just have it finished and done with,' Colin said, his blue eyes searching my face. 'We've got two children now, our little boy and our little girl.'

I gave him a watery smile.

'Sam was born ill; Jo was born early. I'm not sure I want us to take any more chances. Perhaps we are only meant to have two children,' he said carefully, watching for my reaction.

I nodded reluctantly, feeling worn down by it all. The most important thing was to be around for Sam and Jo as long as possible. I felt as though I had this malevolent growth inside me, and I just wanted it gone, to be able to get on with my life if I could.

That evening after the children were in bed, Colin and I went out into the garden. He put his arms around me as we looked at the sky. The smell from the early lilac blooms swam around us and the stars were very bright. 'Look,' he said, pointing upwards, 'it's funny isn't it? The light that we are seeing now was shining thousands if not millions of years ago. It makes you feel very small and unimportant, doesn't it?'

I snuggled into him, strangely comforted by the thought that we were just small dots in a vast picture.

I returned to that moment many times over the weeks while I waited to be called in to hospital.

51

Mum's Illness

'Kathleen, will you help me clear out the cupboard in my room?'
Mum asked softly watching me with her blue eyes that had
faded now to grey. I had popped round with some fresh scones,
to find her ill in bed. With her wispy white hair spread across her
pillow she looked older than her seventy-three years.

Mum had asked me about the cupboard several times over
the past few months. Surely she didn't feel up to it at the
moment? It was becoming an obsession with her.

'Mum, I can't do it tonight,' I said, 'the kids will be wanting
their dinner.' She looked away and I thought I saw tears in her
eyes. 'Are you all right, Mum?'

She nodded sadly, 'Yes, but I'm not well, Kath,' she
whispered.

I stroked her head; it still felt alien to kiss her, but I did. 'I
know. I'll come back at the weekend,' I promised, packing up my
things. 'I'd better get going. You never know what the traffic will
be like.'

I looked back from the doorway, and saw Mum, a shadow of
herself, melting into the bedclothes.

'Try to eat something, Mum; you won't get better unless you
do,' and with that I left Valence Avenue and drove our little 2CV
back to the cottage, Sam and Jo squabbling in the back over the
Matchbox cars that Pat had bought them, my thoughts back on
myself and my own fears. I pushed Mum out of my mind. I
would worry about her after my operation, I thought. I couldn't
worry about everything at once.

The next morning I got the letter through with the date for
my operation. As I opened the envelope my hands shook. I gave

it to Colin when he got home. 'I have to go in on the 7th May,' I said flatly. I was trying hard to hide my emotions.

'Good,' he said, 'it will be over and done with and you will feel better'.

I nodded. 'I hope so.'

Mum continued to struggle to eat, so shortly after my visit she was taken into hospital.

Margaret and I met outside at visiting time and walked to the ward together. We saw Mum propped half up in bed looking very frail.

'Mum,' I said kissing her lightly on the cheek. 'How are you feeling?'

She just looked at me with a faraway look in her eyes.

Margaret gave her a kiss and held her hand.

'Oh Margy.' Mum said softly, and her eyes took on a wistful look.

'Have the doctors been round yet?' Margaret asked, her nurse's training kicking in. 'I'd like to have a word with them.'

Mum shook her head. 'No they've been round already today.' She spoke so quietly I could hardly hear.

Margaret turned to me, 'I'm just going to see if I can have a chat with the nurse,' she said, and I stayed with Mum, holding her hand and stroking her arm. Although she had lost all the plumpness from her body, her skin was still soft as silk. 'Don't worry,' I joked, 'Margaret will get you sorted out, you know what she's like.'

Mum tried to smile, but I could see that she was very weak, and I was getting worried.

The staff nurse was talking to Margaret, and I watched them out of the corner of my eye trying desperately to get a sense of their discussion from their faces. Margaret glanced over at Mum and I and then turned back and continued talking to the nurse. She came back with a thin smile on her lips. She looked paler than usual, but had a slight red flush to her cheeks.

'Everything all right?' I asked as brightly as I could.

She nodded unconvincingly. 'Yes fine. Let's grab a drink.' She looked at Mum, who was starting to close her eyes, and whispered, 'Mum, we're going to get a cup of tea. Do you want us to bring you anything back?'

Mum shook her head almost imperceptibly and drifted off to sleep.

The hospital café was starkly lit and almost empty.

'Why is it that hospitals always have the same sticky, antiseptic smell?' I asked, stirring the grey liquid.

'Mum's kidneys are failing,' Margaret blurted out.

'Is it to do with her diabetes?' I knew that she had been warned over the years to control her diet more carefully, but she had never been very good at being told what to do, and this had resulted in her being put on insulin a while ago.

Margaret nodded. 'I would have thought so. The doctors want to run some more tests.'

'Does that mean they'll be keeping her in for a while longer then?'

Margaret looked down at the remains of her coffee. 'Kathleen, I don't think Mum will be coming home for a good while yet.'

'Well I must admit that's a relief. At least now she's getting the attention she needs, and it will get sorted once and for all.'

Margaret just gave me a strange look and pushed herself upright. 'Sorry, but I've got to go and pick up the kids. Can you say goodbye to Mum for me?'

I nodded, swigged down my horrible coffee and tried to put on a cheerful face for Mum's sake.

52

Falling Apart

The following week was busy. I was desperately trying to get everything ready for my impending hospital stay, and I was also aware that I would be incapacitated for a while after the operation. That was going to be tricky to manage with two young children. None of this was helped by my secret conviction that I was never going to come home again, and the deep, debilitating depression that was beginning to overwhelm me.

I went upstairs to make sure that Sam had not thrown his school uniform on the floor again. He was almost eight and had recently had a growth spurt, so looked even skinnier than usual. His hair had lost its red tinge very soon after he was born and was now a pale golden blond, the same as his sister's. Sam had always been boisterous and lively, and Jo emulated him – she was a real tomboy, and wanted to be with her brother and her cousins at every opportunity. They were always together, the six of them, running around outside, climbing, making dens, playing at pirates, racing drivers, explorers, anything where they could let their imaginations fly. We were so lucky to live out here, with a wild garden ripe for exploration.

Just then the telephone rang and I heard Colin's key in the door. As the kids ran to meet him, I picked it up.

'Oh Kath, is Colin with you?

My stomach lurched. I tried to speak but my throat felt tight, so that I had to cough before I could respond.

'Pat?' I didn't want her to say anything else then. Until I heard the words, life would be the same.

'It's Mum,' she said, 'I'm sorry, she died this afternoon.'

And there it was – boom – the explosion that rocked my core. The floor beneath my feet shifted, and I involuntarily sat down on the bed, hands shaking, barely able to hold the phone.

'Kathleen?' Pat said. 'Kath, are you all right?' I could hear the concern in her voice, but couldn't answer at first. Why wasn't I crying? My eyes stung with the unshed tears.

'Why didn't you call me?' I asked. 'Why didn't you phone?'

'The hospital didn't let us know until after,' she said, her voice heavy with sadness, 'Josie and I had been up to see her this morning, but she slipped into a coma after we left.'

'Who was with her?' I wailed. 'When she died, who was with her?'

Pat didn't answer at first but then said, 'The nurse held her hand; she went in her sleep. She didn't know anything about it.'

Then the next explosion happened, this time it was more like a powerful thud. My mum, our darling mum, had died alone, with just the nurse to see her out of this world. Not one of her ten children there with her to hold her hand, to stroke her silky soft skin, to touch her wispy white hair, to kiss her cheek, to say goodbye. None of us . . . none of us.

Then the tears came, sliding slowly down my cheeks at first, and then the wracking sobs that hurt my chest and throat with a welcome pain. I wanted to hurt. *I wasn't there . . . I wasn't there . . .*

Colin was standing watching me from the doorway, not knowing what to say or do. He was never very good at emotions. 'Just like Mum,' I thought as he came over and tried to comfort me. Sam and Jo had crept into the room now and were peeping round the door at us.

They didn't ask what was wrong. Children have a knack of knowing when not to speak, when words would be out of place. There were a lot of tears then. A week full of them. All of us, desperate that we hadn't been able to say goodbye, angry that we had been cheated of our chance to tell her we loved her, that despite everything, anything that she had ever done, we adored her. Those tears were full of regret, of unsaid words and unasked questions. Mum was dead, and there was an empty space in our hearts where she had once lived. The finality felt too much to bear, and it plunged me even deeper into depression. My world started to crumble and there was nothing I could to do to halt the disintegration.

I had lost my way, and I didn't believe that I would ever find it again. The world had shifted, and didn't make any sense any more; nothing did.

Then there was the funeral.

It was a strange ceremony, so different from Aunty's; a solemn and desperate day. My mum's remaining siblings were there, as were our cousins. My dear friend Anne, who had loved my mum as her own, came and we clung together to withstand the tempest that was blowing through our family. But I took no comfort from it. I was surer now than ever that it would be my children's turn to grieve soon, to feel this same bereft sorrow, because I knew that I was not going to survive my operation, and I would never be there to see them grow up. So I cried my tears with my brothers and sisters, but I cried them for me, not for Mum, and the guilt made it even harder to bear.

53

Saying Goodbye

I looked at the letters I had written before placing them in a box covered in paper flowers. 'These are for you,' I told Colin, the night before I was due to go into hospital.

'What is it?'

'Letters for the children,' I explained, feeling the tears that had become as familiar as old friends to me slip down my cheeks, 'and one for you.'

'Oh Kathy,' he said, taking the box hesitantly, 'you're going to be fine, I just know you are.'

I looked away. 'Please make sure you don't lose them,' I asked plaintively, 'and remember to look after my babies, give them an exciting life, do lots of wonderful things with them, and be patient – they're only little you know'.

I tiptoed into their rooms, Jo's first. It was a blue room. She had chosen the colour herself and had been very clear about what she wanted. She was only three, and still had tiny plump baby hands and feet, but had a strong personality. She was my little fighter and I gently stroked her cheek, and bent to kiss her. Her hair was a little damp still from her bath, and had formed tiny tight curls that stuck to her baby soft skin. She was beautiful, so perfect, like a little doll, and I tried to pour my love into her so that it would sustain her after I was gone.

Then I moved into Sam's room. On the shelf above his bed were the beginnings of his football trophy collection. He loved football just like his dad and played it at every opportunity. I looked down at his sleeping frame, and remembered the heartache of his babyhood. It wasn't fair, I thought, that he was going to be unhappy again. Hadn't he had to go through enough? I bent and kissed his cheek, and he stirred.

'Mummy?' he said sleepily.

'Shhh, go to sleep now,' I whispered, and crept out of the room without looking back.

The apple blossom was out on the trees in the garden as we drove off towards the hospital. I couldn't help wondering if I'd ever see it again. As if he'd read my thoughts, Colin's hand searched for mine as we drove, and we continued the journey in a silence that said more than any words could.

Margaret worked as a theatre nurse in the hospital where I was to be admitted. Although of course she was not allowed to be involved with my operation, she made sure she was there as I started to come round in the recovery room. It was her huge brown eyes peering above a white mask that I saw before anything else when I first opened my eyes.

'It hurts so much,' I muttered through my anaesthetic-induced confusion.

'Of course it does!' she said matter-of-factly. 'What did you expect?' But I was still very glad to see her there. It just seemed right somehow.

My recovery went well, and I was elated when the doctor told me that it was just 'a fibroid the size of a melon!'

The elation didn't last. I couldn't shift my conviction that there was something badly wrong with me and that I was going to die. I didn't realise that I was in the grip of an all-consuming depression.

My friend Anne came over to stay while Colin took the children for a short break camping, and my other friend also called Anne came over too. Each assumed very different but equally essential roles. Anne M tiny, funny and matter-of-fact made me laugh even though it hurt, and Anne D tall, slim, sensitive and kind, cleaned the house and made us food. After a few days I thought I could see a glimmer of hope, but it took more than six months of careful care from my new wonderful GP, and my dear family and friends, before I felt that life might just be worth living after all, and I was strong enough to confront the ghosts in Valence Avenue.

The leaves on the trees which lined Valence Avenue were in full leaf, helping to disguise the growing dilapidation. As our car drew up, I felt a deep sadness and loss that the person who had been a constant presence in this house would no longer be there. I gathered up my new-found strength and opened the car door, waving goodbye to Colin. I wanted to be on my own so that Josie and I could make a start on clearing Mum's room.

I knocked on the front door with the usual family knock, and waited, a host of memories crowding into my head. Aunty's once beautiful front garden had been paved over now so that Pat could park her car, and it made me feel sad that the flowers she had loved were gone forever. The door swung open after a while, and Josie stood there looking rather dishevelled.

'Oh there you are. I wondered where you'd got to.'

As I came in I felt an oppressive weight bearing down on me. I could feel Mum there even after all this time. The house looked different to when I was a child. Pat and Josie had bought it from the council with Aunty before she had died, so at least they had that security now. They had put in a fitted kitchen, complete with a new fridge and an automatic washing machine. The coal fire was gone, replaced with gas, there was fitted carpet everywhere now and a new three-piece suite with reclining chairs. Upstairs had a new bathroom, 'fully tiled' as Mum had boasted, and complete with a washbasin and shower over the bath.

Although I almost resented the changes, I was glad that Mum had enjoyed her 'mod cons' for a while at least before she died. She had never been sentimental about the past, and had been greedy for the new world, including all the gadgets that went with it.

'Come on then,' I said, 'let's get started,' and we climbed the stairs to the landing. As I got to the top I stopped under the painting of the Sacred Heart of Jesus which hung there, looking down at us. It had been there for as long as I could remember, and I had prayed in front of it many times as a frightened child. I said a prayer now, for Aunty and for Mum.

Mum's old room, the box room, didn't look very different from when I had last seen it, not long before Mum died. Colin had helped Pat and Josie to move most of Mum's things to the front room downstairs, so that she wouldn't need to climb up and down the stairs. The wardrobe that blocked the built-in cupboard over the stairwell was still in the same place it had been when I was a child. There was a layer of dust over every-thing, and I ran my finger along the top of the dressing table that held so many childhood memories. This had been where I stored my treasures. The little things that had been so important to me then. All gone now. Josie and I manoeuvred the dressing table towards the bedroom door, and then began to inch the ward-robe out of the way of the cupboard door so that we could open it.

'God, this weighs a ton,' I complained.

'Are you sure you're all right to do this, Kath?' Josie asked. It wasn't much more than six months after my hysterectomy, but I felt fine.

'I'm okay,' I said, 'anyway, we're nearly done now,' and with a final push and a shower of dust, the solid wooden piece of furni-ture moved, and the cupboard door, with its original brass catch painted closed, stood revealed in front of us ready to be opened.

Despite the sad circumstances, I felt an odd shiver of anticipation.

54

The Letters

We opened the stiff cupboard door to a musty smell of age. Inside piled high and draped with cobwebs were boxes, mostly empty, some faded photos in broken frames and a few old bags. Josie's face was red with the exertion of moving the furniture, and tiny beads of sweat covered her forehead.

'Why don't you let me do the rest?' I offered but she shook her head.

'Don't be daft; I'm fine.'

There was a layer of thick greasy dust everywhere, and when Josie reached in and picked up an old black patent bag, it scattered and stuck to her fingers. The bag was now cracked and worn with age and smelt of damp and darkness, but was strangely familiar. As she looked inside she made a little sound of surprise and a knowing look crossed her face. 'I think you should have these,' she said flatly.

'What are they?'

She just held out the tattered bag and carried on sorting through the cupboard, not even glancing in my direction. As I peered inside I saw it was stuffed with faded old envelopes. They were yellowed with age and were all different shapes and sizes. There was even a card, like the ones you attach to a bunch of flowers, all addressed to me. Or at least all addressed to Kathleen Stevens, which is the name on my birth certificate, but not the name I'd grown up with. The postmarks were wrong too. One envelope was dated December 1953 but I wasn't even born until August 1954.

'They're Mum's letters from Thomas. I don't know much more than that, but I think you need to read them.'

'But I don't understand . . .' I started to say. Josie just looked away and carried on with the sorting.

My hand shook slightly as I slipped them into my own bag, and turned back to the filthy cupboard.

'Why don't you put them in date order before you start to read them?' Colin suggested, as I settled myself at our kitchen table later that evening. We had got the children to bed earlier than usual, so now at last I could concentrate on the letters.

'This looks like the earliest.' I held the envelope in my hand and turned it over; it was yellow and had a slight brown tinge to the edges. The writing was confident and sloping and it was addressed to Mrs Kathleen Stevens, as they all were. The postmark was Paddington W2 and it was dated 27 Dec 1953, the year before I was born. It looked as though it had been handled many times because of its worn appearance and crumpled feel. We slotted the rest in place. Seventeen letters altogether, starting around the time of my conception and continuing through to after I was born in August '54, and then stopping dead in July 1955 when Mum must have been three months pregnant with Margaret. I looked up at Colin, and saw the look of sudden realisation mirrored in his eyes. These letters could hold the answers that I had been searching for my whole life.

Mrs Kathleen Stevens. These letters weren't addressed to me at all. How could they be? They were written to Mum.

Although it was early winter and quite cold, I felt a rush of heat course through my body as I gently teased the thin paper from the first envelope and began to read:

27th December, '53

Dear Kathleen

I have something very important I would like to see you about, concerning your present. Could you arrange to see me for certain on Thursday next at 6.30 at Seven Kings. I am going to Newcastle on Monday morning, but I shall be back early on

Thursday. Will you answer this letter by return of post so that I will receive it in good time and please try not to disappoint me again. I have been telephoning you all over the weekend, but you have not been there. I do hope you are now quite better. Whatever happens do please answer this letter and do try and come on Thursday

T

I am enclosing a stamped addressed envelope and paper to make it easy for you

'T must be Thomas,' I said to Colin, trying to control the catch in my voice. 'Josie said they were his letters to Mum, but she didn't know any more.'

'And you believed her?' Colin asked incredulously.

'Yes, I believed her.' I was stung by his suspicions. 'Why would she lie?'

'Well let's face it, your family are not exactly known for their honesty and openness are they?' he said bluntly, 'and anyway, why did she give them to you? It must have been pretty obvious by their age that they were written before you were around.'

'I don't know,' I reflected. 'Maybe she had her suspicions, but wasn't sure about who Thomas might be.' I added, 'I think we both know what these letters could be hinting at . . .'

'Hinting is right; that's quite a leap to make. Open the next one.'

My hands shook as I picked up the next letter.

It felt strange to feel the whisper of past words brush against my face as I continued to read:

30th April '54

Dear Kathleen,

Thanks ever so much for your very nice letter, which I appreciated far more than I can tell you. I am so glad you have decided to consider your doctor's advice over the weekend and

sincerely hope you will decide wisely. I should very much like to
come up and see you, either at your house, or the hospital, and
will endeavour to cheer you up when I come. I hope you will be
your old self again (or young self, I should say)

 I am enclosing £2 which you will have no difficulty in getting
cashed.

 I am looking forward to hearing from you again, so I am
enclosing a stamped addressed envelope and paper, and
perhaps you will be able to drop me a few lines letting me
know how you are getting along, and when I shall be able to
see you again.

 Hoping sincerely you are now feeling very much better
 With my very best wishes and lots of luck

T

'Well, he certainly seems keen, whoever he is,' Colin said. 'What
do you think was wrong with her?'

'My guess is probably just pregnancy. She would have been
about five months gone by this date.'

'Do you think he knew? He doesn't refer to any baby, does he?'

'Maybe he did,' Colin said. 'Remember we're talking about
the 50s. People were more sensitive to that kind of thing, you
know, less open about pregnancy and things.'

The rest of the letters were along the same vein. Thomas
desperate to see 'Kathleen' and often being disappointed, prom-
ises of telephone calls sometimes kept by her and sometimes
not, cheques enclosed, and even mention of visits to films and a
trade show.

'Well there's nothing so far to give much away,' I remarked,
feeling increasingly despondent.

'Isn't that the Disney emblem? On the envelope?'

I shrugged, too tired to think any more. I wasn't sure what I
was expecting, but I knew for sure what I was hoping for – some
clear, unequivocal evidence that T or Thomas as he sometimes
signed himself, was more to Mum than a pen pal!

I picked up the letter that was sent 8 August 1954, a week before I was born – one of the longer letters in the set.

Sunday 8 August '54

My Dear Kathleen,

I was more than delighted to receive your letter on Saturday morning, and was so glad you received your flowers etc. okay.

You really must have gone through an awful time, being still so weak. I am looking forward so much to phoning Bridie on Monday morning to know whether you will be able to come away. I am hoping I shall not have another disappointment. It has happened so often.

It seems, and is, ages since I saw you, and I am looking forward so much to doing so. I am sure it will do you more good than harm if you could come away, as the change, after being in bed for so long, would act like a tonic, so I hope you will do your best to be strong enough to come. Bridie has kept me well informed of your health the whole time, and it has been marvellous of her to come and take my calls every time I have phoned up. You too, must have found her a great help and I am sure she has looked after you well. Tell her I am very grateful, and thank her very much for all she has done.

Well my dear, I must close now, hoping to be able to see you on Monday and wishing you the very best of luck and good wishes

Thomas

There was also a little card from a bouquet of flowers which was sent at the same time saying:

Very much looking forward to seeing you on Monday quite well

Thomas

'That's strange,' I commented. 'That letter and card are dated a week before I was born. Mum would have been heavily pregnant. Surely he wouldn't have expected her to go away with him?'

Colin rubbed his head: 'What do you mean?'

'Well she wouldn't have been up to it I wouldn't have thought, would you? Unless he didn't know . . .'

This was not as easy or straightforward as I had hoped it was going to be. It was like trying to complete a jigsaw without having the picture to follow.

'But you could have been premature,' Colin suggested. 'She was an older mum after all and she had already had eight children.'

'Yes, I suppose that could account for why she was so unwell.' I shook my head, trying to clear my muddled thoughts. 'It's all so odd. These letters have been in that cupboard for a very long time by the look of them. It was just chance that Josie and I happened to find them . . .' Then it struck me like a blow. It hadn't been chance. Mum had wanted to show them to me before she had died. It was like a sudden bolt of lightning. How many times had Mum asked me to help her sort out that cupboard? Four? Five? Maybe more. Were these letters the real focus of her obsession? I knew the answer instinctively. Of course! Mum had known she was dying, and she had wanted to tell me about Thomas before it was too late.

'But you don't know any of this for sure,' Colin tried to reason with me.

'I know,' I said, 'but it's all starting to make sense. The pieces are falling into place.' Then a terrible realisation hit me, and I laid my head on the table and cried, hot angry tears of frustration.

I had denied Mum that last chance to unburden herself, to tell me about the man who was mine and Margaret's father, whoever he was. And so I had missed my chance again. How could I hope to understand the messages hidden in these few hastily written lines? Too late again, too late . . .

55

Trying to Make Sense

Colin had tried to persuade me to leave the rest of the letters until the morning, but I couldn't. I greedily sucked the words from the pages, not just once, but several times. Reading and re-reading, until Thomas's words swam around my head. I had even begun to answer the letters, trying to guess what was in the replies that Mum had clearly sent. 'I'm going mad,' I thought, 'I need to stop.' But it was out of my control now. By the time the children woke up in the morning I hadn't even been to bed. Colin came downstairs and looked at me.

'You look awful,' he said. 'Why don't you try to get some sleep now, and I'll take the kids out?'

'No!' I almost shouted, 'I'm going over to Margaret's. She needs to see these too.'

By the time I arrived Margaret was already up and about. Her children were also early risers, and so they had eaten breakfast and were upstairs playing.

'Well,' she said as soon as I got there, 'what's all this about?'

I pulled the letters from a folder I had carefully filed them in.

'Josie and I found these in Mum's cupboard yesterday when we were clearing it out, but I don't think it was an accident. I think I was meant to find them.'

'Meant by who?' Margaret asked puzzled, obviously surprised.

'Mum,' I stated flatly.

It was only just starting to get light, even though it was nearly nine, as we sat to read the letters together. I hated those long dark winter mornings and evenings. They seemed to cast an air of depression and a loss of hope. There was still a slight smell of hot buttered toast floating from the kitchen, and I suddenly felt ravenous, and realised that I hadn't eaten since yesterday lunchtime.

'Can I make myself some toast while you carry on reading?' I asked, knowing that I could probably recite the contents of each and every one of Thomas's letters by heart.

Margaret nodded without looking up. She was being drawn in just as I had been.

'The last letter talks about a holiday,' she said finally. 'What holiday was that?' 'Listen . . .' she started to read aloud,

Friday 1st July '55

My dear Kathleen,

I am sending you a cheque as promised for £5.

I do so hope you will have a very lovely time away and enjoy a nice rest. I also hope the weather will keep nice and fine for you my dear. I will look forward to having a letter from you so that I receive it in good time to meet you.

With my every good wish for a very nice holiday

Lots of luck

Thomas

'That was written about six months before I was born,' she said, chewing her lip, 'and that's the last one, right?'

'Yes, there are no more after that. Well, none that we know of.'

'But why?' she continued, 'he was obviously expecting to meet her either on the holiday itself or when she got back, so why do the letters stop so abruptly?'

'I think that we need to talk to Pat and Josie,' I said firmly, 'It's time we got some proper answers.'

Pat and Josie had come to visit me most Saturdays since Mum had died. They enjoyed the children's company and in the better weather Josie would bring her watercolours to paint in the garden. The next Saturday they were due to come over, I made sure that Margaret would be at my house so we could tackle them together.

It was almost March and the garden was starting to stir into life. The snowdrops had almost finished, and the bluebells hadn't yet arrived, but daffodils were bursting into life all over the place. Their sunny yellow heads made me feel more optimistic somehow, and I was determined that I would find out just what my sisters really knew about that time 35 years before. Pat was fourteen and Josie twelve when I was born, and they would have been eighteen months older than that when Margaret arrived. They hadn't been young children, they must have seen things, heard things. They must remember something.

I heard Pat's car draw up in the driveway. 'Aunty Pat's here,' Sam shouted, galloping out to meet her, as usual excited at the prospect of seeing his favourite Aunty. When he was about six he had come home after a weekend at Mum's and announced 'Mummy, it's not that I don't love you and Daddy, but I think I would have a better life if I lived at Aunty Pat's house.'

We had all laughed over it, and things hadn't really changed since Mum died. He still adored his Aunty Pat. She could converse with him about all his favourite things, football, cricket, tennis, in fact sports of any kind, and was also very knowledgeable.

I really didn't want the children around while I talked to my sisters, so had arranged for them to go with Tony to the local country park for a spring picnic with Margaret's four girls.

'Can I see Aunty Pat first?' Sam had pleaded when I shared the plan with him.

'Yes, of course, she can help you pack the picnic things,' and so he had been placated.

'Look Aunty Pat,' he said as soon as she opened the car door, 'we've got a picnic basket ready to pack, and you can help me pack it up with stuff.'

Pat laughed at his enthusiasm, and allowed herself to be led into the kitchen saying 'Isn't it a bit chilly for a picnic?'

'They'll be fine,' I reassured her smiling. 'It's not like they'll be sitting still for long if I know them.'

Tony arrived with Margaret and the girls and Sam and Jo bundled into his car excitedly, while Margaret made her escape and came in to join Pat, Josie and me.

'Hello Marg,' said Josie. Margaret had always been her favourite, and I had always been Pat's.

'Are you staying for lunch?' she asked.

'I hope so!' Margaret answered, sitting herself down on the sofa with a sigh. Neither of us got much time to ourselves without the children, so this was a rare treat, despite the serious purpose.

As soon as we had eaten, I made a cup of tea, and then produced the black folder containing the letters.

'What's that?' asked Pat innocently. I looked at her and felt sad. Her hair was going grey even though she was not quite fifty, and she was quite overweight, just as Josie was, and this had the effect of making them look older than they were. When she was very young Pat had been very pretty and a keen sportswoman but had started smoking heavily in her teens, which had put an end to all that. She was such a kind person, never seeing any bad in anyone, never judging, and here I was, about to try to force her to spill all her secrets, and I felt a stab of guilt. What was it that Aunty had always said 'I can't tell you about your father without telling you about your mother.' Her words rang in my ears, but I had to go on now.

''They're some letters that Josie and I found in Mum's cupboard,' I said.

Josie's eyes slunk away; she had recognised them.

'What letters?' Pat asked.

Josie cleared her throat. 'They're letters that Thomas sent to Mum.'

Pat was taken aback. 'Thomas? Thomas who?' I was surprised to see that she looked as though she didn't have a clue who we were talking about.

'Thomas, the man that used to be so kind to Mum,' Josie explained.

Pat went quiet. That was always her defence. She didn't attempt to look at them, in fact her face closed down completely, giving nothing away.

'One of them talks about a holiday,' I carried on, determined. 'It's dated July 1955. Do you remember it?'

Her face relaxed and she smiled. ' Oh yes of course, that was the Isle of Wight. We went there when you were still a baby, just learning to walk. I'm sure you've seen a photo? I'm holding your hand as you're trying to walk along the beach.'

'Oh I'd love to see it,' I answered, and then continued ' Who went?'

'We all did,' Pat said. 'Granny, Me, Josie, Mary and the twins, and Peter of course and you, but it was before Margaret was born.'

'Oh right, and where did we stay?'

'We were camping, Granny and us had a tent together and Mum had one on her own the other side of the campsite.'

This sounded puzzling. Why was Mum's tent so far away? But I couldn't ask – not yet, anyway. Even now we knew if we wanted to find things out it was best not to be too obvious.

'So you don't remember any Thomas?' I asked her pointedly, and she shook her head.

'Don't you remember anything about when I was born?' I asked.

'Look Kathleen, all I remember is a man coming to visit Mum just after you had been born. She was in bed and told me to take the baby downstairs. He came in a big posh car and had a dark coat and hat. He seemed really nice and I remember he gave me 10 shillings! That was a lot of money then which is probably why I remember.'

'And . . .?' I prompted.

'And nothing,' she said, 'I'm afraid that's all. I don't know if he was this Thomas, but from what Josie says I suppose he probably was.'

'Was Mum pleased to see him?'

'I don't know really, I think so, I can't remember.'

'Please try,' I pleaded. 'Did he know there was a baby, did he know I existed?'

Pat didn't look at me. She was getting more and more uncomfortable, but I wouldn't let it go.

'Do you think he was my dad?' I asked outright.

There was a long silence. I could tell Margaret thought I had gone too far, but I didn't care.

'Kath, I don't know who your Dad was, I really don't. I'm sorry.'

I looked across at Margaret whose face betrayed the same disappointment as mine, because the sad thing was, I knew Pat was telling the truth.

56

The Scandal

A few years after Mum died, I had a strange conversation with my niece Sheila. She was my brother Michael's middle daughter and was now married with two children of her own. We had often talked about Mum, and the many secrets that still lay buried, but recently she and her older sister Vicky had become more and more curious. They knew some details of course, but they were muddled about others, and wanted to try to get a clearer picture of why their dad had been put in a children's home, and what had happened there that made him refuse to ever talk about it.

When the phone rang I was out in the garden pegging the washing on the line. Colin called from the back door. 'It's Sheila on the phone.'

I pegged the last towel onto the line, and bent to pick up the washing basket. It was a glorious warm day, full of the promise of the long summer holidays. 'Tell her I'm just coming,' I shouted across the lawn. Sam had thrown his bike down casually, and wandered off to do something else, and I almost tripped over it. 'Damn bike,' I muttered to myself as I hurried towards the house.

Colin thrust the phone into my hands. 'Hi Sheila,' I said distractedly, mentally trying to tick off the list of things I still needed to do.

'I've got some news,' she blurted out. Sheila was ten years younger than me, but despite that we got on very well.

'What news?'

'Vicky and I have been to Valence Library,' she said, barely able to contain her excitement, 'and we've found Nan.'

'What do you mean you've "found her"?' I asked.

'We went there to see if we could find out about Nan going to prison for bigamy. We thought if we could find the date then we could see if it would help us trace which children's home Dad was in and for how long.

'Well we found her in the *Dagenham Post* all right, but not when we expected to. The date of the articles we found is years later.'

I started to pay attention. 'How many years later?'

'Hold on,' she said, 'I'll read it to you.'

Waitress appears on £458 fraud charge

A 41-year-old waitress, Florence Catherine Stevens of Valence Avenue, Dagenham, appeared at Stratford Court on Wednesday charged with obtaining credit over £298 from Mr A F— by false pretence or by means of fraud other than false pretence. She was also accused of similar offences of obtaining £135 and £25 by false pretence with intent to defraud. All the money was from Mr A F—.

Stevens was remanded on bail until 19th September.

'What year was it?' I asked slowly, guessing the answer.

'1956,' Sheila replied.

I held the phone in my hand and said almost to myself, 'the year Margaret was born . . . the September after the letters from Thomas stopped.'

'Yes that's right, but there's more,' she continued.

'Go on.'

'Well, there's another article from the same newspaper. Listen to this one . . .'

Mother of ten gets 18 months for fraud

Mrs Florence Catherine Stevens, 41, mother of ten children, of Valence Avenue, Dagenham, was sentenced to 18 months imprisonment at Essex Quarter sessions Appeal

Court on Thursday for obtaining credit by fraud and money by false pretences.

'This is one of the most extraordinary instances of gullibility it is possible to imagine,' said Miss Nina Collins, prosecuting.

The charges related to groceries and money, totalling £433, which had been obtained from a Dagenham grocer Mr A F— of whom Mrs Stevens had been a customer.

Disguised Voice

Miss Collins said that Mrs Stevens assumed a series of poses, disguised her voice over the telephone, and led the grocer to believe she was a highly paid member of the Walt Disney Film Corporation.

She assumed various identities over the phone at varying times such as Mrs Roy Disney, Roy Disney himself, and attorney to the Walt Disney Corporation.

She persuaded the grocer that he was going to get a contract to supply groceries to the corporation and in that belief he supplied her with groceries and about £122 in money.

At the time she was friendly with an executive of the Walt Disney Corporation and she led Mr F— to believe she was to receive a substantial sum under a will.

Wild Extravagance

Miss Collins said that in that belief the grocer indulged in wild extravagances including the purchase of houses and a car. Evidence was given that Mrs Stevens at the time of her arrest was receiving national assistance and family allowances. Mrs Stevens' legal representative said she was trying hard and loyally to look after her family and temptation came her way. He added, 'She saw this opportunity of getting something for her children and having started the snowball continued. What she did was out of need and necessity.'

I was stunned, but it made perfect sense.

'It was Thomas!' I said. 'He was the Walt Disney executive – don't you see? It all fits, the Disney emblem on one of the envelopes, the different places the letters were posted from, the cheques that he was always sending her, the money she had probably grown to rely on . . .'

'Yes, but why?' Sheila broke in, 'If Thomas was giving her money, why did she need to steal it?'

'Because he stopped! Something happened that made him break off contact with her, stop the letters, the money, disappear from her life, something that we don't know about yet. And because she was desperate, I suppose, because she saw the opportunity, like the solicitor said, and it just snowballed.'

We both stood at our phones, silent for a moment now, our minds teeming.

'There is another one; this time it says much the same things except it also refers to her "two previous convictions", one for bigamy, and one . . .' Sheila paused. 'One for trying to kill herself.'

This time I let the silence grow and lengthen. Maybe some secrets were best left untold.

57

Fragments of a Memory

I arrived at Margaret's house and Tony opened the door.

'Marion's not here yet,' he said, 'but Sheila is out in the garden with Margaret having a coffee, do you want one?'

I nodded my thanks and wandered outside. Sheila and Margaret were deep in conversation as I approached to join them.

'Hello you two,' I said. 'Whew it's hot out here.'

'We can go inside if you'd rather,' offered Margaret, but I sat myself down at the patio table with them, making sure I positioned my chair in the shade. I still got migraines, and the sun was one of my triggers.

'I've brought the letters round, so we can have another look, just to see if they give up any clues as to what happened.' I placed the black folder on the table and sighed at the same time.

'What's wrong?' asked Sheila concerned.

'Oh I don't know, I suppose I'm just tired of it all. We seem to get so far but then every time we think we're getting close to cracking it, it peters out, another dead end.'

Margaret sipped her coffee and said, 'Look, this newspaper stuff is really helpful. We can write to the home office now we have a date; they might be able to give us details of her previous convictions and get exact dates for them.'

'Yes,' I said, 'but how is that going to help us find out if Thomas was our father? I think we're just going round in circles.'

Marion suddenly appeared at the doorway carrying a tray with two cups of coffee. She was wearing a bright yellow T-shirt which was attracting tiny black thrips.

'Tony made me bring these out,' she joked. 'He said he didn't want to interrupt the witches' coven!' and then she stopped abruptly as she picked up on the air of despondency that had settled over us. For once, no one laughed. 'What's up?' she asked, setting the tray down on the table, and brushing at the flies.

'Sometimes I just wonder why we bother,' I said flatly, slumping back in the chair and watching the swifts swoop in circles.

'Marion caught me watching them. 'They never stop, you know,' she said. 'They never rest, they fly round and round apparently in circles, gathering up the insects they need to survive, and that's how it's got to be with us – we've got to keep going, keep looking, keep gathering.'.

Now I laughed out loud, 'You're beginning to sound a bit preachy,' I said good-naturedly, and reached for my coffee. At that moment there was a loud clap of thunder and the heavens opened. We all jumped up and ran for the door, screaming and laughing as the rain thrashed down ferociously. I grabbed the folder of letters and held it close, and Sheila clasped the newspaper photocopies that she had brought with her and we went inside to go through it all over again.

'OK so, we know that Mum had been in prison,' Marion said, 'but I found something else out last week when we went to see Pat and Josie. Pat had taken the dogs for a walk so I managed to corner Josie on her own.'

We all turned towards her in expectation.

'Mum had electric shock treatment, the first time she was in. I think it was quite commonly used for people with depression.'

'Depression?' I asked.

'Why do you think she had depression?'

'Josie told me that she tried to kill herself, but she wasn't sure when, she thinks it was either when she was arrested for bigamy, or maybe before that during the split with Ron Coates.'

'Does Josie think she really was depressed?'

We all knew that Mum had fantasised about a range of illnesses over the years, to manipulate sympathy, and also to try to get money on some occasions.

'Yes, I think she does, and then when I was talking on the

phone to Marge in Australia about it last night, she told me something else.'

She stopped for a moment. It was so quiet we could hear the soft murmur of the children playing upstairs.

I broke the silence, 'What did she tell you?' There was something stirring in my memory, fragments of forgotten moments, a frightening, half-remembered day from long ago.

'She wasn't sure if she should tell you, but I told her you had the right to know. She told me about the time it happened again,' Marion continued 'when she and Josie came back and found . . . the time when you and Margaret were still only little.'

Margaret and I looked at each other and there was a sudden shock of realisation.

'Yes,' I said, 'I think I remember.'

Margaret started to cry. 'I thought it was a dream, a horrible, scary dream,' she sobbed.

Sheila put her arm around her. 'Don't cry Marg,' she comforted. 'She must have been desperate if she was prepared to leave you two'.

'No, you don't understand,' I said. 'She wasn't going to leave us, she was taking us with her.'

No one spoke, and Margaret carried on crying, more quietly now. It wasn't that we had forgotten that day many years before, just that we had chosen not to remember it. Sheila looked more shocked than I had ever seen her, as the colour bled from her face. There was a look of disbelief and horror in her eyes that made me feel ashamed.

'She was ill, she must have been,' Sheila said now, trying to justify the unjustifiable.

I nodded, the one thing that was becoming clearer the more we found out, the more we remembered, was that Mum must have been very ill indeed, not physically, but mentally.

We sat quietly for a few minutes and then Marion pulled an A4 writing pad from her bag. 'I've started to make a timeline,' she said, 'of all the things we know, and I have put question marks where we don't.'

We pored over her work, the four of us, making a few changes here and there as we all chipped in with what we remembered. It took us a few hours, but what we had in front of us for the first time ever, was a sequence of events and information that we hoped would help us to make sense of what we already knew, and help us see what questions we still needed to find the answers to. Whether we would ever be able to do that remained to be seen.

58

A Double Death

As the new millennium approached, I stood next to my husband and daughter on Parliament Hill in Hampstead, surrounded by an eruption of colour and noise.

'I wonder where Sam is now?' I shouted to Colin, trying to be heard above the chaos of celebration. 'Do you think he's all right?' There was a little bit of me that was worried, desperately hoping he was somewhere safe with his friends. At the same time I knew that I had to learn to let go, after all he was nearly nineteen!

'He's probably having a great time. Don't worry!'

By the time we got back home from Sherry's the next day, my teenaged son was lying fast asleep in bed. It was a relief to know that the world hadn't ended with the old century; Sam and Jo were safe and sound and life suddenly felt full of new beginnings.

I was teaching at a local infant school at the time, and enjoying every minute. It was Marion who had first introduced me to the head teacher, and she had initially offered me a temporary job-share. It wasn't long since my Mum's death and the blackest period of my depression, and I was still feeling very vulnerable.

'Come on Kath,' Marion encouraged me. 'It will be good for you, and it's only two days a week.' I had been persuaded to accept because everyone told me it would help, and they were right. The temporary part-time job had now become permanent and full time. It wouldn't be too great an exaggeration to say that the children at that school helped save my life, and I loved working there. Everyone was so friendly and supportive that before long the term that I had originally signed up for became a year, and then another, and before I noticed it I had been at the school for almost ten years and become the deputy head teacher!

Perhaps Mum was right about the devil, or else our run of luck had just been too good to last. First Colin's feisty, independent mum took a turn for the worse. And then I got a call from Pat.

'Oh Kath . . .' she started, clearly very distressed.

'What is it?' I asked, 'What's happened? Are you all right?'

There was a brief moment of silence until she gathered herself together and was able to continue.

'It's . . . Well first I had a phone call from Sarah, our sister Sheila's daughter in the Isle of Man. Sheila's died.'

I gave a sharp intake of breath. I had never met Sheila. The correspondence that we had exchanged many years before had petered out once I had started to ask questions that she didn't want to answer. Now I'd lost a sister I never really knew.

'Oh no. What happened? How old was she?'

Pat sniffed heavily. 'You don't understand, Kath,' she said. 'I phoned Michael to tell him, and Vicky answered the phone. She was hysterical. At the exact moment I rang, the paramedics were trying at restart Michael's heart.' At this point her control gave way and she sobbed.

I was dumbstruck, trying desperately to process the information she had just given me. Sheila *and* Michael?

'They've taken him to the hospital now, but oh Kath, they don't think he's going to make it.'

Then it sank in. I was not just losing an unknown sister, a hazy image conjured from photographs in magazines, a television programme and a few letters, but maybe also Michael, the brother who'd remembered us all those years when he was far away in Spain, sending us parcels and letters. The dear big brother who we might never see again.

'Oh God,' I said crying down the phone. 'What shall we do?'

'There's nothing we can do. Just wait and pray.'

So that was what we did. We waited and we prayed, but our prayers weren't answered. Our brother Michael died on the same day as our sister Sheila, hundreds of miles apart, not having spoken to each other for nearly sixty years and neither of them reaching their sixty-fifth birthday.

59

A New Home and a New Sadness

Over the next few years my depression came and went. It usually manifested itself through symptoms of illness. It would always be so real, so palpable, that even my GP would send me for various tests, just to make sure. There was the pain in my side that came and went, the lump in my throat, the panic attacks that would debilitate me, turning me into a quivering wreck, with clammy hands, palpitations, sweats . . . and all the while I managed to hide it. Teaching helped because I would never let the children be affected, and I never took time off. Being with the children made me focus on them instead of me, and for the most part I managed to keep my depression hidden. I tried a range of antidepressants, cognitive behavioural therapy, counselling – I was so desperate to conquer this curse I would try anything.

My sisters Pat and Josie were both retired now, and living in the same house in Dagenham that we had all grown up in. They continued to come and visit me every Saturday, and I like to think that they thought of our cottage as a second home. We had thought about moving further into the countryside, but although Sam was now at university, Jo was still at school in Brentwood, so we decided we should wait.

As the years flew by we were lucky enough to be able to build a new house next to our cottage, it was big and modern, and easy to live in at first, but I soon started feeling restless.

'Shall we move?' I half joked to Colin, one Saturday morning.

'OK then,' he replied to my amazement.

'Did you hear what I said, I said shall we move?' I repeated.

Colin laughed, 'I knew you would get fed up living here,' he said, 'it's too finished isn't it? Too perfect.'

'Do you feel the same then?'

'Well let's put it this way, I have never really been that keen on this house, it's too big for us now that Sam and Jo have moved out, and anyway, we want to move to the country at some point don't we?'

'Yes! Let's do it!' I exclaimed enthusiastically.

Within a week the house was up for sale, and we were looking for a new home in rural tranquillity.

We found a beautiful old house in a picturesque village in Suffolk. It felt like a fresh start, but not for long.

When Colin's wonderful mother passed away shortly afterwards, I was convinced that our family had had its share of bad news. I was wrong.

Like Mum, Josie had been diagnosed with type 2 diabetes. She had been in and out of hospital a few times over the years, so we weren't unduly worried at first when Margaret phoned to say she'd been admitted. The hospital ran some tests and then she was discharged once again, but it wasn't long before she was taken in again as an emergency.

'She looks really bad,' Margaret warned me.

We arranged to meet at the hospital the next morning, only to find that Josie had been moved to intensive care. She looked yellow and could barely open her eyes. With her fine wispy hair spread across the pillow, she reminded me so strongly of Mum that I shivered.

She was connected to all manner of machines that whirred and clicked quietly in the background and there were the remnants of tears on her cheek. I reached for a tissue from my bag and gently wiped them away.

'Don't worry,' I told her. 'I'm sure they'll get you sorted soon.'

'Kath, I've spoken to the consultant,' she started, and then hesitated before going on. 'He's told me that they won't resuscitate me.'

'What?'

'He said that there would be no point, that I would need someone to look after me all the time; that I will never be able to go home.'

I was shocked and confused. She started to cry quietly again.

'Don't worry, if you need to be looked after then I'll look after you.' I was crying myself now. 'We'll sell the house and buy one that has a little annex for you and Pat to live in. Would you like that?'

She nodded and gave a little smile.

'I'll look after you, silly,' I said again, smiling through my tears, knowing in my heart that I might not be given that chance.

Marge flew over from Australia and she, Marion, Margaret and I stood vigil with my poor sister Josie while she slowly slipped away. We were determined that, unlike Mum, she wouldn't die alone.

We slept on chairs in the room she had been moved to for her last few days, taking turns to rub her legs, stroke her forehead and talk quietly with her. Her nieces and nephews all came to visit, bringing laughter, life and ice-lollies into that little room. We crossed our fingers that Mary would make it in time from Australia, and still Pat wouldn't come. She couldn't bear to say goodbye to the sister who had been by her side throughout her life. The sister she had looked out for in the children's home all those years before, who had been the backbone of our family through so many difficult times. It was she and Pat together who had kept us safe and fed, who had looked out for us, always putting our needs before their own, and now Josie was about to leave us and Pat would be alone.

The morning Mary was due to arrive at Heathrow Josie died quietly, knowing that she was a much loved sister and auntie and that she would be leaving an unfillable hole in all our lives. Mary was distraught when she arrived at Valence Avenue no more than an hour after Josie had died.

Each of our children wrote out a memory of their Aunty Josie. Sam's was her love of travel, which he caught from her; Jo's was of collapsed summer puddings and fairy dolls made from pegs. We cried as we read them, my sisters and I, and after the funeral we gently placed them with the flowers.

60

Finding Thomas

The first couple of years after Josie died were hard for all of us, but the loss also made me appreciate how lucky I was.

'Gem keeping you out of trouble?' I joked with Sam. I had gone up to London to meet him for lunch. He was now living in Hampstead with his partner, a beautiful, clever Australian girl who he had met while working at a political think tank.

'Just about.' My handsome son was almost thirty now, but with the same cheeky grin and sandy blond hair and his grandmother's charismatic personality. 'Look Mum, can I ask you something?'

'Of course.'

'Mum, I've done something that I hope you won't be annoyed about.'

'What's wrong?' I asked nervously. 'What is it you've done?'

He laughed then. 'Sorry, I didn't mean to worry you. It's just that, well, I know that you have always been unhappy because you don't know who your dad is, and I got to thinking about it a few weeks ago, and I thought how I would hate it if I didn't know my father.'

'Sam, what are you talking about?'

'Well, I decided to see if I could help, and I've found out a few things.'

I sat back in my seat. How could my son know anything that I didn't about my past? Who could have told him anything new, after all this time?

'So I rang round a few people, and finally contacted a genealogist. She's been doing some digging and I think we've found him.'

'Found who?'

'Thomas,' he replied. 'Thomas Bartholomew, the man that you think is your dad.'

My hands and head tingled as I felt a hot flush of excitement and trepidation flood over me. The jacket that I was wearing over my new blue dress suddenly felt intolerably hot. I started to take it off, trying to process what Sam had said.

'But I don't understand. How do you know his surname?'

'Well,' he continued, smiling with satisfaction, 'you know your letters – or should I say your mum's letters – well I thought I saw something on one of the envelopes. It was just a trace of a surname, under the label that was stuck over it, he must have re-used it you see'.

'Slow down Sam', I said. 'What do you mean?'

'Listen Mum', he spoke more slowly now, 'I was looking through the letters last time I came over, and saw that one of the envelopes had been re-used. There was a label stuck over the original address. I managed to peel it off.' He laughed again. 'It wasn't easy, I kept thinking that you'd kill me if I tore it!'

'So what was underneath then?'

'His name is Thomas Bartholomew, and his address is Ralph Court in Paddington.'

How could I not have noticed? How many times must I have read and re-read those letters? And not just me, my sisters as well . . .

'I suppose you were more concerned with the letters than the envelopes,' he said seeming to read my mind, 'it was just chance really that I noticed.'

'Thomas Bartholomew.' I played with the name on my tongue. 'So what about the genealogist? Where does she come into this?'

'Well I showed her the name and address, and she did some research, and she came up with a few bits of information. Are you ready for this, Mum?'

I nodded, transfixed.

'Well, I'm afraid he's dead,' Sam started. 'He died in 1960

and I've got his death certificate.' He thrust a brown envelope across the table. 'He was a widower with one son. He definitely worked for a film company, because it's on his death certificate.'

It all fitted. I sat in that busy pub, with people coming and going around me, and thought about a man that I had never, would never, know. A man who might be my father, whose name was Thomas Bartholomew, and who had written so many letters to a woman that he must have cared deeply for.

'1960,' I said eventually, 'so I would only have been five or six when he died.' I suddenly felt relief. All through my life I had imagined that time was running out. That if only I could find him soon, I would be able to ask him the unanswered questions. Now I realised that would never have been possible. I was just a little girl when he died, and I was glad that I wouldn't have to torture myself any more.

'Are you okay, Mum?' Sam asked, and I realised that I hadn't said anything for a while, and was just staring into space.

'Sorry Sam,' I said. 'I'm fine, really. Of course I'm not annoyed and thank you.' I picked up the brown envelope on the table. 'Do you have the name of this genealogist? I think I'd like to speak to her.'

61

Fitting the Jigsaw Together

Over the next few months, with the help of the genealogist, I was gradually beginning to fit the jigsaw of my mum's life together, piece by piece – but there were still some important gaps.

When Marion phoned me and told me that Marge was coming over for another visit it seemed like perfect timing. I was almost ready to share my findings with my sisters.

'I know you've got a lot to tell us,' said Marge, when we were curled up in my living room, 'but I've got some more things as well.' She sat back and tucked her legs under her to get more comfortable.

'Okay,' I began, 'let's start from the beginning. We know Mum married Ron Coates in 1937 when she was just twenty-one and already expecting their first baby, Sheila.'

'Yep, Sheila was born later that year,' added Marion.

'And during the five years they were together they had four children.'

'Just a year or so between each of them,' Marge said.

'And don't forget that Mum was evacuated with Sheila, Michael and Pat. They went to that Lord's house in Somerset,' said Margaret. 'Mum herself told me about that, said how she had been told off for feeding the hunting dogs or something.'

'Yes, I remember that too, and it must have been about that time that things started to go wrong between them,' I continued, 'and we still don't know who Peter's dad was.'

'Aunty always used to say that Peter had gone to find his father in Ireland every time he ran away,' interrupted Marion.

'Hmm, well maybe, but Peter was born a couple of years after Josie, so he definitely wasn't Ron Coates' child.'

'Okay, carry on,' said Marge.

'Well as far as we can tell it was after she had Peter that she went off to London.'

'Yep, to be a waitress.'

'That's when she met yours and Mary's dad,' I said looking towards the twins.

Reg Stevens – the man whose name was written on all of us younger children's birth certificates. I had begun to feel sorry for him the more I found out. Uncle George, my mum's younger brother, had always told us what a nice man Reg was, a kind and gentle Yorkshire man who had fallen head over heels in love with Mum.

I picked up a tiny black and white photo and passed it to my sisters.

'She was so pretty wasn't she?' I said. 'A real Irish Rose.'

The photo showed a beautiful young woman with dark hair, and although we couldn't see the colour of her eyes, we could see the sparkle.

'She could charm the birds out of the trees,' said Marge, wryly sipping her tea.

Marion shook her head. 'It was more than that though. Everyone, men and women alike, were drawn to her. She was so good at listening; made people feel that they were important and had something to say that was worth hearing. Everyone except us, of course,' she added, glancing over at her twin with a pinched, hurt look on her face.

'It was almost as though she was capable of hypnotising them,' I said.

'We didn't need a genealogist to figure that one out,' Marge said with a little laugh.

'No, I know,' I continued, 'but there are some things that she has helped me to find out. For example I have a copy of Mum and Reg Stevens's bigamous marriage certificate.' I took the envelope and handed it to Marge.

'They were married in Sheffield!' she exclaimed.

I nodded. 'Yep, and look at the name!'

'Kathleen Francis Coates – widow!' Marge looked across at me. 'She used a fake name – your name!'

'Well it wasn't my name then; it was nine years before I was born.'

'And her age – look: she says she was twenty-six, but in 1945 she was thirty!'

My sisters all wore the same shocked look on their faces. Mum had always been so good at lying, and here it was in front of us, proof that she was well practised even then.

'But why lie about her age?' Margaret asked.

'Well have another look,' I said. 'Reg was only twenty-six, so perhaps she felt it was a good idea to become the same age as him.'

We sat in silence considering the document in front of us. Had this been the start of the downward spiral of Mum's life? Just when she thought she was getting a second chance at happiness? Or had the descent into misery started long before, when she married Ron Coates?

'So she married Reg, just before the end of the war,' Marion stated, 'and Mary was born about a year later.'

'Yes, but by that time, her bigamy had been discovered, and she was in prison. Holloway we think, as Mary was born in St Mary's Hospital, Paddington. You know they gave her electric shock therapy?'

'Oh God, poor Mum,' said Margaret, letting the tears flow freely now. I got up and got a box of tissues from the table and pulled one out to give her.

'I think we might need a few more of those before you go home tonight,' I said smiling thinly.

'So do you think Reg knew anything about her other family?' asked Marion, looking intently at the certificate in front of her.

'No, I doubt it. She already had five children, but she kept that well hidden. I don't believe he knew anything about her other life. He was a young sailor, just back from the war, and to him she was a single waitress who was fun to be with and had a reckless enthusiasm for life – a shining girl. Someone worth coming home for.'

'When she got out of prison that first time, that must have been when she went up to Birmingham, to Uncle John's?' Margaret added. She was starting to look more and more tired as the evening wore on. She had never been much of a drinker, and the glass of wine she'd drunk had obviously already affected her.

'Yes, I think maybe she was hiding from Reg, because he came to find her. Remember what Dot told us? I supposed she was ashamed . . .' I sipped my wine, and its heat warmed me. 'And then she went back with him, but obviously not for long.'

'Long enough for her to get pregnant with me and Marge,' Marion interjected forcefully, 'and then she must have just dumped us at Valence Avenue with Granny and Aunty and the others. But why?'

'Well reading between the lines, I'm guessing that she either met someone else, and was messing Reg around, or of course he could have found out about her other family. He wouldn't have left her otherwise.'

'Unless something happened to him,' Margaret said.

'I'm guessing she was still waitressing in London when she met Thomas all those years later.'

'Well she certainly wasn't at home with us. Until that day she turned up out of the blue.' Marge took another gulp of wine and I filled up her glass, emptying the bottle.

'I think I'll open another one,' I said and went into the kitchen. I could hear Marion now. 'Yes I remember that too, it was weird, we just stood looking at her. It wasn't long after that Kath was born.' The twins would have been seven and Mary eight when I arrived. 'And do you remember telling our teacher at school that we had a baby sister?'

'Yes, and feeling really upset because she just raised her eyebrows and said, "Not another one!" ' replied Marge. We all laughed, as I refilled our glasses.

A silence descended for a few minutes. It was as though we were trying to ready ourselves for the next part of Mum's story – the part when Mum must have lost all hope; when she felt like it was time for her to give up.

'The letters start the December before I was born, and stop the July before Margaret was born. It would be an unlikely coincidence if he wasn't our dad,' I said.

Margaret was silent. We all knew that we would never know for certain.

'But why did they stop?' Margaret spoke now suddenly. 'Why did they stop before I was born? What happened?'

Marion and Marge exchanged looks, and then Marge broke the silence.

'We were on holiday in the Isle of Wight,' she started. 'Granny was there, we shared a tent with her, Pat, Josie, Peter and Mary, all of us in the one tent with you – except for Mum.'

Their eyes met again and Marge went on. 'You were only about a year old, just starting to walk,' she continued. 'Mum had her own tent the other side of the campsite, we didn't see much of her.'

'There was nothing to eat, I remember that,' said Marion joining in now. 'We had to pick blackberries and Granny cooked them up for us to eat.'

'And then the lady came,' said Marge.

'What lady?' I asked. Why hadn't I heard any of this before?

'We don't know; she was very smart, I do remember that,' said Marion.

'Yes and she asked where our auntie was,' said Marge, 'so I told her, "She's not our auntie, she's our mummy." I suppose I was proud that I had a mummy now.'

Their words jangled around in my head. What did it all mean?

'When we got home from that holiday things got harder than ever,' Marion carried on. 'Money was very scarce. I suppose looking back now it was because Thomas had stopped sending any more cheques. Mum was suddenly around all of the time, but always seemed to want us out of the way – especially us,

Mary and Peter. We still loved her and wanted to please her however we could.'

Marion was getting upset now, and the emotions in the room were growing.

Was Thomas with Mum in that tent? It didn't seem likely, but it was possible. Who was the mysterious woman who came looking for Mum? Could she have been Thomas's wife? His sister?

'The fraud, that's when she was convicted of fraud and sent to prison again,' I said. They nodded.

'She must have been desperate,' Marge said, watching our reactions. 'She had come to rely on the money from Thomas, it helped feed us, kept her in cigarettes, kept her sane, knowing that there was still someone who cared so much about her, even though by that time her looks were starting to fade ...'

'So she used the fact that the grocer had cashed cheques for her over a couple of years,' I said, the pieces fitting together more snugly now.

'And Thomas worked for Walt Disney – she would maybe have had letters from him with their letter heading ... who knows how she managed to convince that poor gullible grocer that she was Roy Disney's wife! It beggars belief, but she did,' Marge finished.

We sat looking at each other.

Did Thomas even know I existed? And Margaret, did he know about her? Were we his children? Or was there always someone else?

I picked out the last remaining sheet of information that the genealogist had given me. I held Thomas's death certificate for a moment and then, trembling, handed it to Margaret.

'I was five and you were three when he died.'

A look of realisation washed over her face. 'Oh no,' she murmured quietly.

I nodded. 'The scary day,' I said and we cried quietly together, each of us swamped by our own memories of that day so many years before. The day we'd chosen to forget for so long.

62

Hidden Truths

When the knock came Mum was startled, her eyes flying towards the front door.

'Come on, quickly!' she hissed through almost closed lips, bending down and grabbing our hands. We got as far as the doorway when we heard a scraping noise; someone was pushing at the tall rusty gate that led round the side of the house to the back garden.

'Come on – run now!' she said pulling us forward and bending down low, so that we fell towards the stairs.

'Come on – up here!' Positioning us halfway up the staircase, she held her finger up to her mouth. It was a tally man, and he was trying to get in the back door while we were crouched out of sight.

Mum was rigid with anxiety, and hung on to us in case we moved and gave ourselves away. 'Don't worry,' she whispered, 'he will go soon if we keep quiet and pretend we're statues.'

We froze, hardly daring to draw breath and wanting desperately to move or cough. There was a loud knocking at the back door and then at the kitchen window. He was banging so hard I thought the glass would break and he would come jumping through all covered in blood. I tried saying some prayers in my head but couldn't remember the words. We waited for what seemed like an age until we heard the back gate clang shut as though he had swung it in temper.

Mum let out a soft sigh. 'Wait there while I peep out of the window.' She slid down the stairs and into the front room, then called to us, 'Come on you two, the coast is clear!'

We followed her back into the kitchen, and watched as she sat and lit a cigarette. Her pale blue eyes had taken on that other look, the one which made us feel like she was being pulled away from us. As she sat in her chair by the fireplace, looking much older than her forty-five years, she told us a story about a bear.

'There was once a bear and he was a friendly bear but had no friends. He was a cuddly bear but had no one to cuddle. He was a kind bear but had no one to be kind to. He was a loveable bear but had no one to love. He was a lonely and desperate bear.'

As she continued we were rapt, listening to her words spoken in a soft voice, drawing us into this other world of longing as we sat at her feet.

'One day as the bear wandered through the forest looking for the things he could never find, he heard something. It sounded like crying, so he followed the sound. Behind a big old gnarled oak tree, with roots that reached deep under the ground, the bear saw that a trickle of water was bubbling and gurgling and forming into a stream, which flowed away into a wide river, which rushed towards the sea.

'He wondered where all the water was coming from, and for a while he puzzled to himself. Then suddenly he realised what the water was and as he looked up he saw the whole world crying. Crying for those who had no friends, no one to cuddle, no one to be kind to and no one to love and to love them back.'

Mum's eyes misted over as she continued the story, not looking at us at all now.

'The bear became sadder and sadder as he stopped and watched, and as he stood there he grew more and more tired out with feeling so sad. So tired that his arms ached, and his head hurt, and he couldn't keep awake, so he lay down next to the trickle of water and the oak tree and fell fast asleep. And as he slept he had a wonderful dream. In the bear's dream he had friends, lots of them, and they cuddled him and were kind to him and loved him, and he loved them back, and he was so happy not to have to worry any more, so he decided that he would stay in his dream forever and never wake up again.'

As we listened Mum's eyes grew brighter, and towards the end of the story she seemed to have cheered up.

'What happened to the bear next?' I asked.

'Well he stayed in his lovely dream, of course,' said Mum smiling.

'But wasn't he sad not to wake up again?'

'No,' said Mum, 'of course not! He had all the friends, cuddles and love that he needed now in his special dream place.'

With that she got up and picked up a worn old green cushion from the settee. It had a smooth, grey sheen on it from many years of use and it had never been washed.

Mum took the cushion out into the scullery and opened the oven door. As we followed her, she smiled at us.

'Come on,' she said, 'let's go and find the bear's special dream place.'

We giggled, excited to be acting out the story, and tiptoed after her.

'Lay your heads on the cushion,' she said. 'It's nice and cosy in there.' And she placed the cushion in the oven.

We did as she asked, and I can remember the feel of the cushion on my skin, and the smell of our dog Pongo's special ointment, from where he had lain on it a hundred times. I saw the stone pillars that cradled the big Butler sink where Margaret and I would stand on a chair to help Mummy wash up or sometimes float orange-peel boats. I looked at the pile of pans under the sink, the fat congealed inside them that smelt of stale, long-past meals. Then I smelt another smell. A smell that I didn't recognise at all and that choked my throat and made me feel sick. Margaret tried to sit up, but Mum said, 'Shh now, try to go to sleep. We will all hold hands and we will all go together to the dream place.'

It was quiet apart from a strange kind of hissing sound, but I didn't like the smell, so Mum sung to us:

> Lulla lulla lulla lulla bye bye
> Do you want the moon to play with?
> Or the stars to run away with?
> They'll come if you don't cry . . .

I felt sleepy and started to close my eyes when suddenly the silence was broken. I heard a key in the front door, and my sisters Josie and Marge came in.

I sat up. 'Josie's home,' I said sleepily, rubbing my eyes.

Everything changed. Where there had been silence and stillness there was now shouting and movement.

'Open the window!' Josie bellowed as she attacked the back door, pushing it open wide. A blast of cold air blew in as Marge pushed at the scullery window, which was stuck tight through years of over-painting. I didn't like the banging as Marge tried to force it open, and I put my hands over my ears as the old bottles and soap dish and jugs that stood on the window ledge were knocked skittering into the sink.

Margaret was awake now and was desperately trying to cling on to Mum as she walked slowly away. I sat on the scullery floor, crying from the shock of it all, with Josie and Marge staring on in silence. All the while I could hear Margaret wailing 'Mummy! Mummy!' and not getting any reply.

63

Missing Pieces

My life has been so full of confusion, so full of an all-consuming need to find out who Mum really was, and why she behaved in the way that she did, who my father was and why he abandoned us. I have found some of the answers, but still have many left to ponder over.

I am not sure if Mum ever loved Ron Coates or Reg Stevens. In fact I am not sure that she ever loved any man, although I like to think that she cared for Thomas. Surely she wouldn't have kept his letters all those years if she hadn't? Or is this just something that I want so badly to believe – that out of all of them, the one that she really loved was my father. Margaret and I knew we were always special to Mum. Perhaps that was because we reminded her of our father. Or maybe it was because by the time we came along she was beginning to realise that the men in her life came and went, but her children would always love her with a fierce adoration, not only until she died, but beyond.

I still have many things I want to know. Was Thomas Bartholomew really our dad? Why did she keep his letters for all those years? Did the news of his death when I was only five years old trigger her desperate attempt to finally escape from the bleakness of her life?

The genealogist has left Margaret and I with a tantalising thread to hang on to, but I don't know whether or not I will ever have the courage to use it. You see Thomas had a son, and we know his name, and that we could find him. But how do you ask a man who probably doesn't even know you ever existed if he's your brother? How many memories would it hurt or destroy?

* * *

Will we ever look into the past again? I'm not sure, but we are determined to find out whether or not we are full siblings, my little sister Margaret and I, and a DNA test should be able to tell us that.

I went to visit my brother Peter not long ago.

'If you had to use one word to describe your childhood, what would it be?' he asked.

I had no hesitation in answering: 'Fear.' The fear that our darling Mummy would leave us; that someone, anyone, would hurt her or that she would be unhappy, or be disappointed in me. The fear that I was different, wasn't good enough, would mess things up. But most of all the fear that I carried with me for so long that I will never truly know the name of my father, and why he deserted us so long ago. As I have written this book I have come to a startling realisation that this is no longer true.

Depression is devious; it has no morals. It will lay in wait for you, and be there ready to pounce when you are least expecting it. It slides into your mind, and corrupts your body with darkness, leaving you struggling and panicked, desperate and desolate. I have learnt to fight back – not on my own, but with the love and loyalty of my wonderful family and the laughter and enduring support of my dear friends without whom I couldn't survive.

Over the years I spent as a teacher I came into contact with many troubled families. What I have come to realise is that the greatest gifts we can give children are love and self belief, because with these comes an enduring tenacity and strength of spirit that will allow them to be ready to stand up to the world proudly, to fight their corner, to know that they are worth something. Family and friends are what make that possible, and I am so glad that I have been given so many of those wonderful people in my life.

I have many failings, faults and weaknesses that I am ashamed of, but there are also things of which I am proud. I still ache with longing to know who my father was, but this is soothed by a kind of calm acceptance. I have at last managed to exorcise my ghosts. Does it really matter whose blood flows in my veins? After all I am still Kathleen, my mother's daughter. I am the sister, the aunty, the wife and mother, the friend . . . despite my past, or perhaps because of it. All of these are what I was able to be with the love of my family and friends. I have at last found a sense of peace and I dedicate this book to you all as a token of my gratitude, and of course to you Mum with thanks for those sunny days when we sang and danced and ate banana rolls.

Acknowledgements

I have only been able to write this book with the love and encouragement of my family and friends to support me. Thank you to my sisters Pat, Mary, Marge, Marion and Margaret, and my niece Sheila – all of whom showed immense patience and kindness, reassuring me along the journey. To my dear husband Colin and our children Sam and Jo (and Gem of course!) thank you for always believing in me and keeping me going when I faltered (and for the copious cups of tea and coffee!). I send my grateful thanks to my friends, Anne and Anne and Sherry – and especially my dear 'partner in crime' Karen who helped me to believe in myself, and my wonderful boss lady Liz who read my work with enthusiasm and made me believe that I had a story to tell. I would also like to thank both my editor Fenella for her kindness, patience and support and woman&home for the opportunity they have given me.

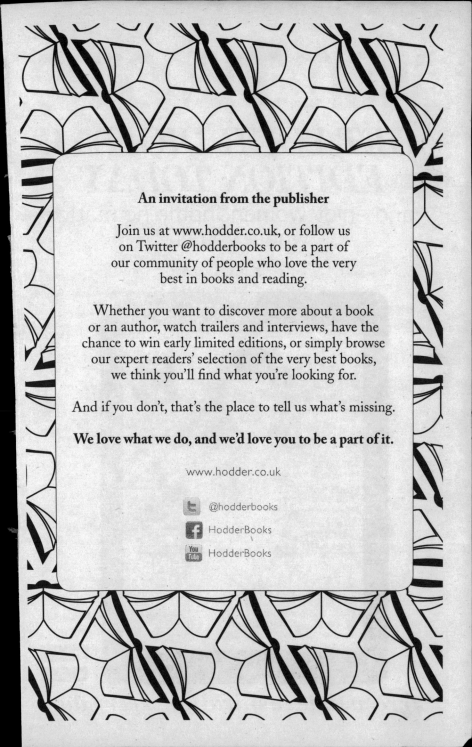

An invitation from the publisher

Join us at www.hodder.co.uk, or follow us
on Twitter @hodderbooks to be a part of
our community of people who love the very
best in books and reading.

Whether you want to discover more about a book
or an author, watch trailers and interviews, have the
chance to win early limited editions, or simply browse
our expert readers' selection of the very best books,
we think you'll find what you're looking for.

And if you don't, that's the place to tell us what's missing.

We love what we do, and we'd love you to be a part of it.

www.hodder.co.uk

@hodderbooks

HodderBooks

HodderBooks

woman&home

GET YOUR DIGITAL EDITION TODAY

and enjoy woman&home no matter where you are!

IPAD ✳ KINDLE FIRE ✳ NOOK ✳ GOOGLE NEXUS

Irresistible inspiration, every day